INSIDE THE FORTIES

To
John Clifford Bayliss
– 'who broke the seas of thorn with me'

INSIDE THE FORTIES

Literary Memoirs 1937–1957

Derek Stanford

SIDGWICK & JACKSON

LONDON

ACKNOWLEDGMENTS

The author and publishers are grateful to the following for permission to use extracts from their copyright material: (page 24) Oxford University Press for *Works of Love* by Kierkegaard; (pages 28 & 110) Poetry London Editions for David Gascoyne's 'Ecce Homo' from *Poems 1937–42*; (page 45) Poetry London Editions for Nicholas Moore's 'The Waves of Red Balloons' from *The Glass Tower*; (page 57) Fortune Press (Charles Skilton) for John Bayliss' 'Letter to DS on his birthday' from *The White Knight*; (page 74) Fortune Press (Charles Skilton) for Charles Hamblett's 'Bun Brene and Requiem' from *A Cactus Harvest*; (page 83) Jonathan Cape for *Mythologies* by Roland Barthes; (page 98) Duckworths for Alex Comfort's 'Wingless Victory' from *Signal to Engage*; (page 108) Oxford University Press for *The Point of View* by Kierkegaard; (page 109) Poetry London Editions for David Gascoyne's 'Noctambules' from *Poems 1937–42*; (page 114) Duckworths for 'Winter the Huntsman' by Sir Osbert Sitwell from *Collected Satires and Poems*; (page 138) Faber & Faber for *In Memory of David Archer* by George Barker; (page 160) Oxford University Press for John Heath-Stubbs' 'Epitaph' from *Selected Poems*; (page 173) Poetry London Editions for Paul Potts' *Dante called you Beatrice*; (page 174) Madame Catherine Guillaume for Richard Aldington's 'Church Walk, Sunday Morning' published in *Images* in 1909 by Heinemann; (page 209) Peter Owen for Rayner Heppenstall's *Portrait of the Artist as a Professional Man*; (page 216) The City Lights Pocket Bookshop for Allen Ginsberg's *Howl*; (page 222) Mrs Wyndham-Lewis for Percy Wyndham-Lewis' *One-Way Song*; (page 231) W. T. Nettlefold for his 'Fan Mail for a Poet'; (page 231) Faber & Faber for Herbert Read's 'Surrealism and the Romantic Principle' in *The Philosophy of Modern Art*; (pages 237–8) Duckworths for Alex Comfort's 'Maturity' from *Haste to the Wedding*.

Special thanks are also due to Charles Wrey Gardiner, who allowed the author to quote extensively from his autobiography, originally published by Grey Walls Press, to Sir John Waller, who lent a splendid assortment of photographs for inclusion in the illustrations, and to John Bayliss, who provided the author with much miscellaneous information and the loan of rare volumes and periodicals of the period covered by these memoirs.

Contents

List of Illustrations

Photographs and illustrations have been supplied by, or are produced by kind permission of the following people and organizations:

Introduction

Permit me to introduce myself: an old gentleman of the 'forties. My wife demurred somewhat at this statement, holding it to be misleading. She pointed out I was not 'an old gentleman' during the decade in question, and am not properly to be recognized as such today. The last reassurance was kindly meant, yet I feel I must none the less stick to my phrase. The 'forties are undoubtedly a long while ago – culturally and socially quite another world – and the intervening years make me sometimes feel quite an ancient person. Indeed, they seem now so distantly remote that I set out to write this book and fix the traces of their presence before all had passed away – mostly a matter of stalking memories hidden in the hinterland of my head.

For all that, I cannot properly think of this book as an individual autobiography. True, I have written it in the first person and given such pointers to my personal life as will assist the reader to know the score. For the main part, though, I have thought of myself as the narrator of something else: the story of my generation, which followed upon that of Auden and preceded the coming of the Angry Young Men. Very broadly, it was Neo-Romantic in tinge – a literary and artistic coloration found between the years 1937–1957 and whose fashionable hey-day was in the 'forties. I have wished to act as informal portrait-painter to many of the figures thronging those years, a great number of whom I knew. Just as Richard Le Gallienne told the tale of *The Yellow Book* generation in *The Romantic Nineties* and Percy Wyndham Lewis did the same for 'the men of 1914' (Eliot, Pound, Joyce, etc.) in *Blasting and Bombardeering*, so I have tried to set down, in autobiographical form, the story of the Neo-Romantic generation in which I was, I suppose, a not unrepresentative figure.

No literary generation exists, of course, isolated in time. It cannot be neatly pigeon-holed within the space of one decade. It has its run-up or practice years; its years of prime and power; its years of decay. So with the Neo-Romantic generation whose fullest gambols occurred in the 'forties but who were rising in the late 'thirties and waning in the early 'fifties. This, I hope, reconciles any apparent incongruity between my title *Inside the 'Forties* and my sub-title *Literary Memoirs 1937–1957*.

To help me out of my difficulties with a title and sub-title which said different things, a couple of friends made useful suggestions. One hot July afternoon, Robert Greacen and I sat at a little green ironwork table near the tea-kiosk in Lincoln's Inn Fields, trying to decide on some umbrella term which would encompass all the years of activity enjoyed by the Neo-Romantic generation. Robert finally came up with *Apocalypse and After* which pleased us greatly. The term Apocalypse – as readers of the Scriptures will recall – signifies a revelation foretelling the future, especially a disastrous future. Then, of course, one of the Four Horsemen of the Apocalypse was War, and since the central years with which my book was dealing were themselves war years, the notions of Apocalypse and Armageddon seemed peculiarly fitting.

There was in addition a further reference which my title might play upon. In 1939, a group of young writers, challenging the leadership of Auden and company, issued a little symposium which they called, somewhat oddly, *The New Apocalypse*, their declared purpose being to express revelations of the human make-up ignored by the older poets. Since these Neo-Apocalyptics were the older cousins of the Neo-Romantics, they merited some reference in my title. 'Apocalyptic' at that time proved something of a joke word. Critics spelt it 'Apoplectic' and gave its possessors the same sort of treatment as had been accorded to those Victorian poets 'The Spasmodics'. The Neo-Apocalyptics were regarded as wild and woolly men; what is worse, as wilfully regressive fuzzy-wuzzies. I have written about them in this book, but finally decided that the reference might prove too recondite for the reader.

The other suggestion came from my friend Kay Dick. Expressing herself dissatisfied with existing titles, she grilled me, over tea in her flat upon the Brighton front, until I produced my description of the Neo-Romantic generation as *The Aesthetic Anarchists*. Kay found this an engaging phrase, though I had to point out that Herbert Read's young men (with the philosophic anarchism received from their master) made up only one part of the Neo-Romantic legions. 'Never mind,' Kay assured me, 'you were an anarchist yourself, weren't you?' I admitted that I had professed anarchism enthusiastically for a period of ten years but during the other ten covered by my book, I reminded her, I had given my allegiance to quite a different political theory. Kay said not to worry; but good as her idea had been, on consideration I thought it not sufficiently representative to serve as a title.

Talking of politics brings me to advice offered by Frederick Grubb. When he learnt that I was writing this informal literary history of my time, he urged me to base it on 'good sound Marxist principles'. This, no doubt, was counsel well intended. The only difficulty was that I was not a Marxist; quite the opposite, in fact.

No longer an anarchist, I still feel all the anarchist's dislike and distrust of Communism (a distrust sufficiently based, one would have thought, upon anarchist experience in the Bolshevik Revolution and the Spanish Civil War.) And this leads me to a personal idiosyncrasy for which I must ask the reader's pardon. The terms 'left' and 'leftist' are used in this book in a somewhat private manner. They are also employed pejoratively. When I use these terms I am resorting to a personal shorthand, implying either 'Marxist' or 'influenced by Marxism'. So 'left' and 'leftist' must be understood according to my own intention which will, I think, become clear on reading.

I should perhaps add that I am not primarily a political animal, the politics in this book being those of *homo aestheticus*. Mostly, these memoirs set out to offer personal chat and literary gossip; a snapshot album of friends and acquaintances together with a few loved a little less well. There is also a smattering of theory in these pages to acquaint the reader with certain key ideas current in the art and literature of the twenty years covered – ideas now tucked away in rare or inaccessible sources.

Lastly, in self-defence, a word of warning. I should be happy if the reader would make a simple act of dissociation and not assume that the opinions I then held are invariably mine today, though in some cases they may still be so.

Seaford, Sussex, January 1977

Prologue – The Day War Broke Out . . .

On the night of Sunday, 3 September 1939, I and my friend John Bayliss were granted a sort of symbolic foretaste of what we were all to experience in the years to come. Our school, Upper Latymer, was being evacuated from Hammersmith; and John's father, a master there, was busy making plans for the move. His parents thought it would be nice for him to stay with me at Osterley until his long vacation was over and he went up to Cambridge again in October. Mine were always ready to welcome him, so we both of us looked forward to several agreeable weeks together.

The air-raid warning on Sunday morning having proved abortive, Jack and I had made arrangements to meet two girls – former pupils from our sister-school, the Godolphin – by Kew Bridge that evening; and, after some hours frolicking on the Thames towpath, had caught a late trolley-bus back from Kew corner.

Black-out and the dimming of lights in public transport had already been enforced, as we climbed to the upper deck and prepared to glide along in a sort of subfusc limbo. As we talked over the evening's amours, we became aware of a far-off rumble. At first, I thought it must be distant thunder; but as it approached, increasing in volume, it seemed that this could not be so since the sound was not audible in separate rolls but came as an almost unbroken booming. Our recognition of this soon led us to construe it as belonging to the actual spear-head of an invasion. If so, the Nazis were acting fast; but that, after all, was what we expected from having seen H. G. Wells' *The Shape of Things to Come.*

Another point against that thunderstorm theory was that there had been no lightning; nothing but an almost uninterrupted growling, creating the image in our minds of German tanks and mobile guns advancing on London as they engaged our forces. When we alighted at Isleworth Station to make our way to Osterley, this premature picture of a *blitz-krieg* was dispelled. Drops of rain now started to fall, and soon lightning lit up the sky. Within two or three minutes the heavens were ablaze with the blue-white glare of continuous flashes; and whereas in a normal storm at night the pattern is one of basic blackness punctuated every so often by light, in this it was the converse: a screen of blazing light as the background with pauses of the briefest darkness. Never have I seen such a storm in Britain; and, years later, I was interested when David Gascoyne showed me a passage in his diaries revealing how this same storm had impressed him. He, likewise, was finding his way home that evening – not, in fact, so many miles away – from Richmond to Teddington. 'The most brilliant lightning I have seen for many years, an uncanny violet colour. Rapid flashes; short sharp detonations. It seemed invariably part of the general situation – just a feature in the "war of nerves".'

The rain was now bucketing down, and we, in light jackets and sports shirts, were drenched. I have always been frightened when out in a storm; much more so, as I was later to discover, than of being exposed to an air-raid. I linked hands with Jack and we ran the odd mile home in record time. Hardly had we changed our soaking clothes than an air-raid siren sounded; but, once again, it proved a false alarm. So ended the first day of our 'phoney War'.

The Saturday before its declaration, we had spent the morning on our bicycles distributing leaflets. These had been given to us by my fellow-travelling friend Leslie Miller, and had been printed by the Communist party. They were anti-War leaflets and, as such, acceptable to Jack and me, for we had taken up a pacifist position.

This was the one and only occasion on which I had assisted the Party which, with the German–Soviet pact in operation, desired to spread its fools' honeymoon approach to countries quite outside the agreement. In doing so, we were assisting the most hypocritical element in modern politics – an element which I had recognized as deceitful and untrustworthy from the time of the Spanish Civil

War. Only our political naïveté could have led us to render even
such humble service.

Behold us, then, as we perambulated the smaller streets of Spring
Grove and Lampton, handing out leaflets to all who would take
them, or walking up the paths of little front gardens, full of the
first autumn flowers – aster, dahlia, Michaelmas daisy – to pop them
through polished letter-boxes. The sun was bright; and I remember
wearing a lime-green Aertex shirt. Tomorrow, Neville Chamberlain
was to announce that Britain's protracted holiday from European
obligation was over.

When Jack Bayliss returned to Cambridge for the Michaelmas
Term just a day or so before my twenty-first birthday, it was agreed
I should follow him up as soon as he had secured me lodgings. I
had already registered as a conscientious objector, and could come
before a tribunal as easily at Cambridge as in London. Before that
occurrence, it was pointless to plan any long-range future activity.
I could spend the interim agreeably in study.

At this point, perhaps, it might be convenient to go back some
years and fill in a few gaps.

Postscriptum

After this book had gone to press, Tambimuttu – to whom in friendship I had sent proofs – objected to what he held to be certain factual errors in my portrait of him. Information making up part of this portrait came to me at second hand – namely, from Julian Maclaren-Ross' *Memoirs of the Forties* (1965) and from conversations with the poet and journalist Charles Hamblett. Both of these sources of information are now dead, and I frankly acknowledge to Tambimuttu that I therefore have no way of checking the validity of their statements and freely assent to his objection that there may be errors contained in them.

I must, however, stand by those portions of my portrait which resulted from my own first-hand impressions. These are purely personal and subjective, of course; but I hope he discovers in them the goodwill and respect I feel for him as a skilled editor and publicist for poetry.

DEREK STANFORD

7th March, 1977

Part One – Prewar

I

Great Striped Tigers

My friendship with Jack Bayliss, who remains my oldest friend, began when we started to sit next to one another in the fifth form at Latymer. His father, my Junior English master, had already commended himself to me by demonstrating, perhaps without intention, the pleasure I derived from poetry. Finding me, on entering the classroom one day, conning over a poem with complete absorption, he remarked that I seemed to be taking it in 'like a cat lapping at a saucerful of cream'. Ah, yes, I thought to myself afterwards, that's what I was doing: enjoying it. Since he was known to have published a volume of poems himself when young, under the name of Edward MacDuff, and appeared to have provided the lower forms with at least half of the anthologies used by them, I was all the more impressed by his pedagogic salesmanship.

Soon I saw, too, that his son had points which I wished to emulate. I was growing tired of being one of the Bad Boys, rough-housing and endlessly larking about. In private, I had written poems which essayed pessimistic modern themes in ponderous and graceless free verse; but whereas Jack had contributed some elegant humours to the school magazine, I had limited my Latymerian muse to an overheated dithyrambic chant which was drummed out to the banging of desk-lids:

GREAT   STRIPED   TIGERS
STALKING THROUGH THE JUNGLE GR–AH–AH–ARSE

The upper case and the first line spacing represent the fortissimo and the pauses integral to correct rendition.

Jack, like me an incipient Swinburnian, regarded it with enthusiastic approval. His own *Punch*like epigrams or Gilbertesque snatches filled me with a generous envy. I felt that from our association respective good properties might rub off on each other. At the age of sixteen he had had a sonnet published in the *Cornhill* and had, with his father, produced a book of one-act plays duly issued by Harrap, his father's publishers. A mutual apprenticeship of one to the other might, I hoped, do us both good, since in one sense between us we represented the heavy note and the light.

Before very long, once or twice a week in my house in Jersey Road, Osterley, or at Jack's in Flanchford Road, Stamford Brook, we betook ourselves after tea or supper to an upstairs room where we read and criticized each other's verse. Playing mentor and cheer leader turn by turn, we went through the poems with a fine-tooth comb. And sometimes afterwards, we would draw the curtains and see the moon bowling along between the clouds like the polished wheel of a racing car or a bright newly minted half-crown. Clouds symbolized our obscurities, imperfections: the moon was an emblem of the clipped and rounded poem.

Another thing we shared besides a love of all the arts was an overriding interest in girls. Perhaps both of us being born in October with Libra as our sun sign, under the rulership of Venus, influenced these two preoccupations.

When in 1937 Jack went up to read English under Thomas Henn at St Catherine's College, Cambridge, I disappeared into the Law. It was not a calling I much esteemed then, but to article me to a solicitor represented my worthy father's idea to secure for me a profession less precarious than the arts. I did not stay much longer than a year, however, before deciding that this was no life for me. For this there were two main reasons: first, it seemed incongruous for a person professing anarchist ideas to follow a legal career (the calling of letters by this time having beckoned me irresistibly away); and, secondly, affairs in my principal's firm had reached such a financial condition that it seemed wise to separate myself before the inevitable *débâcle*.

Not that I had been unhappy in the year or so I spent in Chancery

Lane. I met a number of interesting people; and if I spent almost as much time poring over the outside stands of booksellers in Breams Buildings and Cursitor Street as I did over the pages of Hailesbury's *Laws of England*, perhaps neither activity was wasted. Among personalities from the Inns of Court, the one who absorbed me most was Krishna Menon, later to be India's High Commissioner. He was, in those days, a barrister with chambers in New Square, Lincoln's Inn. His relationship to our firm was twofold, since he often represented us in court but was himself also our client in a case he was bringing against Penguin Books who had appointed him general editor of their newly started Pelican series.

So, quite often, my boss would say to me, 'Nip round with this brief to Old Krishna and tell him we've heard from Penguin.' 'Old Krishna' did, indeed, peculiarly suit him, since although he was young in years (forty in 1937) there was the gloom and bruise of care upon him so that he reminded me of Old Father Time, that boy of preternaturally ancient spirits in Hardy's *Jude the Obscure*. Tall and imposing, with long, almost emaciated features, he had the appearance necessary for a 'people's martyr' as became a luminary of the London School of Economics and a borough councillor of St Pancras in the days of its fiercest fights against depression. There was something of the look of a suffering Christ about him, a Christ nailed on the Cross, who took a pessimistic view of the chances of resurrection. Not that this mitigated his struggle against the Nobodaddy of capitalism. He fought on unflaggingly, but, at the same time, in the realization that Utopia was not to be built overnight.

And so I would call on 'Old Krishna' bringing him business in the form of a brief, and ask him if he would like to call round and have a word with my principal about Penguin's latest letter. Perhaps because he was as much a journalist as a barrister, or because he thought barristers' pin-stripe a bourgeois affectation, he seldom wore a black suit save when appearing in court. Sporting an old tweed jacket, a pair of uncreased silver-grey flannels and a Middle Temple tie, he would walk round with me to Chancery Lane.

'Ah, Krishna, and how are you feeling today?' my boss, a short broad-shouldered Jew, would ask him; to which Krishna would invariably reply that he was not feeling well, or was feeling cold. As likely as not it was May or June, but the gas fire would duly be lit; and Krishna, standing or sitting before it, would stretch out his skeletal hands towards the flame, flexing his fingers and grimacing. Afterwards I would ask my principal what it was that pained our visitor so.

'God knows!' he would exclaim. 'Krishna calls it rheumatism but I suspect he's got the pox.'

As often as not when I think of him now, I see him stand before the blue-yellow flicker while a red glow starts to creep up the bars, and outside, in the pouring rain, a contingent of Welsh miners on hunger march pass slowly along the roadway below to the intoned words of 'Bread of Heaven'.

Not that all the figures of note who brightened my days in that den of law were as lugubrious or dignified as Krishna Menon. Sometimes, in the dusk of an autumn day, I would catch the figure of Count Potocki, with flowing cloak and peakless velvet cap, stepping through the wooden door of the gateway into the court-yard of Lincoln's Inn Old Buildings. Under the faint gaslight and the growing darkness, the robes of this pornographer-poet and claimant to the throne of Poland would produce a half-Titian, half-Rembrandt effect.

Nor were English Pretenders absent. On the steps of the war memorial seat beside the entrance to Lincoln's Inn grounds, Anthony Tudor would stand and address the lunchtime strollers on his own unimpeachable claims to kingship. He was a fair-haired mass of a man, a young-middle-aged bull in his prime, whose features showed a memento or two of that bluff, polygamous King Henry in his heyday. Bluff and amiable was Edward Tudor, happy to answer questions about the predicament of England today and the best policy for tackling the crisis. And every so often he would bring in the name of the scientist J. B. S. Haldane – 'my dear master and friend' – and what apt thing that pundit had said to him. Very likely he saw him as his Sir Thomas More or Cardinal Wolsey. On the credentials of his line of descent, I would not care to pronounce; but I thought he evidenced a pragmatic approach such as character-ized Henry VIII. To me, a collector of lost causes, this seemed refreshingly unusual.

After saying goodbye to my office colleagues, I put myself out to grass among my expanding bookcases at home and the shelves of some half-dozen public libraries. Apart from a casually chanced-on month of work for an Armenian in an art gallery in Tottenham Court Road, I was without an employer until His Majesty's Forces became my boss from 1940 for the duration.

From the run-up summer to the war, I select only one personal image: that of William Joyce, Lord Haw-Haw in embryo. Richmond, its river, its hill, cafés and pubs, was then a haunt of mine, and one evening in May or June, I stopped to listen to an open-air speaker who had set up his rostrum in Heron Court by what was then Mylo's Milk Bar in Hill Street. Joyce had by this time left Mosley's British Union of Fascists after having served his chief as propaganda officer and deputy leader of the party. He had founded, with John Beckett (an ex-Latymerian famous for his seizure of the mace while a Labour member during a debate), his own British National Socialist League, and was now very capably addressing a small gathering. Having listened to so much left-wing oratory, I thought I would sample a specimen from the right; nor can I say that its quality *qua* rhetoric was inferior. Joyce, indeed, was a man of ideas with an educated mind, and a distinctive speaker.

After the questions had been answered and the small crowd had melted away, I told him that I was especially interested in the relationship between art and society, and what his party might have to say about it. He forthwith invited me to a cenacle of inner supporters held weekly in the upper room of a Westminster pub. The group I found there was hardly inspiring, though Joyce and a young lieutenant of his seemed serious and thoughtful people. Apart from an ageing whore with varicose veins (but possibly someone's Diotima), there were no obvious representatives of the *demi-monde* present, nor were there any bullyboys or members of the *lumpen proletariat*. The tone was almost totally lower-middle-class.

The main question I put to Joyce was: Did his party believe in the freedom of the arts? Certainly it did, he answered.

Well then, I put to him next, what did he and his party think about the suppression of pictures by the Weimar Republic artists under the regime of Hitler? This, he explained, was because their paintings were degenerate and, as such, a source of infection and depression. I said I thought this so-called degenerate art reflected the state of contemporary society, and that if it mirrored images of rottenness, then this very mirroring performed a cathartic function.

To this Joyce retorted that an artist could not be allowed to heal himself through his art in public. If he wished to do so in private, this was a different thing; but once he exhibited his disease before others, then social health must take priority over that of his individual well-being. If art, in other words, was to be therapeutic, it was the therapy of society, not of the artist, which must take precedence. This, after all, was very much what Plato would have argued and the fact that I inclined in this matter to an Aristotelian position could not obscure from me the fact that Joyce had formally got the better in this discussion.

Another month or so and he was gone, to become that hated mocking voice upon the air.

2

Two Small Circles

Meanwhile Jack and I had fully kept up our relationship. We wrote to one another regularly and met frequently during his vacations, and I visited him at Cambridge.

A further link between us was the little magazines (limited to three or four handwritten or typed copies) which we edited and circulated among our friends: *The New Poet, Storm, Facet, Lynx, Morse* and *The Richmond Review*, some with exotic illustrations by our friend Pauline Drapier who was studying at St Martin's.

These provided a repository for a group of ex-Latymerians who met at the Dove on Hammersmith Mall, the little green ironwork tables on the terrace looking out over the river being essentially, as it were, editorial office furniture. This small group – with one or two additions such as Dennis Stuart who professed music, hoping for a scholarship in the same but entrapped for the moment in the dull mazes of the law – appealed to one strong aspect of my nature, the aesthetic and hedonistic side which I possessed in common with Jack.

Russell Clarke, who put together one number of *The Richmond Review*, represented the *beau idéal* of such a standpoint. Under his editorship the magazine appeared between dun-coloured covers, the reverse side of a piece of richly figured wallpaper. His own poetry was elegiac and impressionistic, paying formal lip-service to despair. Down at Chelsea, we would visit the Blue Cockatoo on the Embankment (a famous café now, alas, demolished). Our high spirits there would know no bounds, but afterwards Russell would indite a copy of free verse full of scented world-weariness.

At the Blue Cockatoo
We who have lost tomorrow,
Seeing only candlelight on tarnished brass
And ash-grey embers on a littered hearth,
Hearing only words spoken by past loves,
Faintly,
Through the fumes of some long dead debauchery,
We love only the darkness without shadow
And the dull negation of the senses.

This was at a time when I took Edgell Rickword's poem 'For the Passing of the Entire Scheme of Things' to constitute the *ne plus ultra* of what one could expect from a title.

Down at Osterley there existed a very different group who attracted the intellectual part of my make-up. It met at the house of Maurice Moiseiwitsch, nephew of the great pianist and already, by twenty-four, an accomplished professional writer. Jack and I called it 'the Penny Circle', after the name of a character 'Mr Penny' who featured in a regular radio programme written by Maurice.

Two doors away from Moiseiwitsch lived his cousin Leonard Cassini, at whose house I first enjoyed the delights of cinnamon toast. Len was a B.B.C. pianist as well as contributing cartoons to *The Daily Worker*. Leslie Miller and David Stribley, two local teachers, made up the four. All save David – the 'funny man' and Liberal – were members of the C.P. or strong sympathizers. The left-wing argument of this group – an intelligent, sometimes subtle Marxism – provided a valuable whetstone on which I could sharpen my adolescent wits. When Jack and I were irritated by their socializing discussion of the arts, we would refer to them, between ourselves, as 'the Penny or small-change school of critics'.

It was David, largely apolitical, who was, in one sense, the bridge between us. More interested in literature and music than in international affairs, he preserved an unlikely devotion to an unusual trinity made up of Bertrand Russell, Max Beerbohm and the 'Marx Brothers'. Respecting logic, he enjoyed the irrational, and would amuse us younger men by sticking pennies on his bald brow. Later, he followed for some years a career as a general and sporting journalist under the name of David West. In proof of the sanity of Fleet Street, he would point out how, being a serious student of cricket, he had been set by an editor to provide a weekly forecast on soccer, a game for which he had small feeling.

The imaginative ethos of these two groups – the Latymerian aesthetes and the Penny Circle realists – could be assessed by contrasting a short story by Jack Bayliss with one written by Les Miller. Jack's story was called *The Violet Volume*. It was set in Richmond in the 1890s, and borrowed the device of a wonderful seducing book from *The Picture of Dorian Gray*. A young exquisite enters a little antique bookshop on The Hill and taps imperiously on the counter with his tasselled cane. The ancient bookseller shuffles forward, and the dandy demands by name *The Violet Volume*, not on the shelves but which he knows the shop-keeper possesses. The old man, guessing the use it will be put to, pleads with him not to purchase it. The exquisite grows angry and throws down his gold, and the bookseller parts with the beautiful pernicious book. Later that night, just as he fears, he observes behind the curtains of a nearby house two shadows embracing: those of the exquisite and a chaste young woman who has surrend-ered to him, *The Violet Volume* having done its work. Years later, the old bookseller sadly watches the noctambulation of this same ruined maiden, now a prostitute, as she plies her trade up and down The Hill, cursing the bookshop in her passing. All of which goes to prove that the pen is mightier than the penis.

Very different was Leslie's story written in the manner of the Social Realists, and which, after Walter Greenwood, we spoke of as 'Love on the Sewage Farm'. In it a young engaged couple stroll out one summer evening to inspect the new sewage works which are in the course of erection. Their conversation, though intimate, is full of anticapitalist reflections. In a bourgeois society based on money, the young swain explains to his inamorata, your waste, your dead matter, is looked after for you. It is only your life that is left uncared for. Ours, her prospective groom assures her, will be a civilization of the bed – an apt description of the dormitory suburb, but one which we found highly diverting.

At least the story was well written, and more interesting than the lecture delivered at the I.C.A. in the late 1940s by a foremost Soviet theorist on the arts. Polite and poker-faced, he spent most of his time enthusing about the efficacy of vast recent sewage and electric installations now operative in his motherland. This was felt to be cheating; and the audience of intellectuals, no longer mesmerized by that wonder Utopia as they would have been in the 1930s, gave the urbane but puzzled professor something of a rough ride. *They* wanted to know what the latest dialectic had to say about art and beauty, and all *he* talked about were the problems of handling voltage and waste. Unlike the Russians, we had had flush closets and light switches from what seemed like time immemorial.

In those run-up years to the war, literature was not my only recreation. Besides the Dove group and the Penny Circle, there was the Ballet Club – an informal gathering of late teenagers who used to resort to Sadlers Wells together, and to cafés in Richmond and Chelsea, for edifying conversation, flirtation and the reading of short papers.

One of our favourite haunts was the Lombard on the Chelsea embankment (like the Blue Cockatoo, sadly now no more). Here the proprietor kindly put the basement room at our disposal, since the din we made would be less audible to its well-heeled clientele. Down there, it was colder and less well lit but neither of these factors bothered us much. I recall how, after seeing Robert Helpmann in one new production, I contributed an enterprising little essay entitled 'In Praise of the Devil: some ethical reflections on the ballet *Job*'. All grist to my anti-establishment mill.

Most of the girls belonging to the group had been at the Godolphin School. Among the members was Hattie Jacques, though I don't know whether she had been at that school. She was, even then, a wench of goodly girth, and lived with her mother and her brother Robin in a late Victorian villa in Oxford Road, Gunnersbury. Her histrionic gifts were already quite marked, exhibiting themselves in mimicry and the studied affectation of her talk. She possessed a naturally sceptical intelligence and a tendency, at times, to dissolve in tears. I found her highly diverting and shall always remember the evening when she draped herself in some highly embroidered cloth and danced a Chinese mandarin's dance in the front drawing-room in Oxford Road, the desired oriental effect increased by the large inverted lampshade which she placed on her head. The mirth she occasioned amongst us was frequently uproarious, and I recall how her mother would sometimes appear upon the scene to hush us lest we disturbed a mysterious 'uncle' who lived in the house.

As dynamic as Hattie was her brother Robin, who studied art and was later to become art editor of a well-known periodical. Dennis Stuart and I used to meet him sometimes in the tube on the way to our legal dungeons in Chancery Lane. He impressed us with his rakish tweed cap, his pungent French cigarettes and his own cogent line drawings. It might have been a word of his about Gaudier-Brzeska which led me to put a slip in for the two numbers of Wyndham Lewis's *Blast* at the Victoria and Albert Museum Library, a favourite haunt of mine when I had time to spare.

When that magazine – of 'bright puce colour . . . a page area of 12 inches by 9½ . . . in general appearance not unlike a telephone book' – was deposited on my desk its contents struck me like a torpedo. One talked much then about art and revolution and revolutionary art (not necessarily the same thing). *Blast* was certainly the second with a vengeance. Both these issues interested me, but chiefly the later one.

And all the time this aesthetic play-acting of ours was going on, the political situation was deteriorating. On 28 September 1938 the British Navy was mobilized; and then on the 29th came Munich, which gave us a moment's respite, a necessary if unsatisfactory breathing-space, the whole tempo of those days being immortalized in Louis MacNeice's *Autumn Journal*.

It wasn't long, of course, before the writing on the wall was appearing again in firmer, even more lurid, characters. Annoyed by the didacticism of the left, by which I refer to that section of opinion which was Marxist or Marxist inspired, I had responded to the fall of Barcelona with an intransigent short story rejecting the bait of 'commitment'. I did not like one bit the uniform, or Cominform, hectoring tone of fashionable parlour pink pronouncement. I had also read Wyndham Lewis's satirical novel *Revenge for Love* (1937), the best send-up in fiction of trendy international corruption in Spain as engineered by Marxist crooks in London. So, in my tale wherein two young men debate the pros and cons of volunteering to fight for the Republic, the last speaker comes down against any such action. His counsels are those of despair. A few more long-haired boys, he declares, will make no difference either

way. It is now too late to intervene. All one can do is to erect one's
flimsy pleasure tent on the side of the ravine until the cataclysm
sweeps it away. This parable of an aesthete was uncompromisingly
unheroic; and can only be explained as a reaction to 'the preacher's
loose immodest tone' which Auden later recognized he had over-
employed in the 'thirties.

Then, some time within the shadow of Munich, I came across
Herbert Read's *Poetry and Anarchism* (1938) in its bold-lettered
yellow wrappers. Hitherto my strongest public feeling might be
formulated as 'Hands off Art!' What I lacked was a politic which
should be the moral and social counterpart of such an attitude; and
in Read's book I found it.

What I was really looking for was a combination of revolution-
ism and aestheticism. This, I understood from Read, was something
he himself demanded. 'To me it seemed just as important to destroy
the established bourgeois ideals in literature, painting and architecture as it was to destroy the established bourgeois ideals in
economics.' The Marxists, of course, always claimed that their
programme implied exactly this; but in the equation between art
and society, as elaborated by the Marxists, art appeared to me to
obtain a bad deal. In their notion of Socialist Realism they subjug-
ated art to the requirements of society, to the unborn society of the
future. The bourgeois philistine I took to be far less dangerous to
art than the commissar or party boss.

Read held that 'the cause of the arts is the cause of revolution'.
At the same time, he felt that the artist, 'pledged to the shifting
process of reality . . . cannot subscribe to the static provisions of a
policy' or 'come to rest in the bleak conventicles of a politcal
party'. Read recognized that though the artist may require to work
with some social or political bearings, such larger notions are very
different from such 'a static system of ideas' as the Communists
impose on the worker in art.

From the time of reading *Poetry and Anarchism*, I called myself
an anarchist – something I continued to do for about ten years.

When Read wrote his book in 1938 he openly admitted that 'in
the parochial atmosphere of England, to profess a belief in
anarchism is to commit political suicide'. This, I think, was for me
part of its attraction. I saw it as a minority last measure – the last
measure which someone whose individualism was sickened by other

collective political programmes, both parliamentary and revolutionary, might yet be able to accept in good conscience. It was also, I might add, a measure which I did not expect to see successful in the immediate future (what awaited us beyond the coming war was impossible to prognosticate). To elect for it publicly might well be tantamount to political suicide, the ruination of one's political good name. Having no thought of a political career I was not much worried about the first consideration; as for the second, one does not desire to be characterized unduly for common sense at the green age of twenty. Today, with politics being as much a matter of the streets and the shopfloor as of the debating chamber, things are different. Anarchism is now almost an instinctive campus politic, one of a set of conventional gestures which include such odd alternatives as Maoism or meditative esoteric cults. One acquires it as naturally as a pair of adscititiously patched jeans. Then – for an Englishman as distinct from an Italian or a Spaniard, since anarchism had preserved a small traditional hold on Latin countries – it was the almost ludicrous exception. For me, in those days, I took truth and the exception to be synonymous. The minority appeal of anarchism was its chief recommendation.

All that was unusual in the 'twenties and 'thirties, everything not sanctioned by the man in the street, was made into a laughing stock by the daily press and *Punch*, that laughing jackass of the philistines before Malcolm Muggeridge got his enlivening hands on it. For millions, the only thing known about anarchism was represented by the cartoon of Popski, a blackbearded being always on the point of lobbing a smoking bomb as though it were a cricket ball. I believe the *Daily Mirror* was responsible for this bit of public education, and it did its work well for there are still plenty of middle-aged persons who think that an anarchist is a bomb-thrower.

That anarchists *have* thrown bombs in the past and *are* throwing bombs again today is an all too undeniable fact. In Britain in the 'twenties and 'thirties, however, they were not throwing them; and the brand of anarchism I learnt from Read was a reflective philosophic attitude as much as any programme for action. Two other thinkers especially – Kropotkin, a Russian prince, and Proudhon, a French printer – made up the cornerstone of my anarchist principles. Since the political terrorism of the Baade-Meinhof group and the

Angry Brigade in Britain has led to further misunderstanding of what one might call classical or philosophic anarchism, it might be a good idea if I offered a brief synopsis of what a belief in it entailed.

To begin with, anarchism posits a minimum of government control, a reduction of all centralized powers of the State. (Lenin promised to the people of Russia a gradual 'withering away of the State'. Instead, in the U.S.S.R. all the attributes of government have increased a hundredfold. This is the betrayal of the Revolution which all anarchists find in Soviet Communism.) It believes in a devolution of power; in regional rather than national control. It believes in fact, as Read put it, that 'all politics are local politics'. Its economic policy was one of syndicalism: the control of industry by all those involved in it, whether workers or managers, but again on a regional as distinct from a centralized basis. Communally, it held to the notion of an egalitarian society. Quite unlike the Communist idea that the essence of social virtue belongs to the proletariat, and that a Communist society is based on working-class principles, the anarchist believes that the good society is essentially classless. On this issue Read, though agnostic, was to quote from the Christian philosopher Kierkegaard: 'The neighbour is your equal . . . loving your neighbour is a matter of equality . . . the neighbour is everyman . . . everyman unconditionally has this equality.'[1] The thinking here is based, of course, on Christ's commandment to love thy neighbour as thyself: as sons of God, we are all brothers. It is possible to accept the brotherhood of man without the sanction of divine fatherhood, and this is just what the anarchist does. All brothers are not good brothers, alas, but brothers they are for all that. A sense of the fraternal between man and man is an essential part of the anarchist sensibility.

The morality implicit in this notion was elaborated in the idea of 'mutual aid' as being responsible for much that is constructive in man's achievement. Kropotkin's famous book by that name was published before the turn of the century, some thirty years after Darwin's *Origin of Species*, a work whose conclusions seemed to give credence to the remorseless capitalism of the nineteenth century. Kropotkin's *Mutual Aid* reverses this image of 'Nature red in tooth and claw', and seeks to show what a large part co-

[1] *Works of Love*, 1946.

operative effort has played in the animal world between creatures of the same species. The book then goes on to demonstrate the same cooperative effort in human societies (the craftsmen's guilds of medieval cities provide Kropotkin with impressive historical parallels to zoological examples he has gathered). From the evidence of this work, Read claimed that while Marxism was founded on economics, anarchism was based on biology.

Finally, for me, anarchism was the natural choice since it offered so much more – and so much less, of course, others would add – than party politics. Read once descibed anarchism as 'the politics of the unpolitical' and since I saw myself as only a political animal minimally speaking, it appeared to be the best brand for me. Why, it might be asked, did the *homo aestheticus* I took myself to be stand in need of any politics whatever? The answer is that the state of the world (the oncoming war, and the double struggle between democracy and Fascism and democracy and Communism) would not leave me, or any other creative intellectual individual, free to get on with artistic endeavour. Faced with the unavoidable fate of becoming a pawn in political power games, I sought the cover of that position in which my status would be respected if not protected or preserved.

Having said that anarchism provided me with more than party politics, I will try to explain my meaning. Most politics, for their implementation, require committees and committees unending. The dictates of a party must be channelled down from Central Office or its equivalent, and nowhere was this more apparent than in the Communist Party in Britain, whose rulings in the 'thirties were drawn up not here but in the Kremlin. Anarchism offered instead a viable attitude and a way of life with bureaucratic regulations and chairmen's decisions unheard of.

One could begin putting into practice the morality of mutual aid wherever two or three were gathered together. If Marxism was like the synagogue of the Pharisees, anarchism seemed to suggest the informal gatherings of Christ's own ministry before St Paul sought to preserve it by means of legalistic thinking. If red is the colour of Revolution, anarchism appeared to me to offer the redness without the red tape. One could start a cell of 'good living' with any friend or chance fellowman.

For me, anarchism was as much a system of ethics as a political

C

programme. That was why it did not worry me that I saw little chance of it being adopted as the national political system in my lifetime, unless the coming of war should bring infinite changes which no one could foresee. I could none the less practise its teachings day by day and spread its mystique by word of mouth and by my pen.

In February 1939, two months before Franco's final victory, Britain recognized his government in Spain. In the same month, there appeared at the Whitechapel Gallery a large Surrealist exhibition sponsored by the Artists International Association as 'a demonstration of the Unity of Artists for Peace, Democracy and Cultural Progress'. The posters and leaflets proudly proclaimed that 'the Exhibition will be opened by THE MAN IN THE STREET' – a typical Popular Front con-trick, always good for pennies or votes. The main attraction for me, however, was that Read was to make the real opening speech and, never having seen him before, I decided to go.

It was, I remember, a bleakly cold day when I and my faithful lieutenant Dennis Stuart (or Stu, as we invariably called him), with his orange-brown overcoat, trailing orange scarf and cachinnation of a semi-hoarse macaw, detrained at Aldgate East adjacent to the Gallery. The first obstacle to the exhibition lay with that prodigious individual 'THE MAN IN THE STREET' (invisible, possibly, without the capitals). True, no doubt, that Whitechapel High Street, with its then sweet-sour smell of cookshops, horse-droppings, beer, dirt and vomit, was a more 'approachable' terrain than Bond Street or Piccadilly, but the man in the street still felt a healthy, if nervous, wish to stay clear of art and its sophistications.

Three or four passers-by – including a melancholy zombie, his overcoat clasped with a safety-pin at his neck; a plumber with tools protruding from his bag; and a bus driver going home after duty – were invited, in turn, to speak the opening words and declined. Finally, it fell to a little Jewish tailor to act as the people's representative. Whether or not he was a socialist, believing with Read that 'it seemed elementary that a belief in Marx should be accompanied by a belief in, say, Cézanne', he assumed the role proffered and executed it with dispatch. Having spoken the prescribed words, he partook of a quick glass of sherry and vanished, doubtless feeling he had better things to do. At least he saved the day for that not overcrowded *entente* between art and the masses campaigned for by the cultural left.

Then came the star of that Saturday morning, and I recall the slight stir of amazement with which Stu and I observed Read's arrival. Clad in a dark double-breasted blue suit with his navy blue polka-dot bow tie, and attended by a highly groomed posse of begowned and bejewelled squaws, he seemed an oddly incongruous presence among so many bohemian uniforms and the sprinkling of rag-tag-and-bob-tail from the streets. Elegance of dress is, for some, a social gesture; for Read it was more a quiet dandyism – an outward expression of inward and spiritual grace; and later, reflecting on this quietist dandy, I have thought of Lawrence Durrell's apt words : 'Style is the cut of the mind.'[1] Certainly his accompanying chorus, with their wraps and fur capes and pinnacled coiffures, lacked only feathers and dazzling tiaras to appear a group of Lady Bountifuls dressed for some ambassadorial ball and strangely deflected to the soup kitchens.

Nor were Read's first words more reassuring. Looking like an aristocratic rabbit, he addressed us all as 'Comrades' (a term I was not over fond of at the best of times, having become suspicious of its affected inclusiveness). In a modest account of some of the fighting on the Western Front in the First World War, Read had described how, on leading an attack, he gave 'a great inhuman cry', but as he was a man with 'a lazy larynx' his normal utterance lacked volume and timbre. Never have I heard that apostrophe 'Comrades' less resonantly trumpeted – the gentle baa-ing of an over-refined sheep.

Had Read not already been a great name to me, I might have become disenchanted, but the magic of his books had rendered me immune to such small pricks of doubt or irrelevant laughter. I had read his volumes of visual criticism – *The Meaning of Art* (1931), *Art and Industry* (1934), *Art Now* (1933), *Art and Society* (1936) – and was mightily taken with their clarity of approach and systematic division of theme.

As to the pictures on the walls, they came with the force of a personal revelation. I had, of course, seen Surrealist paintings

---

[1] 'Conon the critic, on the six landscape painters of Greece', *Personal Landscape*, 1945.

before but never in such massed numbers. The first International Surrealist Exhibition had been held in June 1936 – 'a month of torrid heat, of sudden efflorescence, of clarifying storms' – but I had not succeeded in visiting it. Then, too, the impact which art makes upon us depends on the context of time and circumstance. In 1936, although the civil conflict in Spain had broken out, there was still a diminishing chance that a major holocaust in Europe might be diplomatically evaded. By 1939 the faintest of such hopes had been dissipated. Events were now acting as a catalyst to unite the spectator and the picture in a conjunction unexperienced before. As I was to write a little later, in a poem, he who portrays the horrors he dreams of

> invents no myth.
> Nightmare is history.[1]

The pictures exhibited showed me two futures: one signposted Doom and Gloom; while the other beckoned with shapes of escape along an enlarging vista of dreams. In the first I recognized what was to come, what was historically now unavoidable; in the second, I saw what yet might chance to be, what latently existed as a reality in that interior world of the mind. Far from being contradictory, the two visions complemented each other. The former spoke prophetically of that environment we must come to inhabit, the latter of that subjective landscape we could enter by turning our attention inward.

In terms of the Time Spirit, the pictures achieved a visual break-through, and if every decade has something like a cultural sound barrier, then that of the 'thirties was emphatically smashed by the paintings exhibited. We were into the war, into the 'forties, into the blitz on London completely. There stood, with uncanny prescience, as David Gascoyne had written about that same time, 'our about-to-be-bombed cities',[2] roofless or half-demolished houses, their interiors exposed in cross-section. Only in one point were these spokesmen of the future incorrect, the artists, like the poet, having envisaged each devastated metropolis abandoned. Art,

[1] 'The Shape of Dreams', *Music for Statues*, 1948.
[2] 'Ecce Homo', *Poems 1937–42*, 1943.

perhaps, is always more extreme, more tragic, more absolute than life.

How I passed the rest of the day after leaving the Gallery, I cannot remember, but recall that, next morning, on removing my pyjamas to dress, a poem began to form itself in my head. Before the last button was fastened, it had amazingly completed itself.

It was certainly not a composition the genuine Surrealist would have approved of, since it was written in rhyming quatrains. At the same time, it came close to André Breton's definition of Surrealism as 'psychic automatism' and was my only piece of automatic writing possible to dignify with the name of poem. A lyric of renouncement and salutation, I called it 'Hymn without Choir and Organ', no doubt because I considered these churchly accompaniments as so much conventional dressing. Such as it was, it appeared, along with a screed by me on the Exhibition, in the pages of a Cambridge magazine.

> In the great days that are endless,
> in the new year to come,
> where the hound sings in the forest,
> and the water-springs are dumb;
>
> where the birds' talk is silver
> and the moon's giggle is gold,
> far from the streets of suburbia
> with boards 'To be Let or Sold';
>
> where daylight falls in a shower
> of rainbow-crystal bliss,
> and the primrose climbs to the lime-green sky
> in a saffron kiss;
>
> where the bee's song sizzles
> with the sun's electric fire,
> and the fountains in plenitude pour us forth
> our nectarine desire;
>
> tired of apples at four pence a pound
> we came to the unpronounceable door;
> we tossed our top-hats away and entered,
> and shall return no more.

At St Catherine's, Jack had become review editor of *Granta*. From time to time he sent me books for review; and often on vacations I would join him in a crawl around the publishers to solicit copies for the magazine. It was thus we came to meet the mysterious Mr Caton who conducted the business of the Fortune Press from a basement in Buckingham Palace Road.

A breeze of perceptible poetic newness had started to blow from these quarters. Wafted from this catacomb of office and storeroom, there appeared a number of slender volumes by the spearhead of the post-Auden generation: Roy Fuller, Julian Symons, Gavin Ewart, Francis Scarfe, Henry Treece and H. B. Mallalieu (later to become a Labour politician). The king planet of this constellation was Dylan Thomas who, very ingeniously, seemed to have parted with the copyright of his *18 Poems* to a couple of publishers in place of the usual solitary one. In this race for the Dylan Stakes, David Archer of the Parton Press certainly obtained a head-start over his rival the Fortune Press – a lead, however, which did not carry him past the post since the Parton Press shortly went out of business while Fortune Press continued to advertise the poet's epoch-making book in their list up to Dylan's death and for some years after.

This first wave of post-Auden talent was followed by a second – a younger wave containing many of my own generation: John Waller, Nicholas Moore, George Woodcock (the anarchist), Tambimuttu, D. S. Savage, Ruthven Todd, Drummond Allison and Vernon Scannell. Jack Bayliss and I also joined the party, our first books appearing in 1944 and 1946. It was this current of freshness which led us to beard the Caton in his den.

A rich eccentric with money stashed away in Switzerland, he was not in publishing for the pennies as far as his poetry list was concerned. (Needless to say, neither were his poets and although Jack and I *were* paid for our volumes, this, we gathered, was very much an exception.) But if poetry was not his fortune, he must have had reasonable returns from certain erotic classics which were included in his catalogue: Huysman's *À Rebours* in translation along with English versions of Pierre Louy's hellenic fantasies: *Aphrodite*, *The Songs of Bilitis*, *The Twilight of the Nymphs*, Marcel Aymé's *The Green Mare*, John Cleland's *Memoirs of a Coxcomb* and titles of that kind. Other slower-selling but steady

works were Montagu Summers's *The Gothic Quest* and his translation of a medieval manual on witchcraft *Malleus Maleficarum*,
not to mention *A Treatise on Ghosts* by Noel Taillepied – three
appropriate titles for a publisher who was to become the Leonard
Smithers of Neo-Romanticism. His real money-spinner, however,
was *Fourteen, a Diary of the Teens by a Boy of Fourteen* and
followed by *Fifteen* and *Sixteen*. It was said to have proved so
successful that he thought of extending the series to cover all
other adolescent phases before starting again with *Diary of a
Boy of Thirteen and a Half, Diary of a Boy of Fourteen and a
Half*.

It may have been the thought of such publications which made
his reception of callers, to say the least, exceedingly wary. Down
the unwashed area steps one went to ring at the basement door.
The bell was one of those enigmatic buttons which offer the ringer
no auditory proof of having functioned at all. Then, after some
moments' pause, one saw through a grubby window a figure
emerging into the stone-flagged vestibule from some inner pene-
tralia. At length the door would be opened, possibly after it had
been ascertained that the caller was not a man in blue or some
other suspect intrusive personage.

Before entrance was granted, further stages of inspection or
recognition must be gone through. 'Who's there?' or 'What do you
want?' Caton would enquire suspiciously, a hat, as like as not, on
his head, his shirt without collar, his cheeks unshaven. After first
credentials had been offered, he would open the door less churlishly,
and perhaps for several minutes one would converse on the doorstep. Generally after such an interval, he would beckon one in and
repair to his office. This was probably in a shambles, with books
and papers everywhere. Sometimes he would proffer an explanation
for its state of utter confusion: 'Alterations . . . Re-wiring . . .
Waiting for the painters.'

Caton was certainly more weird than sinister, though there was a
palpable suggestion as of some unclean presence about him. I
remember once, some time in the 'fifties, meeting the painter Ithell
Colquhoun by chance in Great Russell Street. Ithell was a wartime
friend of mine and now asked me if I would act as escort to her in
a visit to the Fortune Press.

I would not have described Ithell as unusually apprehensive of the male, yet the dweller in the basement in Buckingham Palace Road seemed to have rendered her singularly uneasy. Apparently she had sent Caton some prose-poems which he was considering publishing. As he had not replied to her letters requesting him to come to a definite decision she had called round to see him in person. After routine scrutiny at the portals, she was ushered in, only to observe him carefully bolting the front door before returning to his office. It was then, by the light of the naked bulb which burned in the chill hallway, that she noticed his trouser flies were unbuttoned; and since he carefully shut and locked each door before sitting her down in his office, she concluded that assault or rape might have been on the programme. Excusing herself as quickly as she could, she had made her getaway unharmed, but without a verdict on the prose-poems.

I could have told her that the unbuttoned dress signified no condition of urgent virility but was, in fact, merely a part of that casual toilet which Caton favoured. However, I offered my strong-arm service (equipped as I was with an umbrella), and once more we descended those baleful steps and stared in, after ringing, through the fusty window. Once more we were met by open flies, open collar and bristled chin. We may even have been treated to a final insult – watery tea from cracked cups and saucers. As to the typescripts of Ithell's prose-poems, he couldn't, as he said, lay his hands upon them without some prior notification; but eventually she did receive them back by post. This unfavourable impression I have given would falsify the truth unless supplemented. Caton was a complex character. Mean in some ways he indisputedly was. Travelling first class to Brighton at weekends (a favourite hunting-ground of his), he would walk the whole length of the train to procure a discarded newspaper rather than pay the odd pennies for one. But if he was something of a literary miser, a poetical miser in the true sense he was not. One might compare him with Leonard Smithers, the *risqué* randy publisher of the English *fin-de-siècle*, who was ogre-ish enough, but Caton was a very mild sort of Smithers, pale and colourless even, one might say.

I believe him to have been a lonely man – to use George Darley's term, 'a solitudinarian' almost. In a sense, he was something of a spider, the generally unlaundered state of his quarters suggesting the murky filaments of a web. From its musty centre he did not need to beckon young poets into it. All that was necessary was for him to wait; sooner or later they mostly made their way to him. In his feeling for these younger poets there may have been more than one element. It seemed to me that he was not without kindness, but that it was a kindness powered more by curiosity than by any ready fund of natural affection. When I went to see him from time to time, to procure some book for review perhaps, or to deliver someone's typescript poems for his consideration, it seemed to me that he fed hungrily on such scraps of gossip, such tit-bits of news or talk as I brought him about those poets. It was as if he lived like a man cut off, deprived of information about his kind and the more eager, therefore, to receive it when available. I am glad that so many of the titles in Caton's interesting list have today been taken over by Charles Skilton who has likewise preserved the Fortune Press imprint.

But whatever the benefits conferred on humanity by Caton's publication of *Tortures and Torments of the Christian Martyrs*, Lili Bródy's *Kept by His Wife,* or *Boy Sailors* by Gundry Grenville Hearne, it was the appearance of *The New Apocalypse*, 'An anthology of criticism, poems and stories', which struck tinder for me. Its wrapper was a rather drab grey, the lettering of the title a bold black. Black, too, was the binding of stiff cloth, publication being the summer of 1939 before wartime economies ruined book-production. All save two names of the contributors – Dylan Thomas and Pablo Picasso – were more or less new to me. I think it was Jack Bayliss who had sent it to me for review in *Granta*, and I found it called for more than the quick flip through which critics often patronizingly bestow. My copy received a thorough underscoring, in addition to page-top and margin notes.

With no false modesty the blurb announced: 'This volume, comparable in importance with NEW SIGNATURES and NEW COUNTRY, is the first attempt made to display the influence and show the progress of the work done by experimental writers since the advent of the Auden–Spender–Day-Lewis triumvirate'; and what excited me most was its attempt to steer a path between the stringencies of Social Realism (Socialist Realism's little English sister) and the excesses of the Surrealists.

The watchword of this group was 'organic' – a quality they

stressed in opposition to the programmatic writing of the former
school and the irrational automation of the latter. J. F. Hendry
(a philosophic Scot and the T. E. Hulme of the movement) lumped
Eliot, Wyndham Lewis, Auden and even Neville Chamberlain all
together as 'machine men'. All, he considered, had allowed themselves to be hypnotized by certain objective systems: rationalism,
logic, the State. He quoted from Louis MacNeice that 'Wyndham
Lewis is basically a pessimist, thinking of human beings as doomed
animals or determinist machines. . . . Eliot is always stressing the
nightmare quality of machines.' He argued that those who permit
their sensibility to be bludgeoned by established systems can only
escape by retreating into others. 'The impact of scientific rationalism on modern society', wrote Hendry, 'leaves machine-men like
Eliot, Allott, Auden and Lewis bewildered. They enter the Church,
the B.U.F. [British Union of Fascists], the Communist Party.' This,
at the time, had my full support, since I did not then wish to land
up in any of the three specified havens. Only a little less was I
delighted by Henry Treece's assault on the sacrosanct doctrines of
the Surrealists. It always seemed to me odd that a group so licenti-
ous in artistic practice should bind themselves so tightly with the
red tape of official theory. Most mini-churches are authoritarian,
however, and 'the Breton boys' were no exception.

I have spoken of my considerable sympathy with Surrealism, and
how the Whitechapel exhibition some six months earlier came as a
revelation to me. By the time I received *The New Apocalypse*, I
had acquainted myself with the thought of the movement, and
observed, even then, certain shortcomings: unselectiveness as to
thought and style was the cardinal defect. In his *Memoirs of a
Public Baby* (1958), Philip O'Connor put his finger on this.
Speaking of his own interest in the group, he noted how 'it
condoned my very apparent lack of technique in verse and paint.
In fact I found most of my weaknesses as considered adornments
by the movement.' What the Surrealists needed was a filter, and in
Dylan Thomas, Henry Treece believed he had found it. Thomas,
whose gruesome tale *The Burning Baby* (incest plus a species of
suttee for good measure) together with a poem ('How shall my
animal . . .') appeared in *The New Apocalypse*, straightaway
became the movement's cynosure. It is doubtful whether this
embarrassed Dylan, but almost certainly it amused him since, as he

wrote, 'putting little trust in most of the poetry written today, I put a great deal in mine'.[1]

Splendid poet as he was at his best, Thomas had his fuliginous phrases, his opaque tenses, and was a worse model by far than Auden. For whereas Auden by his modish example led others without his intellect to streamlined intellectual pretension, Thomas was the cause, in all too many without his imaginative gifts, of a baroque facetiousness. Indeed, the New Apocalyptics must answer for encouraging this rhetorical farrago, their own coryphaeus J. F. Hendry being particularly prone to it. The truth is, as Thomas recognized, that he was an expert at aping his own moods. Others, impressed by his virtuosity, engaged in the same gymnastic contortions and ended up spreadeagled on the poetic mat.

Another slogan of *The New Apocalypse* was 'myth'. In his Introduction Hendry wrote:

> I drew up in collaboration with Henry Treece a preliminary manifesto, in which several points were made, the most significant of which were first, that myth is today of extreme importance, both psychologically and pathologically, for the re-integration of the personality; and second, that the 'machine' age in which we live, with its terrifying objectivity, has revived the myth as a mode of release from the object-machine, whether state system or rationalism.

This talk of myth I found most stimulating. It seemed to promise a middle path between the dry sticks and dusty bricks of Social Realism's documentary writing and the Surrealists' wallow in the slough of unreason. Amongst the Pylon poets and their prose counterparts, only three had attempted myth in an interesting way: Auden, Isherwood and Rex Warner. Auden, as always *sui generis,* produced his own heady compounds of the Icelandic sagas, Tom Minx, the school Cadet Corps and the psychologies of Freud and Homer Lane. Rex Warner assayed allegories of power, responsibility and motivation in *The Wild Goose Chase* and *The Professor* – novels whose fantasy was, perhaps, undercut by the political slanting of their thought. Isherwood, in *Lions and Shadows,* had

---

[1] To Henry Treece 23 March 1938, *Selected Letters of Dylan Thomas,* ed. Constantine Fitzgibbon, 1966.

given us the unbuilt-on foundations of a myth in his story of 'Mortmere' before leaving that fascinating private world for swamis, gurus and Hollywood studios. I thought, therefore, that the Apocalyptics should find plenty of room in the field to hold their own gymkhana of myth.

Among the new names to whom *The New Apocalypse* introduced me was that of Robert Melville, later to become perhaps the leading authority in Britain on the art of Picasso. In his essay *Picasso's Anatomy of Women,* Melville did something of a John Berger on the artist. It was though, one might say, a Berger in which Havelock Ellis was substituted for Marx and Freud as providing clues to the drawings. I was certainly taken by Melville's formulation of Picasso's rendering of the vulva: 'a notched board, a peach, a piece of V-shaped channelling, a broken milling cutter, a flower-pot and a shape like a grocer's scoop'. I had somehow never thought of it in that way before.

Another name destined to be more widely known was that of Norman McCaig who had four poems in *The New Apocalypse.* Nicholas Moore, son of the philosopher, whom I was shortly to meet at Cambridge also appeared in its pages. All in all, I decided to keep a benevolent eye on Apocalypticism.

Part Two – War-Time

3

At the Dorothy

Within a week or so of his return to Cambridge, Jack Bayliss wrote to say say he had secured rooms for me in a little street off Trumpington Road. On 11 October 1939, my twenty-first birthday, my mother had taken me out to lunch and bought me a handsome tweed jacket from Simpson's – quite the smartest I ever possessed – so I was able to flaunt myself along King's Parade and in the Dorothy and other Cambridge cafés and pubs with a requisite coxcombry. I regarded Cambridge as my spiritual home, an affection I have preserved despite the popular identification of that place with F. R. Leavis and his crabbed iconoclasts. I recall how that 'sea-green Incorruptible' had once asserted that he and his followers knew they were 'the real Cambridge', whereas, for me, they were the veriest Redbrick. Every ointment contains its insect. Oxford, after all, was infested with its Critical Positivists.

After breakfast I would leave my comfortable lodgings and make my way, across the water-meadows and up Mill Lane, to Jack's rooms in St Catherine's. The clear Cambridge light pearled on the dew, raindrops or hoar frost adhering to the grass of the water-meadows as I approached the churning waters of the mill-race by Mill Lane. Later in the morning, at that same spot, we would sit outside on the parapet with the sunshine winking on our mugs of cider. During the day, I would spend my time in the English Faculty Library or sitting in Jack's study before the fire. Sometimes we would walk out to Grantchester or drink in a pub by Byron's Pool. A few times I borrowed a gown and attended

lectures on the Jacobean drama. (I preferred the Jacobeans as being more gamey and decadent than the Elizabethans.)

I went to a number of *Granta* tea-parties where the policy and
plans for the next week's issue were deliberated. From these meetings I recall the serious-minded editor Eric Hobsbawm, now a
lecturer in political and economic studies at London, and can it
have been Mark Holloway, later to be the author of a book on the
history of Utopias, who came to one such bun-fight bearing a medieval lily in his hand? The poet George Scurfield was there certainly,
having penned a line about the conscript 'saluting his sergeant on the
bathroom floor' – so much for military love at Cambridge, unless
some sexual signalling was intended. Another who I believe was
present was Gervase Stewart, an Apollo in tweeds, reading theology
at Fitzwilliam House. His poetry showed enormous promise, but
his early death in the Fleet Air Arm destroyed that 'bough which
might have grown full straight'. His laurel wreath, a tiny one, is a
volume of verse published by Fortune Press entitled *No Weed
Death*. In verse, Gervase was to Cambridge what Drummond
Allison was to Oxford.

In the evenings, we would go out to various functions
announced by little white cards which were propped up on
the mantelpiece. It was at one of these, a *soirée* of the Cambridge
Poetry Society run by Joan Murray and the poet Stephen Coates,
that I first met Nicholas Moore, elder son of the philosopher G. E.
Moore whose *Principia Ethica* is said to have provided the
Bloomsbury Group with its exiguous stock of moral notions, and
himself at that time the most widely published poet in Cambridge.
In fact, it would probably be true to say that he was the most
widely published poet under twenty-five in Great Britain, for
whatever 'little magazine' one picked up there was a poem or two
by the ubiquitous Nick.

At this gathering, on that autumn night, there was a bevy of
belles from Bedford College, its members having been evacuated
from the metropolis. Their presence in Cambridge was a godsend.
The Bedford girls were freer and more sophisticated, more
jocund and *soignée* than their serious Cambridge sisters who, with
one or two exceptions – Molly Panter-Downes, later to be the
author of an excellent book on the home life of Swinburne and
Watts-Dunton at No. 2 The Pines, Putney, springs memorably to

mind – were inclined to be over-earnest and inured to the chaperon system, a pretty girl trailing a plain girl as escort.

Chatting with these late-teen London beauties, I remarked that this meeting in Trinity would give them the opportunity of seeing the Rupert Brooke of the Second World War. (Moore, like Jack and myself, was a pacifist; but I thought his undergraduate fame sufficient to justify the statement.) All agog with virginal excitement (most women students were virgins in those days) they asked me if I knew this cynosure and would I point him out to them? Now, at that time, I had never set eyes on Nick, though I had heard he would be coming later in the evening. Not wishing to keep these fair Amintas waiting, I promptly introduced Jack Bayliss to them under the guise of Nicholas Moore. This entailed some straightening out when the rightful appellant arrived, but since Jack had a certain beaming comeliness while Nick favoured a more owl-like look of meditation, I considered my substitute had been well chosen.

I got to know Nick a little better when he, Jack and I, and some score of others, were working on the land in the summer of 1940 for the Cambridgeshire War Agricultural Committee. In the Dunkirk summer, while we were engaged on hedging and ditching, Nick seemed in depressed spirits. He said he wanted to get married, but there was parental pressure against it. His mother was a dominating figure who used at times to smoke a pipe. She would pin up the day's orders in the kitchen, such as one would find in a camp, allotting everyone his task. One did not lightly escape such rota duty. It is probable that she was running true to form and that philosophers' wives who have a family are apt to get like this. Somebody, after all, has to organize things while father sits in his study engaged in a difficult endless honeymoon with the Categorical Imperative or whatever.

Henry Treece spoke of Nick as 'little Christ' which should have made him John the Baptist, a rather extraordinary role for the Captain of the Apocalyptic first eleven. Why, I could never understand, for Nick was not a diminutive creature, having a rather large body. Nor was he of the persuasion of Jesus, being a left-wing secularist. Gentle, patient, forbearing . . . was it the notion of some such attributes which led Treece so to christen him? 'Gentle' he probably was; but how about the virtue of patience?

D

All I can say about this is a story told me by Jack Bayliss who, shortly after his marriage, was living at Nick's house, 86 Chesterton Road. Jack, Nick and several other guests were sitting down to dinner, waiting for the dessert to be served while off-stage the wives could be heard nattering. Well, despite the exhortations of St Paul, even the more forbearing Christian male reaches his own patience threshold. Even sooner a Marxist or pan-Marxist, however modest his everyday demeanour. So, suddenly rapping the table with a spoon, Nick bellows out the one word 'Pudding!' – once only proving enough.

Talking of wives and Marx, this brings me to Priscilla, Nick's first wife and famous for the number of poems dedicated to her by her loving spouse. She was the niece of Lord Craigavon, Governor-General of Northern Ireland, and one of those debs who adorned the Communist Party and would make today's Dr Rose Dugdale look very much the frump. Later they parted, but while she reigned, the poems poured out: some good, some indifferent, some moving, and some silly: 'Darling, you see between my legs,' one such addressed to Priscilla began, proof at least of an uxorious nature. I remember, too, how Wrey Gardiner, with whom Nick worked on *Poetry Quarterly*, told me how he had once submitted to him a poem with the topical title 'A Very Young Soldier posts a Letter to His Girl' which began with the evocative lines:

> I stuck it in, I stuck it in,
> I stuck it in the letter box ...

Of our own egregious permissive society, Nick was a pioneer, albeit a mild and, I would say, a chaste one. The loves he celebrated were not promiscuous, but were of the type which Coventry Patmore hymned in *The Angel in the House*. If one needs to be both porno and nasty to be in the running as a Sex Hero of Modern Letters (Genet, Burroughs, Nabokov), then Nick was a non-starter, being that old-fashioned thing, a genuine life-enhancer somewhat along Laurentian lines, and should rightly have received a decoration of the Victorian Order since I take it that the loves of the hearth are assumed to purify the muse Erato.

Nick was also a precursor of other interests which have become fashionably developed since 1939. One of these was the link he established between poetry and jazz. Writing a poem in praise of Wallace Stevens, he instinctively likened him – with his virtuoso verbal performance in mind – not to other poets but to solo jazz musicians:

> For all the pretty noise I found him foremost,
> The four past masters of the trumpet nothing
> To his green line of verse.[1]

Right in the thick of things throughout the war and just after, he withdrew from publishing in the 'fifties, going to live at Tunbridge Wells with his second wife and devoting much time to landscape gardening. Then, in 1967, Covent Garden Books, run by the enterprising Dr Nothman, republished *The Glass Tower* (his largest collection of poems), and he burst on the world of the Sunday papers with some dozen odd versions of a sonnet by Baudelaire which *The Observer* had set as a contest. This brief hour of reappearance was followed some time later by a letter in the *Times Literary Supplement* about *Poetry London* and *Poetry Quarterly* in which he disassociated himself from Neo-Romanticism, maintaining it had all but never existed. This was rather like Blake saying there were no such men as Coleridge or Byron.

Cambridge in the 'thirties was famous for its literary criticism. Since the time of I. A. Richards, it had been the home of 'practical criticism', pioneering a pragmatic as distinct from a speculative approach. In a sense Richards was the founding father. When, just before the war, he started a series of lectures, the lecture room was packed – standing room only; by the end of the course his listeners could be numbered on two hands. He was away above the heads of most undergraduates.

One day, walking with Jack in Petty Cury, we passed a smallish man who might have been a gas-fitter save that he wore an academic gown – a gas-fitter who read Bunyan, be it said, and had graduated from chapel culture to old-fashioned Labour debating societies. Or, perhaps to exchange a social for an artistic image, I would say that he reminded me of Joseph the Carpenter in Millais' *Christ in*

[1] 'The Waves of Red Balloons', *The Glass Tower*, 1945.

the House of His Parents. This was the great Leavis who had not yet quite assumed the Gladstonian dignity of a Grand Old Man. Jack had no great love for him, since in his dismissive manner he had dealt over-briefly with Housman's 'Loveliest of trees . . .' from *A Shropshire Lad*. I, however, had already read his *New Bearings in English Poetry* and been rather impressed by his talk of the need for a modern sensibility. On each subsequent rereading, I should add, I have found more grounds for disagreement.

In his essay on Walter Scott, Bagehot paints a picture of the 'Cavalier' personality as 'open to every enjoyment, alive to every passion; eager, impulsive, brave without discipline, noble without principle, prizing luxury, despising danger, capable of high sentiment'. 'Over the "Cavalier" mind,' he tells us, 'this world passes with a thrill of delight; there is exultation in a daily event, zest in the "regular thing", joy at an old feast.' Reverse the coin, and you have the Puritan character. Subtract from that character its religious faith, and you have Dr Leavis.

It was an Oxford girl student who, replying to Robert Graves's question of whether she had enjoyed a certain poem, remarked primly that 'poems were not to be enjoyed but interpreted'. This little anecdote dates from the 'fifties, and by then Dr Leavis's restrictive notions had spread from the Granta to the Cherwell. By the 'sixties, they had penetrated half the grammar schools of the country as well as finding a paperback mouthpiece in the six-volume Pelican *History of English Literature*. Yet still Dr Leavis preserved the tone of one crying in the wilderness; shrill, admonitory, without grace or sweetness.

But if Leavis, with small regard for Coleridge, appeared as no encourager in the growth of Neo-Romantic taste, there were other Cambridge figures who certainly took the opposite line. One such was Hugh Sykes Davies, Fellow of St John's, an original signatory to the English Surrealist group and a contributor to the Faber anthology of *Surrealism* (1936); even more, by association and production, he might be thought of as an English Romantic. Kathleen Raine's first husband, he had published a curious Neo-Gothic romance called *Petron*, an inscribed copy of which he gave to Jack Bayliss who went to him for supervision. The hero of this narrative prose-poem suggests a rewriting of 'Excelsior' by

Mervyn Peake – the young man and his 'banner with a strange device' becoming a twin brother to Titus Groan:

> He passes on along the darkening canyon, its sides veined with curious ores which, catching the failing light, cast lurid and unnatural gleams across the gloom. . . . The coppery sun sinks in a swirling mist, and in his bloody light we catch our last glimpse of Petron, now climbing ledge to ledge the dizzy wall, groping for footholds in the living rock. The clouds sweep down into the abyss, and he is lost to our sight.

This 'Johnny-head-in-air' aspect of Sykes Davies was not the sole one. He was a capable academic and fell foul of some of the lazier teaching dons who were members of the English faculty. In 1943, while working in the Ministry of Food, he brought out the first of his three volumes of *The Poets and their Critics*. This was an anthology in which the poets from the time of Chaucer pronounced judgement on their peers; and, since the first of the series appeared in the then cheap Penguin Books, its accessibility was unlimited. To this Sykes Davies's colleagues in the English Faculty objected, its existence causing them to organize their supervision in a more strenuous fashion. Previously they had been able to tell their charges to go away and read up what the poets and critics had said about Wordsworth, say, or Dryden or Donne. The dons argued that Sykes Davies's book discouraged the spirit and practice of research; what they really meant was that students would now look to them for more than library lists and the checking of references.

I. A. Richards's famous book *Practical Criticism* appeared in 1929. In it he related how tests he had carried out with students revealed the part which preconception plays in our appreciation of poetry. He would, for example, distribute sheets of poems by major or minor figures of the past, with the name of the author removed. In such cases, he noted, the response was quite different from those in which the name was given. We visit the attributes of the brand name on the brand. This new light on the poems of the past was applied by Thomas Henn, the great Yeats scholar of St Catherine's, to silhouette poems by the students themselves. On Tuesday evenings, he opened his rooms to any young tyro who cared to attend. Each brought an unsigned typewritten poem which was handed to Henn on arrival. We then sat round a long table, and Henn distributed the poems anew. These were read out and assessed by all, free from prejudice or personality. Such, at least, was the theory: actually the poets often knew the authorship of the piece in question. Undergraduate typewriters were frequently, in those days, vintage models with characteristic typefaces and defects. Jack and I, who attended these evenings, had great fun puffing our friends' poems, at the same time making discreet reservations so that our eulogies should not appear suspect.

Tom Henn was cast in a large mould – 'big-boned and hardy-handsome' like Felix Randal. He was an Anglo-Irishman, the son of a doctor and small landowner, and as conscious of his Irish charm as he was confident of his English good manners. My Sussex neighbour Reginald Rees, who had him as a supervisor a year or so before Jack, told me a story that illustrated the good conceit Henn had of himself. Convinced that he would prove the easy winner, he abetted the idea (which started in Newnham or Girton) that the girl students should hold a ballot to vote for the most popular male don. As it transpired, the vote went against him, and he was not even among the first three. I suppose, too, some few found him snobbish, though this was not the impression I received. Perhaps one should distinguish between an air of high courtesy and crude condescension. To quote Hopkins once more, Henn was a 'mannerly-hearted' man, and I shall not readily forget the hospitality with which he wined and dined me at high table when I went to talk to the Shirley Society on Dylan Thomas following the publication of my book on that poet in 1954.

At the time I first met him, he had done very little save publish an edition of Longinus on the Sublime, but his knowledge of Yeats, on whom he was later to write much, was already a byword. He helped Ault (who came to a tragic end by suicide) in his compilation of Yeats's letters, and encouraged Patric Dickinson (then at St Catherine's) in his own poetry. He was also a poet himself, though few people knew of this, combining a poetic sense with that which often proves its opposite: a feeling for the speculative and philosophical. I remember, ten years or so before his death in 1974, how his poetic sense was characteristically manifested on one occasion. Henn was giving a lecture on Yeats at the Royal Society which Jack and I attended. He had suffered some serious illness but was still an impressive figure, broad-shouldered and florid, with a fine clarion voice. His address was plentifully studded with quotations from both the verse and prose of Yeats, stitched most carefully together with a commentary or exposition of his own. Now as he richly enunciated each word, I found it, again and again, almost impossible to distinguish between the citation and the comment, since the lecturer's poetic spirit had fused them to a like consistency of speech.

The title of his talk was 'Yeats and Ireland'; and the Irish experience, in literature and history, was something very close, very dear to him, with strong personal ties and vivid associations helping to support and exemplify it. I particularly recall how he told us about being driven to the local station when a boy on his way back to school in England. This was at the time of 'the Troubles' – the fighting for supremacy between the Republicans and the Free-Staters. Little Tom Henn sat beside his mother in the trap when, as they approached a cross-road, she pulled his scarf up over his face, telling him to shut his eyes. The sight she wished him not to see was blood on the surface of the road – the relic of a recent killing. 'Not to see' was surely the common preference of the Protestant Ascendancy in Ireland. At the same time, coming from a country doctor's family, Henn was brought up in a knowledge of the misery in which so many of the Irish still lived. The loyalties of the imagination are subtler than those of the citizen and patriot; and I think it was the tension between English and Irish allegiance, imaginatively speaking, which made Henn so sensitive a guide to the world of Yeats. It is difficult, however, to satisfy all opinion in Ireland, and he used to maintain that the burning down of his old family home, although then in the hands of another owner, might be construed as the working out of some obscure vendetta.

After Henn had finished, Jack and I went up to congratulate him. His performance had been exceptional and the applause tremendous and sustained. We saw, though, how it had taken his strength; and he sat now red faced and mopping his brow, with his veins so painfully distended that I feared he might be in danger of a stroke. I never saw him after that, but I sent him my books as they appeared which he invariably acknowledged in the most generous fashion. As became a Yeatsian scholar, Henn had a special fondness for the 1890s; and since I had written somewhat abundantly on those 'Companions of the Cheshire Cheese' – poets with whom Yeats had learned his trade – as well as on the prosemen of that period, there was this pleasant link between us.

But all this was far away from Cambridge during the phoney war when I first went to his house on late autumn nights to hear my verse praised or attacked by poets who, supposedly, did not know the authorship of the poems they were assessing.

One of the young Cambridge poets very much in the Yeatsian camp, even to a lock of black hair carefully trained forward over the right eye, was Maurice James Craig, now an Inspector of Ancient and Historic Monuments in southern Ireland. This tress which its owner encouraged in wayward wantonness so annoyed Colin Eccleshare (today an eminent light of the Publishers' Association and for long a power in the Cambridge University Press) that he once set fire to it with his lighter, a gesture redolent of the singeing of the King of Spain's beard. I remember Craig's romantic figure well from the time I first encountered him, wearing a dark cloak with a golden clasp, on Armistice Day 1939 when I went before my Objectors' Tribunal at the Shire Hall on Castle Hill.

That same morning a procession of about three hundred people carried banners demanding immediate peace negotiations, a cessation of the 'imperialist' war (a trademark of the Communists participating in the protest) and an improvement in social services. A wreath was laid by them on the war memorial, bearing the inscription 'They Died in Vain' – words which were quickly erased by the police. I might also claim 'He Argued in Vain', having just been struck off the Register of War Objectors. The setback left me feeling in need of some small gastronomic compensation. This took the form of lunch at the Blue Barn whose excellent Chinese cuisine I usually regarded as beyond my means. Afterwards, with Jack Bayliss, I repaired to Maurice's rooms in Magdalene where we listened to records of Respighi and Dohnányi. Jack and Nick Moore had that very morning been given complete exemption from any war service by the Tribunal, their cases having been based on moral grounds. In retrospect, however, I cannot complain that my judges treated me severely since I was not a true pacifist.

At Latymer I had been a member of the League of Nations Union and had engaged in those activities – speaking, debating and writing for peace – which Aldous Huxley called 'preventive pacificism'. When I came to read his brilliant pamphlet *What Are You Going to do About It?* (1937), I realized that I could not undertake the activities of 'combative pacificism' which is concerned with the gesture of 'non-violent resistance to violence'. This is a pacificism for for the few – for those who have the patience, dedication and courage (in a word, the heroism) to serve the cause of peace at this higher level.

I had become a member of the Peace Pledge Union some time in 1938; but the real grounds for my pacificism lay in my anarchist principles. I distinguished, somewhat naïvely I now recognize, between the two notions of 'the people' and 'the State'. The second I saw as the oppressor of the first, the creator of all tyrannies, military or civil. As it was the State that ordered conscription, to disobey was to serve the cause of freedom. Whatever the merits of this logic, it is not essentially pacifist. There were not a few people whom I would have been prepared to kill. The verdict of the Tribunal against me was in no way harsh or unfair.

So the days and the light in the afternoon dwindled, the Michaelmas Term wearing on to Christmas. The man with rooms above Jack Bayliss played a record of *Je t'attendrai* almost without cessation. He was a Federal Unionist, but had, I suppose, grown downhearted about the prospects of 'Union Now' – as Street's much discussed book was called. Certainly the mood of the time was not one in which the prospect of an alliance between the North Atlantic democracies seemed to guarantee total salvation. We went up and drank a sherry with him, but he did not push his Federal wares. *Je t'attendrai*, with its elegiac insistence, its mournful note of waiting for better times, seemed more congruous with these late autumn days.

Then there was something called Essentialism which advertised itself as under :

What is Essentialism?

IT IS –
  The NEW ECONOMIC SYSTEM based upon
  A NEW CODE OF ETHICS establishing
    A NEW SOCIAL ORDER propounding
      A NEW DYNAMIC PHILOSOPHY acknowledging
      PAST, PRESENT and TO COME assessing
        CUMULATIVE SELF-MERIT introducing and organizing
  A MIGHTY SCHEME OF MUTUAL SELF-HELP

One was urged to read *Essentialism* ('obtainable everywhere: 5*s*
or direct from ESSENTIALISM, 7 Park Lane, London, W.1'). I
never heard of anyone who *did* send for it, but a review copy,
massive as a telephone directory, landed up on some Cambridge
editor's desk. He handed it to me, whereupon I wrote a not too
discouraging notice provided the irony was discounted.

Christmas, and still the phoney war continued. Would it, we
wondered, flicker out, or what? Then, with the spring, things got
under way. During the Lent Term vacation, Hitler invaded Nor-
way, an event I always associate with a freezing walk which Jack,
I and John Grover (a pacifist who later became a Commie) took
along the towpath from Kew to Kingston. After we had
exhausted the icy morning's grim topic, we turned to some of
David Gascoyne's poems included in an anthology we carried.
As we paced along the river bank with its white, hoary grasses and
hard-frozen ground, we read aloud one of the poet's Surrealist
pieces, 'The Supposed Being':

> Supposing the sex
> a cruelty and dread in the thighs
> a gaping and blackness – a charred
> trace of feverish flames
> the sex like an X
> as the sign and imprint of all that has gone before

There was a curious contrast between the glinting chill of the day
and the imagery of fire in the poem. Fantasy though it was, the

poem seemed somehow to point forward to that incendiary
devastation that was being prepared for us in the wings.

In June Jack Bayliss obtained his degree, and he, I and John
Grover went to work on the land just outside Cambridge. The
foreman of our party and the warden of a youth hostel run by the
Cambridgeshire War Agricultural Committee was a relative of Sir
Roger Casement – rather an odd choice, one might think, for
someone in charge of a band of pacifists and other dissidents. We
were, in truth, a strange assortment, for along with us objectors
there were quite other elements: Jewish and Arab students of
agriculture putting in a little practice before going back to
Palestine or Egypt, refugees from the Continent, along with English undergraduates waiting, or not yet due, to be called up. Among
those who had escaped from the maelstrom was Stephen Korner,
later Professor of Philosophy at Bristol. Nick Moore, as I have
said, was of the party; and other names with other faces, whose
features return to me as if wreathed in smoke from the bonfires
attendant on hedging and ditching.

David Thompson, a comely Cambridge giant, had christened
our foreman 'the Creaser' because of his reputed slave-driving
ways. In fact, he was, by instinct, a tolerant sad-natured man whose
relative's defection seemed to have cast a shadow on his life. Perhaps he felt his own loyalty suspect unless he professed a need for
patriotic labours beyond his inclinations. I, at least, recall no
oppressive treatment from him.

At a tribunal in Westminster, I had appealed against the Cambridge decision and been granted service in a non-combatant
corps. Knowing, therefore, that I should shortly be one of His
Majesty's khaki inmates, I thought I would say farewell to the
land and make my final adieu to London. My friends back there
were whooping it up, and I felt it would be nice to join the party
while there was still a roof on the house. There were rave-ups at
Rose Cottage on Richmond Hill and dionysian revels at divers
other places. To miss these would be a pity. There was, too, a girl
I wanted to see who called me by the name of a character from a
Wyndham Lewis novel *Snooty Baronet*. I was known as Old
Snooty, while her role and nickname was that of Old Val. In
Lewis's novel Snooty was an old soldier with a troublesome wooden
leg which required to be unscrewed before he indulged in love-

making. Such a predicament as this should surely be avoided. Once more I felt confirmed in my reputed pacificism.

So I left Cambridge, not to see it again till 1948. But for long after my sojourn there, it remained my El Dorado. King's College Chapel, luminous with sunshine; the daffodils flaring along the Backs; King's Parade, magnificent and misty in autumn, despite the penetrating fenland cold – again and again in later days these images confronted me. During my five years' spell in khaki, I dreamed of Cambridge as one dreams of a woman, planning to return one day and live there – a romance which did not come to pass.

4

'Nancy-Elsie'

Called up and told to report at Liverpool on 12 September 1940, I
spent my last night of the London blackout enjoying a full-scale
air raid. Things in the north-west were much the same: it gave
Merseyside a home-from-home feeling.

On the following morning, while breakfasting at a reception
centre, I watched the next man at the mess table prepare for his
repast. We had just collected, severally, in dixie and mug,
porridge, bacon, and tea, together with a crisp hot slice of fried
bread. My neighbour remarked this was 'fucking good grub', to
which I replied that it seemed fair enough. Thereupon he placed
his bacon on his bread over which he poured his ration of
porridge. The whole steaming heap he tackled with relish, des-
patching it with no false niceness.

Registering his noisy gulps and swallows, I was glad he found
the food so 'fucking good'. One could read in his shrunken face
and figure a record of that malnutrition from which about a
quarter of Great Britain suffered. And now, after indifference and
neglect, his country decided they needed him. It would fatten him
up since it wanted him to fight, while he wanted food – so both
were satisfied. I was happy to see all these forgotten men
restored to self-respect. With the worn suits, caps and mufflers
they took off, they put off some of their humiliation. There is
worse dress, sartorially speaking, than the King's uniform. Wearing it gave them a new status. As an anarchist and pacifist, I
lamented the end intended for them; but that thirty per cent of

these men at that moment were better off than in civvy street was something that could not be disputed.

Next came the army process of separating the sheep from the goats – the 'bloody conchies' from the conscript soldiers. My neighbour at the breakfast table was one of those social derelicts who was joining the Pioneer Corps. Our crowd – our 'shower' – were rather a different proposition. They tended to fall into three divisions: Bible-punching fundamentalists along with more conventional Christians, moral idealists, and revolutionaries. The first group represented most of the Christian sects and churches, the second could be called 'nice young men', and the third were political hot-heads, egg-head theorists and temperamental rebels. These three groups did not mix much, nor did they agree. The first and the third tended to be mutually antipathetic. To a Plymouth Brother, a socialist might well appear as an image of the Anti-Christ, while to the socialist a Plymouth Brother might seem a bigoted reactionary ignoramus. Such were the ranks of the Non-Combatant Corps or, as we were first called, N.C.L.C. – Non-Combatant Labour Corps or 'Nancy-Elsie' to genuine warriors. Later, when we became the N.C.C., the wags rechristened us the Nigerian Camel Corps. Our officers, commissioned and non-commissioned, were provided by the Pioneers, though later we were able to nominate our own section leaders.

It was, naturally enough, the long-haired boys who interested me most. For several years, I went about looking for potential delegates to some large hypothetical conference that should spend its time debating World Reconstruction. From No. 12 training Centre, Liverpool Old College, I wrote to Jack Bayliss giving him the news of some I had marked down as possible candidates:

. . . There are some half-score interesting people here – two [university] types from Cambridge, one from Oxford, one from London, one from Leeds and one from Manchester. The Leeds man heads the bunch with ease – a half-Irish Anglo-Catholic Right-winger and a philologist. In appearance he looks like a highly cultivated mouse with ecclesiastical pretensions and a knowledge of Machiavelli. His laughter is pure disembodied humour; aerated, volatile barbs of helium. We have also a delightful medievalist who bats his eyelids whenever anyone speaks to him like some neurotic Venetian blind, and appears like a butterfly looking for somewhere to land.

Although I can hardly say I relished my five years in the Army, I feel that I benefited from them. Perhaps my khaki confinement was too long and a shorter sentence of two or three years might have taught me, more profitably, what I had to learn. For learn about life, my own country and countrymen was certainly something I needed to do.

Like most middle-class youths whose families were in easy circumstances, I had only the sketchiest idea of how the other half lived. True, my period in the law had acquainted me, on the surface at least, with the outward existence of many, sometimes poor, Jewish clients who dwelt in the East End. I knew, too, a number of shady Soho characters whose interests we represented in a variety of criminal cases. Then there were those living in much hardship whom we advised once a week at the St Pancras Labour Party rooms – the sort of voluntary work that a young solicitor frequently takes on with the blessing of the Law Society.

But knowing about people and hearing their stories – more often, tales of woe – is not the same as living with them. This is a lesson which identification or coexistence can truly bring about : a lesson which the Army enforces. In these new circumstances I discovered I was not without the common touch (always a reassuring recognition for a brash young intellectual). I found, for example, that I got on quite well even with our rough or uncouth N.C.O.s, who mostly regarded us with less sympathy than the commissioned officers, being separated from us by class and education as well as attitude. I found that cheerfulness and humour, with a controlled degree of fantasy and clowning, entertained these honest men, who were more subject than us to the weary vistas of military boredom. In return for jokes and fooling, and a little coaching in the art of writing an amatory epistle, I was lucky to hit on a corporal who undertook to darn my socks, since I have always proved a moron when it comes to using my hands. In short, I became a 'character', a card.

My own generation of the 'forties was, I feel, fortunate in receiving this initiation. Remembering his Baudelaire, Stephen Spender could write, in his book *The Destructive Element*, of the need to immerse oneself in 'the bath of the multitude'; yet when he came to write about the unemployed in such admittedly beautiful lines as

> In railway halls, on pavements near the traffic,
> They beg, their eyes made big by empty staring
> And only measuring Time, like the blank clock

he sees them entirely from without – not detachedly, but not at close quarters. One might take as the explanatory motto of all the Pylon poets of the 'thirties these lines from Spender's 'The Uncreating Chaos' :

> Whatever happens, I shall never be alone,
> I shall always have a fare, an affair, or a revolution.

The first signified privilege; the second, love within one's own class; and the third, a theoretical *rapproche* – a paper commitment to the proletariat. When I read Spender's admirable autobiography, *World Within Worlds*, I am confirmed in my feeling of how the 'Pink Triumvirate' (Spender, Auden and Day-Lewis) and so many of their associates, for all their talk of Marx, were more securely sealed off in their class envelope from the experience of the common herd than were we poets of the 'forties who made so much less song and dance about 'the Revolution' and who were labelled offhand as 'escapist' because we were 'romantics'.

I always remember the stupid remark made to me, some years later, by George Orwell's future wife Sonia Brownell. I met her at a party given by Charles Wrey Gardiner; and, talking of the war poets, she declared she thought most of them no good. As they were busy fighting in the desert, they did not have time to read all the latest important books. I was so flabbergasted at this critical apophthegm that I remained speechless. I had thought that encounter and experience counted for something in poetry. It was nice to know a publisher's catalogue was the infallible way to inspiration.

In any case, once we of No. 4 Company of the N.C.C. were settled down for a stay of any duration, packets of books from the London Library would arrive for those of us who were members, while the N.C.O.s would grumble and fume at the number of volumes stuffed in our kitbags.

Just before my birthday on 11 October 1940, I received a letter from Jack Bayliss which I took to be a suggestion that we both renounce our non-combatant status and participate in the war more fully. It was couched in the form of a poem, making reference to our hedging and ditching days together and my tendency, wherever I was, to initiate discussion.

Letter to D.S. on his Birthday[1]

From this dull haven in the coast of days,
watching the clouds like tramps go slouching by,
I send this poem in lieu of answer
stabbing with pen this drowsy holiday.

To you who broke the seas of thorn with me
in the blue fever of our early wars,
greeting in your monotonous grey hell,
and may there be no tournament of stars
to drown the peace of your nativity.

Now you have gone we have no argument
save what the wind or weather bring to us
or ditch or field will furnish, or tired minds
will scratch up like bad-tempered animals,
even the would-be lecturer is stilled
and silent faces see no drifting gold.

Therefore I ask your help, though falling towers
hammer and ring about you, though the street
only reflects your weariness and tars
your mind with darkness like my own at night.

Is all our quiet gone? Have we no time
to drive the dark invader from our sight,
or must we now admit that we are tame?

[1] *The White Knight*, 1944.

E

Actually I was incorrect in the interpretation I placed on it. 'The dark invader' who must be driven 'from our sight' was not Hitler's cohorts but personal depression, while the last line merely expressed the thought that we were 'tame' or craven if we allowed circumstances to triumph over spirit and imagination. It was, in other words, a plea for maintaining the supremacy of mind.

On another plane, however, the poem did appear prophetic, at least as far as Jack was concerned. On Jack's twenty-first birthday in October 1940, Nick Moore gave a party for him at which he met Amalia Edita Fleischerova, a Jewish Czechoslovakian girl who had come to this country as a refugee, her mother having died in the gas chamber at Auschwitz. He fell in love with her almost immediately and they were married at the Cambridge Register Office the following June. This new affinity led him to feel more closely with Hitler's victims in Europe, and he eventually volunteered for the R.A.F., though he was not called up until 1942. But when he wrote the poem, as he told me afterwards, no such ideas were in his mind.

Wherever Jack's subconscious thoughts were turning when he penned this piece (and he experienced much unease at the ending of the phoney war and the unleashing of the *Blitzkrieg*), I was not minded to change my status. At the end of a dark indefinite tunnel, there glimmered an aperture of light – the far-off image of post-war society. It was on this that my hopes were fixed. I felt I must prepare myself – by reading, writing, talking and thinking – for that future epiphany. Social, political and philosophical blueprints must be drawn up, canvassed and examined. This, admittedly, was not heroic; but all the virtues, such as I have, are of a contemplative order. If such contribution was but a poor thing, it was the only one I could usefully make. When, on the other hand, Jack made his decision, I honoured him for it; it seemed, in the context of his marriage, both a logical and right thing to do.

A day or two after my twenty-second birthday, our Company moved south to Virginia Water. We were billeted in what had been the Prince of Wales's favourite golf club at Wentworth, and our task was to aid in the construction of large underground offices intended for use if Whitehall were abandoned.

Both my personal and cultural life now seemed to promise a lively change. Some fifteen miles or so away in Osterley was Dorothy Chandler, a girl with whom I had had an intermittent romance since my early teens. Then in camp things started picking up. We organized debates, discussions, readings, concerts, sing-songs and carol parties. One day our Major (an ex-cavalry man and a Hatton Garden diamond merchant) sent for me to Company Office. A Jew, with that Jewish sense of publicity, he thought it a pity not to make the most of our Company's talents. If he could hardly sell his charges as grade A warriors when he dined at neigh-bouring houses or messes, at least he could boast about our brains. What was needed, he said, to put us on the map was a Company magazine. He declared he would arrange to have it well printed and distributed to shops in the neighbouring Thames-side towns.

Since the Major appointed me editor, it was decided I should join the dining-room staff, my position behind the serving-table being highly conducive, he believed, to my function as talent-spotter. So there I was whacking out great loads of mashed potatoes, creamed swedes or 'duff', the while I peered with anxious eye at all the hungry faces that passed, in the hope of detecting appetite of a more intellectual order. An editor requires an assistant editor, so I was joined at the orderly table by my friend John Bate – later to join a Bomb Disposal unit, to edit the magazine *Oasis* and to land up as librarian and lecturer of Napier College, Edinburgh, and author of a useful students' guide, *How to Find Out about Shakespeare* (1968).

John, at the serving-table, looked like a Shelley in dirty denims. Armed with a ladle, he could be seen staring into the porridge dixie as if he glimpsed Utopia beneath the oaten mixture. As a server, he was hardly popular. Liberal as were his helpings, they were deposited too erratically, and not a few breakfasters received on their boots the ration intended for their plates. Remonstrated with, John would reply with the utmost mildness of demeanour: 'I'm dreadfully sorry, my dear fellow, I was thinking.' So we put him on to serving friend bread. He made less of a mess on the floor with that. As my editorial number one, however, he was all a harassed talent-spotter could have asked for; and, no doubt, helped to sweeten my own acerbities and prejudices.

Of all the faces filing past me, whose owners were to contribute to the magazine, I will name only three: Michael Gough, the actor, who combined an aesthetic appearance with rumbustious behaviour; Michael Hewlett (nephew of the historical novelist Maurice Hewlett) who was later to enter the Church; and Christopher Fry the dramatist. It was Mike Hewlett (who hailed from Shipton-under-Wychwood where his father was the vicar and where Christopher Fry had just gone to live) who tipped me off about Fry. Up to that time Fry had published very little, though he was known in the world of the theatre. He had directed the Tunbridge Wells Repertory Players and put in a spell at the Oxford Playhouse. His first drama *Youth and the Peregrines*, written at the age of seventeen, had seen the light of day at Tunbridge, being presented on the same evening as the première of Bernard Shaw's *A Village Wooing* which Fry had secured for the company. Besides this 'modern comedy with a strong vein of fantasy' he had written a chronicle play about Dr Barnardo and a pageant play *The Tower* for the Tewkesbury Festival. Of all this dramatic activity, however, only one feature had become print – a verse play, *The Boy with a Cart*, written in the village of Colmans Hatch and later enacted in the grounds of the Bishop of Chichester's Palace. Recognized by Gerald Hopkins, a literary adviser with Oxford University Press, it was published by them in 1939. Not being a man of the theatre myself, I was lucky to have Mike Hewlett to put me in the picture about Christopher, who had arrived with a fresh intake.

I asked him how I should recognize Fry. 'Oh, you couldn't mistake him,' Mike assured me. 'A little man as brown as a nut.' This description fitted perfectly. Christopher was good-looking, of shortish stature but well proportioned. Dark, too, he certainly was, with that almost Phoenician darkness sometimes to be found in people from the west of England. He was born in Bristol, and I wondered if Carthaginian merchants, trading in Cornwall in pre-Roman times, had contributed anything to his stock. As to his height, when I got to know him better and realized the calibre of his work, I could not but think of the story of David and Goliath – a David whose exactly aimed words struck their target with tremendous impact. There was such a quiet compact force in him, such a conscious undissipated purpose, that it was hard to be with him without registering its presence.

Christopher was a friendly man, a man of goodwill. He was well liked by a circle of his friends and respected by those who were merely acquaintances. I remember him willingly taking a hand in amateur Company concerts, tap-dancing and singing cabaret songs, one or two of which were his own compositions. Within our small khaki confines, he was soon made a section-leader, wearing the additional bright button on the sleeve of his tunic. A section-leader, in our non-combatant world, was something rather like a prefect, and prefects, of course, come in many different sizes. Christopher Fry was not one of the 'hearty' species, who were much better represented by his friend Michael Hewlett. Neither did he fall into that other camp: the self-advertising aesthetes with their cultivated affectations. Indeed, for a man of the stage, he was surprisingly untheatrical and this is perhaps the more surprising since his poetic comedies abound in finely rhetorical gesture; it was as if that spirit of panache was entirely absorbed by his work.

There was also another element which I learned to recognize in him, a special dimension of self-containment into which he could retreat from the stress and strain of collective living. There were Quakers in his family, and the Quaker cult of inner silence was obviously not alien to him. I remember how he once told me of a serious-minded aunt of his who used to read the Bible or *Pilgrim's Progress* to him when he was only a little boy. She was a good reader and made her recitation interesting. At the same time, she insisted that young Christopher kept perfectly quiet and remained on his chair without the slightest movement. Allowing for the tendency of small children to fidget, loll or screw themselves about, it must have proved a severe regimen for her one-man audience. Although Christopher enjoyed listening to her, he sometimes found himself becoming obsessed with the immobile state of his limbs. Then, very surreptitiously, he would try to flex a finger or wriggle a shoe-capped toe. It is a wonder that this enforced outer stillness did not spoil for him the charm of all calm inner control.

Well, I was fortunate. Christopher said he would let me have something for *Bless 'Em All*, as our magazine was to be called. Indeed, he was as good as his word, and this much-valued contri-

bution was all set to be published in our second issue. Why it never
appeared, I will now relate.

One Sunday morning, I was drinking a sherry in Dorothy
Chandler's house in Jersey Road, Osterley, having cycled over from
Virginia Water on a day pass. The first number of *Bless 'Em All*
had come out a day or two before and was already selling at W.
H. Smith's at Staines and at other shops in Chertsey, Sunningdale
and Egham. I had not brought a copy with me because I thought
the somewhat pungent 'men only' flavour of some of the pieces
might not commend itself to Dorothy's mother. As we sipped and
chatted, Charles, her father, skimming through the pages of a
paper whose patriotism professed itself chiefly through its
interest in abortion and sexual exposure, chanced on an article
which denounced *Bless 'Em All*. The writer described it as
seditious, defeatist and obscene, and asked that something be done
about it.

To take the last of these charges first, it was admittedly obscene,
but only in the mildest manner as would not offend a maiden aunt
at a T.V. showing today. It was merely a case of giving the troops
what they wanted – what they expected. And what they got was
very bromided. Writing under the pseudonym TOM CAT, Mike
Gough had concluded an imaginary letter with a pun on our location 'Yours till Virgins Water'. There was really little more than
things like that. As for the seditious element, that again was inno-
cent enough. A news item by Mike Hewlett was apparently what
was disturbing the Press:

The following communiqué was issued by the Air Ministry
late last night:

'There was no bombing on either side on the 24th and 25th
December. In the morning of Christmas Day a squadron of
Seraphim, believed to be British, was seen flying very high in
the direction of a north-western city. Cherubim were sent up
to intercept, and a good time was had by all. Later in the day a
mass formation of Angels came over in waves, and was heard
singing: "Glory to God in the highest, and on earth peace, good
will towards men." One of the Angels, who made a forced
landing over the Wheatsheaf [our local pub] owing to a strained
pinion, was arrested by the Home Guard and subsequently

interned, on the ground of singing subversive slogans pre-
judicial to the war effort.'

I suppose my short sketch 'Armistice' might conceivably have
been considered defeatist (though in a moral not a military sense).
I had, at least, intended it as an impression rather than a piece of
propaganda.

Dorothy's father glanced questioning at me, and I replied that
it was all nonsense, all a huge joke, and would be good for sales.
When I got back to the camp, however, and was drinking cider in
the canteen, the only sergeant who disliked me assured me I should
be in the Bloody Tower tomorrow; and other well-wishers or indifferent members among the N.C.O.s looked grave.

Next morning, as I was taking down the blackout shutters in the
men's mess, the Major stamped in and accosted me in a bluff but
not unfriendly fashion. 'Stanford, you've put me in the shit all
right.' He then showed me a letter from the War Office, together
with a form which he had to fill in, asking what disciplinary steps
had been taken against the editor. 'A load of bumf, of course,'
he remarked, 'but I'm afraid it's put pot to *Bless 'Em All.*' Later
in the day, a jeep from Whitehall arrived to take away all copies
we had, all proof sheets, typescripts and material selected for the
second number. Surreptitiously I managed to retain certain of the
more interesting items, including Fry's contribution.

For myself, I did not mourn the passing of *Bless 'Em All.* It had,
for me, been a bit of fun, not to be taken seriously. In a letter to
Jack Bayliss I had described it as the 'resultant offspring of a
rendezvous with the Muse in a public urinal; lewd, illiterate,
localized and boorish'. The only person I felt sorry for was the
Major whose brain-child it had been, and who, from its inception
to its decease, had behaved so generously about it.

5

On Leave in Soho

Until the autumn of 1945 my life now became a sort of khaki–civvy street concerto, long stretches of army existence alternating with spells of leave or punctuated with the more poignant day or forty-eight-hour pass. Our Company wandered about the country engaged in a variety of tasks: demolition work in London, fire-watching in the Liverpool docks or loading wagons in a vast marshalling yard in preparation for the Second Front.

I had been put in charge of the men's mess and the mess orderlies, and promptly proceeded to organize them as a simple anarchist cell of good living. By this I mean that what I sought was not to indoctrinate them with anarchist ideas so much as to establish a climate of fraternal cooperation. 'Mutual aid' had been Prince Kropotkin's slogan, and the smallness of our numbers (varying from four to seven) made the group ideal for such practice. We used to tease the Company Office staff with being 'blancoed bureaucrats' since they wore battle-dress and gaiters while we worked in slippers and denims. Ourselves, we proclaimed, were 'functionaries' (not perhaps the best term since public servants are referred to thus), the intention being to distinguish between the paper-wallah and the practical performer – the red-tape merchant and the man who did things.

I seem to have looked on life in the Forces as a training ground for the New Society which I felt must follow after the war. Reconstruction was my keyword, and I would even terminate my letters with the phrase 'Reconstructively yours'. But it was, of course, time away from camp that counted most. In London, there were bookshops, parties, girls, poetry readings – all the fun of the fair.

I recall a Saturday afternoon at the Dick Shepherd Centre in Bayswater, listening to Herbert Read gently expounding the relationship between Existentialism and Anarchism. David Gascoyne sat quietly by the wall, replying only with a monosyllabic word or two when addressed. Later, when the meeting was over and I was waiting for a bus to Marble Arch, he glided past me like a ghost in cap and dark blue raincoat on his way to the tube station. I thought of him, on that sunny late autumn afternoon, as being like Orpheus descending into Pluto's kingdom by way of lift or stairs to underground darkness. Somehow his exit seemed to enact, in loose contemporary terms, these lines from his book *Holderlin's Madness* in which he portrayed Orpheus thus:

He sleeps with the broken lyre between his hands,
And round his slumber are drawn back
The rigid draperies, the tears and wet leaves,
Cold curtains of rock concealing the bottomless sky.

There was something of a sleepwalker, a *buveur de lune*, I decided, about Gascoyne; and some time later his poetry and his image were to mean even more to me than they did then.

Another Bayswater haunt was the International Arts Centre at 22 St Petersburgh Place, whose patrons included Stephen Spender, John Lehmann, John Piper and Sybil Thorndike; and I remember murky ramblings through the blacked-out streets in order to hear John Heath-Stubbs (another sacrificial figure though in what sense I hardly then surmised) recite his poetry by candlelight. There, too, I met Michael Hamburger, as melancholy as he was good-looking despite the recognition of his precocious talents as a translator.

Then there were the bookshops of Charing Cross Road, above all Zwemmer's, where the great Rudolph Friedmann presided. There one could stock up with volumes and magazines which were like a powerline to one's khaki outpost. Ruthven Todd, poet and art historian, acted as Friedmann's first lieutenant – a lieutenant whose superior officer played the martinet. When young writers on leave called in at Zwemmer's it was Ruthven they wanted to see; and there he would talk to them with his hands behind his back so that Friedmann would not notice that one of them held a cigarette. Smoking by the staff in the bookshop was rigorously forbidden. Cigarettes were not Ruthven's only problem. He suffered from stomach ulcers, but claimed to have 'burnt them out' with whisky and brandy.

A tall dandified figure in a blue striped suit, Friedmann was a culture snob of the deepest water. One commentator of the period has described him as 'meditating, handling the books carefully, lovingly, a man of books who hates the vandal, the goth, the destroyer of delicate book-jackets.'[1] I recall how one day while visiting his shop, a lower-middle-class mother came in to enquire whether Zwemmer's stocked any books for children about trains. 'Books about trains?' intoned the princely Friedmann. 'Books about pysch-Ology, phil-Osophy, the-Ology; but books about trains for children, no, madam. Over the road to Foyle's.'

Was it, perhaps, his webbed fingers – and hence his civilian status – which made him sometimes emulate the manners of an Army officer? Unlike most wartime intellectuals, Friedmann was a staunch right-winger and a respected luminary of the Surbiton Conservative Club. There was a certain glacial aspect to him which made it difficult for him to form or preserve relationships. In a little book on Kierkegaard that he wrote at the end of the war, he undoubtedly analysed himself, under the guise of the great Soren, as a schizoid personality. Muriel Spark featured him as Baron Stock, a piece of paronomasia, in her novel *The Comforters*. Some time in the late 'sixties or early 'seventies he took his own life.

So far I have not mentioned the part that the London pubs played in cementing the life of servicemen with the continuing life of art and letters. This has been done so well by Maclaren Ross in his book of stories *The Nine Men of Soho* (1946) as well as in his *Memoirs of the Forties* (1965) that most of what I could say would be a flat précis of it. And like the narrator in those tales, there was Maclaren every night propping up the counter of the Wheatsheaf in Rathbone Place. Accoutred in camelhair overcoat with a silver-topped cane in his hand, he was present whatever the season or

[1] Charles Wrey Gardiner, *The Dark Thorn*, 1946.

weather, whatever the year, all through the war; and on every single leave I took, I never failed to find him there.

In those days, I carried a snuffbox but never dared offer the paltry thing to Monsignor Maclaren whose own, I felt sure, must be pure Georgian. Not that I found him at all unfriendly. He seemed to me one of those people who are genuinely kind and approachable behind their armour of affectation. During the first three years of the war I had published nothing save in 'little magazines' but when my essay on Percy Wyndham Lewis appeared in *The Fortune Anthology*, in which one of his own short stories 'Five Finger Exercises' was printed, he congratulated me on my piece in the most genial fashion. This from a man with fiction published in *Horizon* and *English Story* was the very sweetest ambrosia of encouragement. Then there was the storyist Fred Urquhart, as fair as Maclaren was dark, who was also a part of the Soho circuit. Fred, in fact, might have been described as a sort of Maclaren in dialect, doing for the Scottish scene, and for his bouncing land-girls, prisoners-of-war and odd characters north of the Border, what Maclaren was doing for the *demi-monde*, the bohemians, the servicemen on leave in London.

I remember clearly one of his tales called 'The Matinee' which appeared in *Scottish Short Stories* (1943). A boy of fourteen gets back into his shorts in order to get in half-price at the cinema. He takes his young brother with him so that if he gets a lucky number with his ticket (for which prizes are given) he can send him up to receive it. When the main film comes up, the boy sits fascinated. His little brother wants to go to the lavatory and doesn't know where it is. The boy refuses to take him and makes him sit it out. At the end of the programme he has drawn a prize with the lucky number on his ticket, but his little brother cannot go and fetch it since he has thoroughly wet himself. Fred was a wonderful mimic, and after he had impersonated someone, he would roll his eyes up to the ceiling in a gesture that paid tribute to human stupidity and pretension. When the war came to an end, he and a friend founded a literary agency oddly entitled Windsor Towers.

But not all the denizens of that district were as agreeable as Maclaren or Fred (and Maclaren himself was resented by many who were jealous of his grand manner). There was one, a noted artistic illustrator, who had a nasty gambit all his own. This was to

wander the pitchblack streets of Soho and lie in wait under cover
of some doorway. When the chosen victim came by, he would step
out and ask for a light; as the passer stopped and fumbled
for matches or lighter, he would be hit over the head with a small
hammer specially carried for that purpose. No theft or further
assault was attempted, and what satisfaction the nut-with-a-hammer
derived from his actions nobody knew. As this was before the
days when fixers prowled the West End like jackals, his delin-
quency was all the stranger.

In those wartime days, the pubs of Soho were the young intellectual's club. It was there he might expect to meet friends who had
come on leave suddenly without time to notify him, or who were
enjoying the pleasure of an unlooked-for short pass. And there,
too, rank counted for nothing, pips or stripes being forgotten in
the freemasonry of art and letters. Pubs, like parties, were also
places where one made fresh acquaintances. It was easy to
recognize the likely type. There at a table might be seated a young
second-lieutenant with a pint of wallop beside him. Then came
the give-away feature. Beside the beer was a book or magazine,
either of which he might actually be reading. It was this non-
Sandhurst note which bespoke a sprig of the Muse in disguise;
and I recall so encountering in the Swiss, one sunny winter
morning, the young dramatist James Forsyth who was then writing
a play in verse.

The York Minster (the 'French pub'), the Helvetia and the
Fitzroy were other essential ports of call – Villonesque taverns
where we held court. Nor must I forget that curious institution
the Coffee An' (abbreviation for 'coffee and . . . ?') approached by a passage off Flitcroft Street between St Giles Church
and Charing Cross Road. Here, in the late 'thirties, one might well
chance to be present at a punch-up between Mosleyites and Com-
mies, who attested zeal from their respective causes in this way,
especially on Saturday nights. With Oswald's followers in the Isle
of Man, such occasions for fisticuffs were considerably reduced,
but the bohemian criminal underworld still did its best to keep
things lively.

The Coffee An' was an irreplaceable refuge. There was
nearly always room at some table dotting the spacious floor, and

Boris's food was the cheapest in Soho. In this den of thieves and poets, there appeared two incongruous reminders of Jesus Christ. One was a large wall-painting depicting Him on the cross, all actors in the drama being kitted out in contemporary dress. Instead of the high priests, the artist had given us black-coated capitalists complete with money bags, while the Roman centurions and legionaries were represented by booted Nazis with breeches and armbands. Somewhat strangely, they also wore gas masks.

The other reminder was a figure who sat in a wheel-chair, a blanket covering his legs – a handsome long-faced man with fine eyes and flowing beard, but pale and dreadfully emaciated. I thought he bore a distinct resemblance to the notable spiritualist scholar F. W. H. Myers who himself might well have stood for a nineteenth-century interpretation of an Italian Renaissance Christ. But if his appearance suggested this, the small duplicated newsletter he peddled accorded somewhat oddly with the holy image. If I remember, it was called *Soho Weekly*, and was largely a neighbourhood news-sheet purveying fact and rumour concerning the denizens of the district. One column reported on certain local ladies then in hospital – a useful tip, I suppose one could say, as to past or present serviceability.

Later, when I returned after the war, I found the Coffee An' had become a machinists' workroom and warehouse.

From Jack Bayliss came the news that Russell Clarke's stay in the R.A.F. was blessedly to be short. Of this I was glad, even plain envious. 'His mood', I wrote to Jack, 'was always too moon-mild for his present environment. You and I who have often worn the mask can accommodate ourselves better, whereas the single soul is beaten.'

Soon, at 34 Priory Road, Bedford Park, Russell was throwing open his doors in a series of high-spirited parties. What matter that the house lacked a bathroom (despite its being built by Sir Norman Shaw) and was possessed of a ghost in the attic, the generous drink our host provided made us all boldly spirit-proof!

Russell, the mini-Maecenas of our group, had already sponsored a little booklet *Call Wind to Witness*, a 'Quartet of Romantic Poets' which was published by him 'at the sign of the Capriole,

34 Priory Road, Chiswick, W.4'. This contained verse by Jack Bayliss, Alan Lewis, Emmanuel Litvinoff and Charles Hamblett, with a prose introduction by me. Campaigning as I always was in those days for 'a United Romantic Front', I struck off a thumbnail definition of what made poets romantic. They were, I declared, those 'who seek behind authority for a personal law that should serve them as home; poets who gainsay the spoken word, the herd testament of the common hour; poets who record the age at its turn'. Such a statement of intransigent individualism was, I suppose, fair enough as far as it went. Certainly it reflected the predicament of the 'free spirit' in the straitjacket of Forces life.

To come to one of Russell's parties after having been 'cribbed, cabined and confined' was an emancipating experience. As the front door opened, one would be met by a great gust of music, ballet or jazz or straight dance numbers, from a record-player, an exhilarating aphrodisiac. Russell had the kindly habit of presenting me at the evening's beginning with a half-bottle of rum. This was my current favourite, and the bottle represented my basic ration. Russell used to call me 'our South American agent' because of my appearance at that time; and I sustained the Spanish connection by calling the drink I had invented (a combination of rum and cider) Toreador's Tipple. Perhaps it was partly because of the glow of this liquid sunlight inside me that the memory of those I met at Russell's parties was always so genially vivid.

Whenever Jack Bayliss and I could manage to synchronize our leaves, we did so. He was now married to Lia, a pretty, fair-haired endearing creature who became my trusted confidante. One source of happiness in life springs from the degree in which we are able to impose our personal myths on to reality. Now Jack had always been in search of what I called his 'gold princess', a blonde girl of fairy build, not too firmly of the earth earthy. In Lia he seemed to have discovered this Platonic original; willow-slim, foreign and supple, with hair like sunlight on the running corn. Friendships often end with a marriage. In Lia I secured another friend, and gaiety, laughter and fantasy illumined those early days when we three met together. From the 'sixties onwards, she was often a sick woman, and she died with tragic suddenness in 1966, just before Christmas.

A couple to whom Jack and Lia introduced me at one of Russell's parties were the artists Ithell Colquhoun and Toni del Renzio. Ithell, who later became noted for her Celtic and occult lore, was then painting Surrealist pictures, while Toni, though he also painted, was more of an ideas man. His own Surrealist magazine *Arson* was conducted in a spirit of what I believe he called 'incendiary innocence'. It was certainly a fiery-hearted affair, as the following editorial note from its first and only number makes fully evident:

It was the middle of March that saw blossom some of the finest flowers of the Roman revolutionary tree, the assassins of Caesar. It is not without significance that this month, the first of the old Roman Kalendar, should witness in 1942 the appearance of a *spectral review*, glowing with its own light. It is a Surrealist review, testimony of a vital life lived among the ruins not only of bombed houses but of exploited people.

Its contributors are alight, ignited by the spontaneous combustion of the imagination's flaming spectres. They are violent, ardent and without humility. Above all, they are combustible. Their eyes shine in the dark, projecting the living beams of their own

ARSON

The same page carried a chain of dedications to members of the Surrealist movement, scattered by the war, throughout the world. In the last it named four dear departed: 'Sade, Rimbaud, Lautréamont and Lenin in the concentration camps of heaven.'

All this might truly be accounted an example of higher-prose bombast; but the magazine had some first-rate contributions (Nicolas Calas, Robert Melville, Pierre Mabile, Conroy Maddox, Giorgio de Chirico and an interview with Breton). Toni, too, was a man of parts; and when the temperature of his writing was lowered, his skill in the manipulation of ideas and his wide reading became evident. He was also a mystery man. Even after her marriage to him, Ithell could never establish his origins. He spoke of being related to the Romanoffs – a fondness for aristocratic connections being no uncommon thing among the revolutionary Surrealists. He also claimed to be the Count del Renzio; but when, after the war, he and Ithell travelled to Italy, the ancestral estates were not to be discovered. Had they been confiscated or were they part of the Surrealist dream?

Ithell also was an exotic figure, though her credentials were perfectly valid. Born in Assam and artistically the product of the Slade and Paris, she was *petite*, with large bright eyes in her small head with its page-boy bobbed hair. It was these eyes with her colourful way of dressing – she would not infrequently wear a *sari* – which led to my forming an image of her as some twilight-hovering pollen-sipping moth.

They had, in those mid-wartime days, a studio with its living quarters in a gallery surrounding the ground floor at 45A Fairfax Road, just round the corner from Russell's. Here I would sometimes stay the night after a party or junketing. Mobiles were to me then strange contraptions which I thought of as 'dingle-dangles', and flashing my torch from a mattress on the floor, I would catch these slight-stirring aerial toys as in a searchlight amid the general blackout.

Nor were these the only attraction in that odd artistic hangar. One of Ithell's pictures, which I never tired of regarding, depicted a naked standing male figure. From every high point and opening of the body radiated out in circling curves a line of of circling astral force completely surrounding the man. The colouring was rainbow bright, and the effect of the picture as a whole was both extremely sensuous and ethereal.

A true Lenin of the arts, Toni, like most ideologists, found it difficult to square the claims of doctrine and the demands of reality. Thus when he wished to marry Ithell he may have wondered whether this was not a reactionary and bourgeois thing to do. Love fortunately found a way by giving him a phrase (from Engels, I believe) which would hold the scorn of the *avant-garde* at bay. To be united in 'revolutionary monogamy' was obviously a permitted thing to do.

I much preferred Ithell, and found her most attractive; but could well understand how she felt drawn to Toni in their first years together. He was tall, well-made, and looked Gallicly fetching in a sort of matelot's striped vest which he favoured. When not being supercilious and contemptuous of English culture in general (and I very much suspect he was at least partly English), he was an interesting talker from whom I departed stimulated. It was he who introduced me to Nicolas Calas, a Greek Surrealist critic living in the United States. Reading his essays in *Confound the Wise* (an American edition which Toni lent me) I found myself provoked to challenge almost every declaration made. Thus, when Calas wrote that he affirmed 'without the slightest hesitation, that poetry *begins* with the transformation of the Parthenon into an arsenal and *ends* with the blood of Marat spilt by Charlotte Corday', I was led to affirm the opposite. Calas's own theory that art is consummated only in action incited me, some few years later, to attempt the adumbration of an anarchist aesthetic in which the aesthetic and political elements both received a freer, libertarian treatment.

Some time after the war, Toni and Ithell were divorced, and I lost track of him. For a while he was a luminary of the Institute of Contemporary Arts, and wrote the earlist article I recall on the revival of Charles Rennie Mackintosh. Later, at the end of the 'sixties, he published in Wimbledon a book on the Flower Children. From my earliest knowledge of him, I expected he would occupy more of the limelight.

Another face I would see at Russell's was that of Charles Hamblett who, like his host, had seen the inside of the R.A.F. establishment before being returned to civvy street. Charles then had a job at *Tribune*, working in its picture library and writing articles in its book pages in support of the Neo-Romantic cause. I had first met him at Cambridge when he contributed short stories to *Granta* which earned him the name of the Viennese Damon Runyon, being partly central European by birth. On a cold winter's morning, I had been hugging the fire in Jack Bayliss's rooms at St Catherine's when Charles knocked at the door. He seemed a little bemused – he had, as he pointed out, been drinking – and remarked to me in a rather puzzled fashion: 'You're not John Bayliss.'

I admitted this, and introduced myself. He told me he had just hitch-hiked from Newmarket, where he lived. Like myself, he was not a member of the university; but having attended the Cambridge College of Art and Technology, now came to deliver his copy, pick up books for review and drink with his pals. Charles

F

had fair wavy hair and suggested a strange amalgam of the Duke
of Windsor (when Prince of Wales), a young Austrian cavalry
officer and an early edition of the poet Rilke. He had a fund of
enthusiasm, a loquacious manner and the ghost of a stammer. In
all, I found him an attractive friend, keen to advance his own
interests and those of writers whose work impressed him. Like the
clever journalist he was, Charles had a flair for recognizing new
growing points in society and culture. I was always overjoyed
to see how he would invariably quote just those phrases which
seemed to me most telling in some review or article I had written.
A friendship on those terms could hardly go wrong.

At Russell's, Charles would turn up with the beautiful
Jacqueline Stanley, who had once been Tambimuttu's wife. Possessed of long gold hair, falling in heavy rivers from the crown
of her head (that head which her friends described as egglike),
Jackie had flawless smooth pink cheeks, full lips and large blue
eyes; the total impression being one of voluptuousness without
carnality. With all this beauty and a natural social ease, Jackie was
cursed with diabetes, from which she died while still young. She
left a tiny scattering of poems, with two or three published in
little magazines. Charles, one of the poets represented in
Russell's anthology *Call Wind to Witness*, had written a piece
which spoke of their love-making in an air-raid :

> When horror stalks these rooms and floorboards rock,
> Your fear is lost in mine, becomes my strength;
> Let the ceiling fall across my heart
> Beating for you, beating only for love;
> Let the moon-cooled branches scream
> As babe eyes, filmed with golden laughter, guide
> Dark treasures to my branded lips and fill
> My open pulse with blood.[1]

The experience must be one that rings a bell with many; and was
there not, too, that fine old popular saying : 'Then you can take me
out and shoot me.'

How one recalls trivial happenings concerning those we have
known who are dead! One sunny summer evening, Jack Bayliss,

[1] 'Bun' Brene, *A Cactus Harvest*, 1946.

Lia, Charles, Jackie and myself were strolling down Hammer-smith Mall bound for the tavernous comforts of the Dove. Jackie and Lia sauntered ahead, while Charles walked between Jack and me, his arms lightly thrown over our shoulders. Charles, who was much enamoured of her, winked to signify his sporting intention, and exclaimed so that she should hear: 'Look at little Jackie waggling her bum.' Without a moment's loss and without looking round, Jackie's retort came back: 'And look at little Charlie hugging his boys.'

Charles and Jackie had split up before her death. Jackie began to complain that he returned later and later in the evening, and very often drunk. In return for this treatment, she took to party-going on her own; and her admirers at one time included Alan Ross, Vernon Scannell, and the Oriental writer and lawyer Subramanian. One day, some months after Charles had last seen her, he was drinking with Tambimuttu at the Hog in the Pound in Oxford Street when the latter informed him with oriental fatal-ism that Jackie was dead and had been lain to rest in Highgate Cemetery. Charles was knocked sideways by the news, but Tambi assured him he would have a Rolls and they would go to pay their respects to her together. As it turned out, the Rolls was just another of Tambi's pipe dreams. But the thought, they say, is every-thing.

After Jackie, there was Joanna. She would play a very individual game when we were all out walking together. Each of us had to take turns, spitting up into the air while the rest sought to avoid its descent. She claimed this a good warming sport in winter.

Another incident concerning Charles also springs to mind. Rayner Heppenstall, who had once been a member of the Com-munist Party, had just written an essay about his life in the Artillery with the provocative title 'I am not in favour of the Working Classes'. Screwing his monocle into his eye, as he stood on the floor of the Wheatsheaf, Charles jabbed the offending article and proclaimed it to be in 'very bad taste'. There was an assumption of angry hauteur about his words which I found most amusing. Here was Charles, with his aristocratic air, censuring Rayner, whose origins were impeccably working-class, for satirizing the proletariat. Indeed, his disapproval of the essay was very like that of some old-fashioned colonel who had found a subaltern reading *Das Kapital* in the mess. Of course, in the cultural climate of the 'seventies, I may well be accused of bad taste for even presenting this paradox.

At the end of the war, Charles wrote a moving elegy for all its many dead :

> Some flew on the singing suns of morning
> Some drowned to the music of day-break on a reef
> Others sleep in the sweet corn soil
> *They are your daily bread.*[1]

He, too, is now part of that communion. His death in the spring of 1975 came as a great shock to me, not only on account of the affection I bore him but because of the unusual circumstances in which it occurred. I had not seen him for over a year, though we had corresponded. Having written to him in March, I was surprised one day to hear the voice of Joanna, his first wife, on the phone. She told me he was out of the country, and that she was going in two days' time to join him in New York and furnish an apartment for them both. After being divorced for twenty-five years, she and her much-married Charles were coming together again.

The next thing I heard, about two weeks later, was a report in the *Evening Standard* that Sarah Churchill had been held up in the completion of her autobiography since Charles Hamblett, who was helping her with it, had died suddenly. I wrote to Joanna but received no reply. I suspect that dear Charles had been hitting the bottle, as he was prone to do from time to time, but I had no idea he was anywhere near his end. He was a well-prized, hard-working journalist employed by the Independent Publishing Company, and had made a name for himself as a Hollywood biographer, publishing several books on the stars. His real love, however, continued to be poetry, which he continued writing to the end, a number of which late fruits I possess.

I should like to think that he will be remembered by students of the period for his anthology of the Second World War poetry entitled *I Burn for England* (1966) which contains five of his own poems. In a characteristic introduction he made the sort of state-

[1] 'Requiem', *The Cactus Harvest*, 1946.

ment about poetry which causes Dr Leavis's hackles to rise and is accordingly worth quoting:

Poetry is, in any case, a kind of lunacy. It attracts misfits, arouses prejudices, creates controversy, influences drunkards, consoles cowards, humbles the pompous, pricks the proud, lubricates lovers, soothes widows, baffles duffers, inspires sermons, bamboozles bank managers, turns tea to wine, breaks ice, levels social barriers, and is readily understood by mariners, fliers and soldiers on midnight sentry-go. . . . You can lock up the fools who write it, but you will never stop people from reading it.

In this same introduction, he relates a meeting with the poet Alan Lewis which seems to me to express a great part of what we were all then feeling:

Alan Lewis telephoned me. He was in transit through London. We met briefly in an A.B.C. restaurant. Over tea and buns we maintained an almost complete silence. We had corresponded. There was nothing we could add to our tragic intuitions of the world in which we were playing out our lives. We paid the waitress and on the pavement shook hands. We noticed, and knew the other had noticed, that we were close to tears.

In 1973 we had tentatively planned *A Festschrift for the Forties*, with contributions from that period's survivors. Charles had even taken it up with his publishers, W. H. Allen, but they had said 'All in good time. Let's have your next Hollywood hero first.' Charles was worldly wise and knew where his own interests lay; but always there was that siren voice beckoning him back to highbrow semi-bankruptcy – a temptation he must have found hard to resist. That same year he had written to me: 'Despite my flashy writing about the stars, my astronomical eye is increasingly fixed on the poets and philosophers.'

In a world where we wrestle with the fleshpots for success, it is hard to preserve the faculty of wonder, something born in childhood and nourished by inactive meditation. Charles had kept it, however, along with his irrepressible relish for life. 'I am

basically unchanged but have achieved greater clarity,' he wrote to
me in May 1973.

> It's quite strange and wonderful the way life is moving along, a
> constant movie show which still has me on occasion gripping
> the sides of my seat. Today is the wedding anniversary of my
> third marriage and I'm surrounded by strange brilliant children
> I have spawned.

For me, it was this conjunction of worldliness and wonder which
made Charles so attractive a personality. His sophistication was
more than skin deep. When he died he was in the process of writing
The Confessions of a Professional Names-Dropper, a book of
reminiscences from which I should dearly have liked to pilfer.

Months after I had written this account, and while I was awaiting proofs of my book, I was called upon to add a postscript of
even sadder nature to Charles's story.

I was lunching in the Strand at the old Gaiety, now a little
Italian restaurant, with Jack Bayliss, Wrey Gardiner and Denys
Val Baker – up from his hidy-hole in Cornwall for a medical
check. I had told him and his wife Jess, the previous May, about
Charles's death when we met in Bristol for the annual get-to-
gether of the West Country Writers' Association. Now, on the
name of Charles's first wife Joanna being mentioned, and with my
bemoaning the fact that I had not heard from her after her promise
to write, I learnt the tragic tail-end of Charles's matrimonial saga.

Denys and his wife knew Joanna and her daughter, because
they had lived near them in Cornwall. They had not seen the
daughter Caroline for some time, but when they encountered her it
was to learn of Joanna's despairing end. Within three weeks of
my hearing from Joanna that she was flying out to join Charles in
New York he was dead. The culminating stroke followed swiftly.
Joanna had phoned her daughter in England, telling her she was
booked in to some New York hotel (whose name she refused to
give) and that she was about to take an overdose of sleeping pills.
Charles's death, she said, had been too much for her. She could
not go on living.

6

The White Horseman

But for all the intermittent sweetness of such infrequent company, I and my friends in the Forces were mostly sustained by what we read. When the long or short goodbyes had been gone through, it was only books and magazines, not friends or girls, one could take back to camp. It was certainly easier to study while doing a stint of service than to compose anything save the briefest pieces. I remember Christopher Fry, at Pershore in the early summer of 1941, going down during a period off duty to the banks of the Avon with the manuscript of his tragedy *The Firstborn*, which he was then struggling to write. He left in no elevated mood, and returned even more dispirited. When I asked him how much he had written, he said, one sentence but he didn't like that much either and would probably take it out. Wilde could speak with affected levity of spending a whole afternoon in the placing and removal of a comma, but Christopher was near to despair. Even so, the play somehow progressed; and one act of it got staged at a Y.M.C.A. in Blundellsands when we went to Liverpool for fire-watching in the docks.

So whether we read for entertainment, for information and instruction, or even with a definite view of nourishing our own writing, it was an easier way of spending time than getting down to writing itself. During my five years in khaki, I must have filled some thirty-odd notebooks with extracts copied from the books I was reading. To these I pretentiously affixed a generic title: 'Cells for a Future Synthesis' (C.F.F.S. for short). The content of some of these cells I will now try to recall.

Of all periodical publications of the 1940s, none was so commercially successful as Penguin New Writing. But among the younger generation of Neo-Romantic writers, it was not all that welcome. The reasons for this were twofold: first, it was associated with the Social Realist movement of the 'thirties; secondly, and more to the point, it did not often print their work when they were most in need of publication. After they had become established (at the end of the war) it opened its doors to them somewhat too late to earn our gratitude. Ideological and economic factors thus combined to create a minority Opposition Front to New Writing's Left Establishment.

So far was this dislike of Social Realism carried that I remember it influencing a plan that Jack Bayliss and I had to publish a volume of selected stories of the 1890s. We intended to include tales by Crackanthorpe, Dowson, George Moore, George Egerton and others, and I noted that such a volume 'would serve to illustrate the contrast between the Individual Realism of that time and the Socialist Realism of the 'thirties, helping to weigh the scales against all that Left-wing reportage by firemen, engine-drivers, miners and navvies'. As it happened, we never completed our selection; and when I did publish such a volume (Stories of the 90's) in 1968, the dichotomy I had earlier envisaged found no place in my Introduction.

It was to Reginald Moore's Modern Reading that we looked for active support. Moore printed work by us as well as by a wide range of highly individual authors to whom we were sympathetic: the fine American subjectivists Henry Miller, Anais Nin, Conrad Aiken; such older romanticists as Lord Dunsany; and such unclassifiable talents as Jack Clemo, Rhys Davies, Michael McLaverty and Oswell Blakeston.

Then, too, there was Life and Letters which, through the welcome extended by its editor Robert Herring, became the nearest thing to a Neo-Romantic periodical we were able to find. It was Robert Herring who printed one or two closely guarded poems by Christopher Fry which Jack and I had channelled to him. An apprehensive perfectionist, Christopher had a small stock of verse that we were always urging him to release; but only occasionally were we successful.

Other magazines of smaller scope and magnitude were George Woodcock's *Now*, in whose pages anarchist and pacifist factions fought out a long battle, the former at length emerging victorious; John Waller's *Kingdom Come*, associated with the contributors to *Eight Oxford Poets*; Neville Braybrooke's *The Wind and the Rain*, a Catholic and liberal periodical started by him while still a boy at Ampleforth; and John Atkins's shortlived *New Saxon*, another manifestation of 'the anti-materialistic renaissance'. Through John's position as literary editor of *Tribune*, that journal was also then favourable to us. Then there was Denys Val Baker's small publication *Opus*, to be followed later by the larger *Voices*. Finally, at the end of the war, came Kay Dick's *The Windmill*, a spacious periodical as became its Heinemann imprint.

Over in the United States the Neo-Romantic poets were welcomed by the *Providence Sunday Journal* (whose editor was opposed to Auden) and the more lavish, well-illustrated, pan-Surrealist *View*, edited by Charles Henri Ford in New York. In 1940 we were even being published by the Japanese magazine *Vou*.

As much perhaps as these magazines, anthologies which ran to one or more numbers helped to define the climate of the time. The appearance of each one seemed to indicate fresh paths opening in the literary landscape; and if by chance today I happen on one such on secondhand shelves (especially if in its original wrappers) some of that pristine excitement comes back.

How well, for example, do I remember the yellow, black and green covers of *Lyra: a book of new lyric* edited by Alex Comfort and Robert Greacen, with a Preface by Herbert Read. It represented a combination of forces: that of the Ulster regional poets selected by Robert Greacen and that of the New English Romantics marshalled by that whizz kid Alex Comfort, a prodigy who had proved himself in the field of classics, poetry and medicine.

Herbert Read's Preface, in which he declared his own 'premonitions of a poetic renaissance', stimulated me critically as much as the poems between its covers appealed to me imaginatively. Read maintained that 'by the end of the Spanish Civil War, the poetry of action had fought in the last ditch. To put it another way, action had overtaken poetry, and a new front had become necessary.' This 'poetry of action' I took to be the verse-arm or wing of literary Marxism. If the shortsighted Marxist believed that it was action, triumphant action, which validated the arts, then the defeat of Marxist action in Spain, by their own logical argument, involved the defeat of that art which had been its propagandist expression. The propaganda of a defeated cause cannot claim the justification of art. As Auden himself had written – in a poem he later repudiated:

> History to the defeated
> may say alas but cannot help nor pardon.

The new poetry, Read seemed to suggest, would still be 'reconstructive' (a word he preferred to 'revolutionary'); but its reconstructive energy, its reconstructive vision, would proceed not from objective dogma but from subjective experience. It followed that a poem based on a dream, which the Social Realist might dismiss as escapist, could none the less be 'reconstructive' in its imaginative implications. Of the poets in *Lyra* Read wrote: 'They have realized that even in the midst of war this reconstructive effort must be made, and their poetry is therefore projected away from the immediate struggle into the new world which has to be created out of the ruins of our civilization.'

Of all the anthologies of the war period – and I think particularly of *Transformation* and *Crown and Sickle* – none can have proved so influential as *The White Horseman*, with its plum-coloured cloth covers and green spine. Edited by J. F. Hendry and Henry Treece and published in 1941 by Routledge, the subtitle proclaimed the book to be 'Prose and verse of the new apocalypse', while for an epigraph, the editors selected a passage from D. H. Lawrence:

> The rider on the white horse! Who is he, then? . . . He is the royal one, he is my very self and his horse is the whole MANA of a man. He is my very me, my sacred ego, called into a new cycle of action by the Lamb and riding forth to conquest, the conquest of the old self for a new self. It is he, truly, who shall conquer all the other 'powers' of the earth.[1]

[1] *Apocalypse*, 1932.

Turgid and repetitive as most of Lawrence is in his prophetic vein, it is clear why this passage appealed to the young writer under the lock and key of war. Despite appearances, it assured him that he possessed within himself something more potent than all the armed and hostile world outside. In a universe which reduced him to a number in a paybook, he could still believe his inner selfhood was more significant.

It was this notion of the essential self that led to the concern of these apocalyptic writers with myth and with the part which myth might play in the work of social integration.[1] Since the rise of rationalism, myth had seemed an element which we needed to reduce or destroy; but now that rationalism and its two offsprings, science and technology, as instruments of war, were themselves in jeopardy, it seemed that myth might prove to be not some replaceable illusion but rather a social adhesive, a communal fixative of positive value.

We all know about the myths of the past – Hercules the Strong or King Arthur the Just – but how, we might ask, are fresh myths of a valuable nature to be born? Clearly, there is no single answer, but the Apocalyptics and the Neo-Romantics believed that myth might emerge from imaginings or dreams on to the plane of social existence. Certain individual imaginings or dreams might contain within themselves seeds of collective significance, and works of art were one of the means by which these might be communicated at the social level. As Roland Barthes, the French semiologist, has written: 'Myth is a type of speech.'[2]

What Barthes next goes on to say helps to explain the difference between the creative starting point of the Social Realist and the Neo-Romantic writers. 'What must be firmly established at the start is that myth is a system of communication, that it is a message. This allows one to perceive that myth cannot possibly be an object, a concept, or an idea; it is a mode of signification, a form.' Now a dream, that most basic Romantic act, *is* 'a communication' (from the subconscious to the preconscious). It is, also, of course 'a signification'. The aim of Apocalyptic poetry could, then, be stated in the following formula: *Myth out of dream via work of art.* In contrast, one might say that the Social Realist writer obtains his

[1] J. F. Hendry, 'Myth and social integration', *The White Horseman*, 1941.
[2] *Mythologies*, 1973.

picture of the world not from some starting point in dream or imagining but in an act of intellection. The framework of society which his imagination inherits comes to him secondhand from *The Communist Manifesto* or *Das Kapital*. Somehow he must square the findings of his sensibility and the creative movements of his mind with the blueprints of doctrine to which he has assented. This is a simplified account, but does at least suggest two very contrary ways of working on a poem or story.

In his introductory essay 'Apocalypse in Poetry', G. S. Fraser sited the movement midway between Surrealism and Social Realism. It denied, he argued, the former's 'own denial of man's right to exercise conscious control . . . of the material offered to him as an artist by his subconscious mind', just as it repudiated the latter's acceptance of the control of consciousness in accordance with external principles (the dogma of Marxism).

The Apocalyptics were followed by a somewhat younger generation commonly spoken of as Neo-Romantics, and in their first collective manifestation in *The Fortune Anthology*, Jack Bayliss (one of its three editors) made much the same point as that stressed by Fraser. 'We proclaim', he wrote, 'that we are the representatives of the Centre Movement in literature.' Writings by 'Soldiers and C.O.'s, Catholics and atheists' were all welcome. This alliance between Christians and non-Christians sprang from what might losely be termed the antimaterialistic aspect of Neo-Romanticism. Writing in a personal diary about Russia, J. F. Hendry remarked that 'it is less likely that the Revolution occurred in Russia because Capitalism was weakest there, than because spiritual revolt from materialism was strongest there'.[1] The 'spiritual revolt' against materialism was an aspect of Neo-Romantic thought. It did not, however, believe that salvation from it was to be found in Communism, which it believed had merely substituted an economy of state capitalism for one run on *laissez-faire* lines.

It is amusing to reflect today that in rejecting an economic answer as the only operative way to salvation, the Neo-Romantics were now at one with the 'new born' American Christian Auden, once their most hated enemy.

[1] 'The Soldier's first entry', *Leaves in the Storm*, ed. S. Schimanski and H. Treece, 1947.

7

Poets as Publishers

Literary movements, especially in Britain, can subsist on a bare
minimum of theory. Far more indispensable to them are willing or
sympathetic editors and publishers. In this way, Neo-Romanticism
was served by two distinctive personalities: Tambimuttu, editor
of the magazine *Poetry London* for the firm of Nicolson and
Watson, who also produced, under his guidance, a number of
volumes with the imprint of P.L. Editions; and Charles Wrey
Gardiner who edited *Poetry Quarterly* and ran the Grey Walls
Press.

I first encountered the latter at Hammersmith tube station during
one of my Army leaves. Jack Bayliss and I were to meet there to
escort him to a party being held just over Hammersmith Bridge in
a block of flats opposite a pub, known by bus conductors as the
'Boiler Arms', its French name proving intractable. I recall how
disappointed I was to find myself introduced to a quiet-looking
man in a neat double-breasted brown suit who carried both those
emblems of a City gent, a small suitcase and an umbrella. Up to
that time I had met no large numbers of editors in general, and no
editor at all who could claim to deal almost exclusively in verse,
and doubtless I felt that rather more Parnassian panache should be
manifested. The bohemian appearance of long-haired Tambimuttu
(not shoulderlength in those days, but otherwise profuse) would
have accorded better with my naïve notions.

I had not long been at the party, however, where we were joined
by Nick Moore (enamoured of the interminable records which

our hostess's young sister, a jazz virgin known as Dondo, played to him), before becoming aware that many still waters run deep. Wrey (as some of his friends called Gardiner in preference to Charles) was essentially an introspective being though provided with a rare gargoyle wit. Though he may have worn his heart on his sleeve as far as women were concerned, he was only knowable by degrees. The reasons for this were twofold: first because he kept his guard up until he learnt that one was not hostile, and secondly because he largely existed in a world exclusively his own. If any man had a temperament naturally solipsist, it was Wrey. That is why after having already written five autobiographies – *The Colonies of Heaven, The Once Loved God, The Dark Thorn, The Flowering Moment* and *The Answer to Life is No* – he still remains a misty complex figure. G. S. Fraser once said of him that he was the sort of man who would vanish if you took an aspirin. There was something nebulous about him, so that he might have appeared as the hallucination of a fevered mind.

This strange haziness of his psyche was communicated in the way in which he wrote. All his autobiographies consist of longer or shorter passages of instant impressionism. Each paragraph conveys its own world, but these little atmospheric sentimental worlds are so many microcosms and do not, in a sense, snowball. One of these diary-like jottings admits to the feeling of not getting through:

> Kenneth Patchen's wife writes to me to say that I haven't really put much of myself into my books. She is right. I haven't. Who are we, and what are we beyond the tick of the clock? The telephone connects fools with fools.[1]

'The telephone connects fools with fools.' Many of Wrey's maxims, indeed, read like epigrams discharged in a bell-glass: apophthegms uttered in a sealed and shuttered room.

Put in another way, what Wrey demanded was not 'the common reader' but a readership of poets. He tended to divide mankind into two opposing camps between which, he thought, there could be little trafficking: the camp of the philistines, vast and vulgar; and the camp of the creators, small but select. This sense of hordes of

[1] *The Flowering Moment*, 1949.

the artistically indifferent sharpened his fear and contempt at times into misanthropy. In moods such as this, solipsism seemed the most natural and purest stance. 'The group soul is a form of death by spiritual asphyxia. . . . To be alone and to be other than the others with my own reality is all my endeavour.'[1]

Not only did Wrey envisage for himself and those whose work he published in *Poetry Quarterly* a reading public of poets and artists, he also claimed that he had created in the Grey Walls Press a publishing firm staffed solely by poets. The man in the street, blissfully unaware how exceedingly inefficient many publishing staffs of non-poets have proved, may throw up his hands at this imagined spectacle of dreamy chaos, but, actually, Wrey's team of Nick Moore, Frederic Marnau and Sean Jennett had things tied up shipshape and Bristol fashion.

At Avenue Chambers in Vernon Place, just off Southampton Row, Wrey and his editorial assistants went about their work in a crow's-nest office looking down on the traffic through their *art nouveau* windows. Just round the corner, two doors away, was a little café with marble-slab tables where they and visiting poets congregated to drink coffee and partake of fruit trifle and cream.

Of the team, Nick Moore was the least certain member. The long journey back to Cambridge and the thought that bombs might demolish his Liverpool Street lifeline to Priscilla finally led to his self-rustication; though, by the end of the war, he was ensconced as Tambimuttu's number one in *Poetry London*'s Manchester Square sanctum. In one of his autobiographies, *The Dark Thorn*, Wrey provides an excellent account of what it was like to work with him:

> Nick is a stranger still. Giving me a poem the length of one of Eliot's Quartets every morning, and each one more curious and eccentric than the last, smoking his pipe of scented tobacco or black gold-tipped Russian cigarettes. From day to day his mood varies. . . . One day he believes in an imminent turn for the better in his fortunes. The next he can hardly speak with depression. And always so much hidden like a green, silent river snaking through the trees, ominous, dark and rather sad, or rippling with silent laughter. He is as mysterious as the extra-

[1] *Ibid.*

ordinary detective stories he reads, will talk interminably about himself, but diagonally, or in a roundabout way, by implication, so that finally one wonders if he has said anything at all.

Frederic Marnau (always known as Fred) was the obvious poet among the office wallahs of Vernon Place. He had the outward properties, the poetic physiognomy. Dark hair, large sad dark eyes, a dark visage and a black velour hat. Added to this melancholy charm, there was the exquisite courtesy of his manners. Fred was a continental, his world being that of the Austro-Hungarian Empire, though he inherited it by race memory and family reminiscences, not by direct experience. Fred's politics were romantic, linking the past with the then trendy present, in that he proclaimed himself to be an anarcho-monarchist. The best of all impossible worlds! He wrote in German and his poems were translated by Ernest Sigler who, still in khaki, feared that with the coming of peace he would be called back into the family silk-stocking business. One very good test of the rung occupied by a poet is to see how he frames up to ethical issues in his verse. There is nothing like morality for exposing the unoriginal platitudinous cast of a poet's mind. Subjected to such a test, Fred comes off reasonably well:

> The man who does not doubt the heart.
> The man who does not tire of love.
> The man who adorns grief with joy
> And does not fear the future company
> Of the dead, and is brave for right
> There beats the heart.[1]

His best-known books published in England were *Wounds of the Apostles* and *The Drowned Cathedral*.

Another foreigner from nearer home was the Irishman Sean Jennett. I believe he once told me he was a Protestant, whether from the south or the north I cannot remember.

First-rate typographer as he was, I found his own verse correct but colourless, and his judgements on poetry lacking the flair which Wrey, his employer, evinced. Yet because the latter was a dreamer,

[1] 'London Elegies', *New Road*, 1943.

a man who was often 'away and somewhere else', and above all because he was not disputatious and regarded argument as a grinding bore, Sean was able to override editorial decisions which Wrey had come to in private. A case in point was Wrey's acceptance of Jack Bayliss's romantic eighteenth-century novel *Chiswick House* which he found 'miraculous'. Nick Moore had also responded to it with enthusiasm, by no means his most characteristic reaction. He found it 'amazing', 'surprising', 'thrilling', and was enchanted by its 'peculiar dreamlike quality'. With these praises ringing in his ears, Jack departed with the R.A.F. to India, only to return in 1946 to have his book come back to him. It was Sean, too, who was instrumental in rejecting Jack's long poem of the war 'Venus in Libra' which Wrey had provisionally welcomed.

I also suffered from his draconian editing. Wrey had commissioned me to write a book of essays on the 'post-Auden-and-After' poets: David Gascoyne, Sidney Keyes, Alex Comfort and some others. I also included studies of Nick Moore and Wrey himself, and, at Sean's insistence, an account of his own poetry and a joint chapter on John Heath-Stubbs, Vernon Watkins, W. S. Graham and Jack Bayliss.

When the typescripts were received at the office, Sean appointed himself reader; and, not liking what I had said about his poems slashed the pages through with a blue pencil. I myself was content with the removal of the essay, though I had endeavoured to deliver polite and fair comments on the poems within it. Sean, however, now decided that the supplementary chapter must be omitted also. 'It would make the book too long', etc; and as head of the production department, his opinion carried the day. It is to his goodwill, also, that the dedication of my book *The Freedom of Poetry* to my friend Charles Hamblett carries only the cryptic offering 'To C.H.'

When Wrey Gardiner's Grey Walls Press combined with Peter Baker's firm of Falcon Press, Wrey's boasts of running a publishing business 'for poets by poets' was largely valid. Roland Gant, a translator of Verlaine and other French poets, joined the staff, fresh from a parachute regiment. He suffered from chapped lips half the year and used to employ a stick of lip salve which, of course, was quite permissible in an ex-paratrooper. He was, in addition, a

G

brilliant mimic and used to mime the entry of the various poets into
the office.

His wit, at times, was of the prettiest. I recall how, when
Christopher Fry's play *Venus Observed* was running, Roland
declared its title to be a West End euphemism. It should have been
called *Penis Preserved*, since its real theme was the adaption of the
Duke's virility to the less pressing demands of a sexual St Martin's
Summer.

He is now married to a French author, and is a leading editorial
director at Heinemann.

I do not know many poet-accountants, but Paul Scott was one
such. The accounts department of a publishing company generally
has to bear the brunt of authors' anger at the firm's small or dilatory
payments; but so amiable and sympathetic was Paul Scott that even
other poets spoke well of him. Later, he joined a famous literary
agency and became the author of a best-seller, *The Love Pavilion*,
and other successful novels about the decline of British rule in the
East.

Even dear old Major Mead (late of the Persian cavalry – 'the
most poetic people in the world, the Persians'), who joined the
firm towards its last days, had published a book of verse. But this
is to anticipate.

The early phase of Wrey's publishing venture was both rustic
and idyllic. He lived at that time in one of two large seventeenth-
century houses which he owned off the village street of Billericay
in Essex. Having taken over *Poetry Quarterly* from a man who was
editing it down in Plymouth, he decided to offer it for sale in the
front room of his house, which he had converted into a little shop.
Along with the magazine he sold surplus books from his own
extensive collection and other secondhand volumes that chanced
his way. Why not, he thought, produce books of his own which
could be simply marketed there? Thus originated the first Grey
Walls Press titles, the name appropriated from the name of the
house, and the first emanations from this bucolic publishing house
– *Lyra: a book of new lyric*, *The Nature Diaries of Richard
Jefferies*, and *One Plum More: lesser known poems 1586–1903*
(the two latter edited by S. J. Looker), *Into Egypt: a miracle play*
by Alex Comfort, *The Last Refuge: a modern masque* by Wrey
Gardiner – all bore this unusual Essex address.

The name, too, of Alex Comfort among its early authors is important since that volatile versatile youth was attached as a medical student to a nearby hospital and was often to be found at Grey Walls, seeking to infuse the publisher with his own brand of romantic anarchism. (This, no doubt, is how Wrey came to include the character of 'an Anarchist' among the *dramatis personae* of his *Modern Masque*.) It was 'his enthusiasm', Wrey admitted, 'which turned me away from the old towards the young.'

Born with the twentieth century itself, Wrey was over forty before he became actively involved in contemporary verse; before, as he said, he was turned by Alex Comfort 'away from the old towards the young'. The least stuffy, stiff-shirted of editors, he evinced a rare sympathy with poets just beginning to write. The war numbers of *Poetry Quarterly* contain very little work of the over-thirty-fives; and most of the poems were produced by poets between twenty and thirty. Tambimuttu, unlike Wrey, would often include veteran poets such as Walter de la Mare, and Andrew Young and the famous rebellious Stephen Spender in the pages of *Poetry London*; but apart from an occasional review by Herbert Read (the founding father of Neo-Romanticism) '*P.Q.*' – as we called Wrey's magazine, for short – was reserved largely for new or unknown talents.

Wrey was in the publishing business, particularly as far as *P.Q.* was concerned, almost solely for the poets and poetry; and the profits, if at first they marginally existed, were a very secondary consideration. Far from being a businessman, he looked on the publishing of verse as a kind of extension to the writing of his own poems, and the poets he published almost as a projection of his own personality. *The Dark Thorn* illustrates this curious assimilative solipsism which was one of his characteristics in both his literary and his private life:

> Like God I create my own world. When my son Peter was being born Mimi had a kind of vision under the anaesthetic. She saw me coming to her, getting larger and larger. 'Oh! My God!' she said. 'I am God,' I replied. This is commonly supposed to be one of the hallucinations of madness, but it is my creed that we are all gods and create the world we live in by means of our wills.

If the poets became for Wrey like so many extra limbs to his body, this sympathetic absorption was not without its drawbacks in the smooth, prompt, efficient running of a business. It meant that he must mete out to those employees of his who were poets the same consideration for the operation of their creative gifts as he would permit himself. Here is one of his own accounts of such a predicament:

> It is a beautiful spring day and there is a lot of work to do and I feel like doing it. Nicholas [Moore] has taken to typing poems straight on to his typewriter now. The office table is covered with his yellow paper. I go on with my work. He excuses himself, saying he is composing. He knows I would be the last person to stop him doing that. . . . I had a vision of a great deal of important work, parcels of fifties being taken in a taxi, jackets for travellers, but it has all evaporated.

Since the end product (the books and the poems) and the producers (the authors and poets) were the only things in publishing that interested him, he was hardly in a position to lead his staff by a more businesslike example. The daily chores of his office were a burden to him. 'Doing up parcels here is not poetry,' he noted. 'What has happened to me? The string gets caught round my leg, the paper is not the right size. . . . The problems of G.W.P. weigh me down.'

He complained that publishing took up all his day. 'It is only at night that I can work, and then I must be alone.' Work, here, meant writing – either verse or prose; and to this priority he was prepared to sacrifice domestic bliss. 'That is why my sex-life is odd,' he remarked. 'I have arranged it so that it is not cut out altogether, but does not interfere with my work.' 'Not cut out altogether' was a magnificent understatement since the female attention he contrived to obtain would have flattered and satisfied two or three men abundantly. But if Venus certainly received her libations, it was at the altar of Apollo, god of the arts, that he consciously worshipped. Women came, or did not come, by chance. What he held steadfastly in his sights were the figures of the Muses.

'The nicest young fellow – in dreamland' was Rossetti's verdict on the young Burne-Jones. Wrey, I feel, could properly be considered a subject of this cloud-cuckoo kingdom; and it was something of a miracle that the Grey Walls Press titles were so produced.

Not by any imaginative elastication could Wrey be called a *remembering* man. He forgot things – names, appointments, faces. From time to time he forgot his own actions, so that two reviews of a book of verse might appear in the same number, or a poem be attributed to the wrong poet, or appear in two numbers of his magazine. Once when I had known him some years on a friendly drinking and visiting basis, the following incident occurred.

We were sitting talking in his office when the phone rang. Wrey picked up the receiver and replied to whoever it was.

'Oh, yes, it's you.' The caller obviously wanted to see him.

'No, I'm afraid I've got somebody with me now.' The caller was also curious.

'No, I don't think you know him.'

To me: 'What's your name? I can't remember.'

Wrey himself, I freely admit, could easily turn this tale against me, as – when living in Kensington – I once rang him up from a public call-box to ask what my telephone number was. Perhaps our memories had a way of sidestepping reality. Despite which interior obstacles, *P.Q.* came out regularly four times a year – a feat quite beyond Tambimuttu's periodical *Poetry London* with its splendiferous Henry Moore 'Lyrebird' cover.

About Wrey swarmed the young wartime poets: servicemen and women, civilians, nurses and land girls, conscientious objectors, those in reserved occupations or classified as unfit. Up and down the staircase in Avenue Chambers, or seated round the table of the Olympia Café, they might be seen, as I, amongst them, often saw them. Wrey's autobiographies provide a lively gallery of polyphotos of the poets in their interminable comings and goings. With his generous permission, I have rifled his pages, and the many quotations come either from *The Dark Thorn* or *The Flowering Moment*.

Here, then, is Ruthven Todd, looking depressed, 'his large eyes staring blankly' out of his narrow white papery clown's face. . . . he has given up drinking his two and a half bottles of whisky a day, his rats having become almost pink. . . . His wife has left him largely, I should think, because when he sees a book he wants he just buys it with, I imagine, disastrous results to the family budget. . . . So when Ruthven plays the mountebank I know why. I know the dark patch between his eyes and the world.

And here is Nick Moore, descending the steep staircase of the Redfern Gallery 'like the god Neptune holding the catalogue in his hand as though it were a trident of bronze and with a glassy look in his eye', or talking at lunch 'in a loud penetrating voice about aristocratic frigidity'.

Wrey and Fred Marnau argue with the deaf poet David Wright 'by means of odd bits of paper drawn from the bosom of the irate listener. . . . David has refused to take his holiday, to leave London till the bombs have stopped.'

Then there is Denise Levertoff who, like Ruthven Todd, emigrated to the United States after the war, having a rebirth as a poet following her marriage to the American writer Michael Goodman.

The inevitable knock on the door. . . . I shout 'come in' savagely, then have to relax because it is Denise smiling at me from the passage. She is dressed in a leafy kind of green . . . has eyes like ripe but unplucked fruit on an upper branch. Fugitive, resting, glancing, swaying in the wind . . . She is the only person ever to have caused me to write a poem.

Denise, being a nurse in Essex, had met Wrey in the days when *Poetry Quarterly* and other Grey Walls Press titles were sold from the front room of his house in Billericay.

Nor must one forget the egregious Tambimuttu. 'The same smile, the same benign grin. . . . There is something in him that takes one over to the realm of poetry. Something indescribable.' I, too, had felt this 'something' – an aura, a glamour; not charm, since that, perhaps, implies a partly willed characteristic, whereas the quality exhaled by Tambi existed without moral or social effort. Trying to locate this element, I told him once that he made me think of the Pilgrims' Chorus from the opera *Sadko*, an anology with which he found no fault.

There was, with Tambi, the reverse of the coin. 'Those fights. Tambi being thrown out of everywhere one went with him because of them', and one more famous than the rest which had taken place in the Swiss pub in Soho when the Indian writer Mulk Raj Anand 'poured the contents of an ash-tray into Tambi's beer. It was poor Tambi who got the worst of it and was slung out.'

Along with the poets were the short-story and fiction writers of the period, though they were more often met in pubs than on the stairway of Avenue Chambers. Maclaren Ross would appear, the emblems of his ego consisting of his 'marvellous coat and the sheen of his tie'. Tall and amusing, he enters a bookshop where Wrey is talking to the proprietor and pretends to show him round an imaginary exhibition of new painting. ' "Board with Nails", "Apotheosis", "Coming of Spring" – a bucket and brush, pointing all the time to real articles in the room. The painter, he said, was one Chrim.'

Another one is Subramanian – an Oriental, trained as a lawyer, and owner of the above bookshop. 'When he smiles the whole of his face lights up like a tropical dawn and his fine eyes become human, gazelle-like, and one understands partly the reason for the troupe of adoring females.'

Kay Dick the novelist (now living at Brighton, not so far from me) is one whom Wrey and I both remember and whom I still see.

Kay is tall and wears a shirt open at the neck like a man in summer. She bends forward slightly towards you as if she would dominate you with her blue eyes like the small flowers you find on the very cold heights of mountains, but which soften and deepen in certain eerie lights. Her beloved period is the nineties and she lives on her nerves and books.

I remember being introduced to Kay Dick in Wrey's office with her friend Kathleen Farrell who also writes fiction and whom he described as 'small with large eyes' and running 'about the flat to a great deal of purpose exactly like a squirrel, a nice homely squirrel intent on the efficient harvesting of the moment'. Talking too late at night to jog back to Billericay, Wrey stayed with them at

Hampstead, fascinated by their domestic pet. 'They have a dachshund called Hamlet which sleeps like an old woman covered up with its long nose and melancholy eyes looking out of a fold in the stuff.'

Other names could readily be added, particularly after the editorial office was removed to Crown Passage, Whitehall. There came David Gascoyne, his tall figure and melancholy good looks suggestive of Gerard de Nerval's ill-starred Prince of Aquitaine; Alan Ross, young, fresh-cheeked and handsome in his uniform of a naval officer; the bearded inward-seeing painter Cecil Collins; and Paul Potts, an Irish-Canadian poet, his big head and large profile prompting different likenesses : at one angle, the funny man, the clown; at another, a Shakespearian tragic actor; and at a third, some ruddy-faced farmer, a sort of semi-Celtic John Bull.

And finally, what is this that Wrey has written? 'Derek Stanford's domed half-bald forehead, large eyes and sensual lips are so very like the portraits of Shakespeare.' For 'half-bald' now read 'bald', alas.

Of all the figures of younger writers of whom Wrey left thumbnail sketches, none was so important for the development of Neo-Romantic thought as Alex Comfort. After Herbert Read, with whom he differed on certain issues, nobody did so much to provide the movement as a whole with a political and social theory. He had also the most powerful (I do not say accurate) intelligence of any within its ranks, as well as wide reading in many varied fields. Moreover, whatever he read he remembered and was able to quote to his purpose. Since this purpose was a unifying one, his opinions, taken as a whole, possessed an imposing consistency, and one gained the impression (by no means wholly true) that Neo-Romanticism was not just a matter of so many individual poems, stories and paintings, but a body of work produced beneath the umbrella of a clear cohesive theory.

Then, too, Alex proved himself a polemicist of capability. Charles Hamblett christened him 'the Voltaire of Neo-Romanticism'. Pick up any journal of the time, and there was a good chance of finding a letter from him correcting the editor or his contributor on some point. Nor did it appear to matter what the overt subject was – French films, American poetry, harassment of pacifists or the

Second Front – Alex would have something to say favourable to the furtherance of the anarchist and Neo-Romantic positions.

Without his forceful array of talent, Alex with 'his pale face under that appalling beret', would have been seen as 'one of the most curious figures of [the] time'. There was not a small amount of the schoolboy in him – the boy prodigy in the school laboratory conducting precocious experiments with 'stinks' – and he had in fact blown off a finger while playing with chemicals when young. Wrey noted his 'leering white face . . . and his rude cheerful remarks', but what struck me most about him was his amazing conversation. Indeed, he talked like an angel who has swallowed an entire set of the *Encyclopaedia Britannica*, digested it and made it his own. Neither was it mere facts and details he dealt in. His talk drew copiously on this knowledge presenting it as so many parts of an intellectual mosaic or jigsaw, the completion of which would constitute a pattern of the good society.

Everything that came his way had to be allotted its proper meaning, since man needed to be rescued by meaning (a man-imposed signification) from the cosmic meaninglessness surrounding him. For Alex, to use Wrey's good phrase, 'the *materia medica* of the sane' was made up of the arts. Psychology was also a useful prescription, and I remember an occasion when he interpreted its findings in an unexpected, if brash, fashion.

Alex and his wife had chanced one day to meet me near Lincoln's Inn. We sat on the white stone seat just opposite New Square, and I was turning the pages of Sorel's *Reflections on Violence,* seeking to find some pencilled passage which I wished to shew him when I cut my finger on a razor blade, all unwrapped, which I had left in the book. The blade was intended to serve as a pencil-sharpener and a page-marker; but while his wife bound up my bleeding finger (she had, in fact, qualified as a nurse), Alex read me an analytic lecture. The blade, he said, was clearly the knife of a masochist who was secretly hoping to hurt himself. Who else, he asked, could I possibly name who carried round a naked razor blade in this fashion?

Alex was a sort of one-man New Left. An aesthetic libertarian with a social conscience, he differed from today's breed completely by his dismissal of Marx. Like most anarchists, he regarded Marxist–Leninism as a bureaucratizing of the revolutionary

instinct; but, unlike most literary anarchists, he parted company
with Herbert Read, particularly on the issue of violence. His novel
The Power House (1944) was set in Nazi-occupied France; and
the policy of destruction (the wrecking of trains, etc.) which his
characters performed in its pages could be regarded as heroic feats
of patriotic resistance fighters. Unlike Read, Alex believed that the
battle for freedom should be fought out in the streets, and the
populist politics of demonstration and civil disobedience were
voiced by him in the war years. It is amusing to think that the
chanting rabble of today, vociferously reiterating their cries of
'Heath, out' or whatever, will almost certainly not have heard of
this literary pioneer of the march and the demo.

During the First World War Bernard Shaw published an article
in which he said that the best thing which could happen would be
for the other ranks on both sides to shoot their officers and return
home. Alex had a better idea than this. He knew it was not the
officers who instituted wars but the politicians, and that they should
be the legitimate object of any act of popular vengeance:

> There is one freedom only –
> to take the hands of men called enemies
> and you and they walking together go
> to seek out every throat that told you kill.[1]

Some may find this simplistic – not so much logically immature
as out of accordance with the reality principle, with what one can
expect from human kind *en masse,* always making allowance for
its vast ignorance and vaster inertia. At the time, however, it
appealed deeply to the frustrated intellectual serviceman, and to
quite a few sane but simple souls who were far from being
intellectuals.

I remember talking to an Italian prisoner out with our section
on a work party. We had knocked off for a coffee break and were
showing each other those prized possessions, photographs of our
women. From this we passed on to politics; and my companion,
a sensible peasant, came out with the following summary:

'Mussolini – No good!
Hitler – no bloody good!

[1] 'The Wingless Victory', *The Signal to Engage*, 1946.

Stalin – no fucking good!
Churchill – no good!
You good. Me good.'

Alex would have been delighted.

Naïve as he might have been in any anticipation of popular retributive action, Alex, unlike most revolutionaries, was a pessimist not an optimist. He did not expect the realization of any secular pie-in-the-sky which has inspired so many socialists. In fact, he once said that the only two activities of man which convinced him that the world was not a huge lunatic asylum were poetry and medical science; and before long he was to be engaged in deep geriatric research which Wrey described as 'something to do with a rare species of snail which carried a light on its tail'.

But this is to jump ahead several years. In 1942 or 1943, when I originally corresponded with him, he was collecting material for the first number of *New Road*, an anthology which he was editing with Jack Bayliss, and in which I played some part.

8

Shadows at Coleorton

Meanwhile our Company had moved from Pershore up to Liverpool, settling in not uncomfortable billets a few miles out of the city. Blundellsands was a quiet enough suburb on the Mersey estuary. There was a good bus service which carried us, despite the toll of the bombing, to quite a Mecca of north-west culture: bookshops, theatre, concert hall and gallery. I and my friends in the Company now took to calling on bookshop managers, asking them to take, on sale or return, various publications which flew the Neo-Romantic ensign: *Lyra*, *The Fortune Anthology*, *Poetry Quarterly* and titles in the *Poetry London Pamphlet* series – Nicholas Moore, Anne Ridler, G. S. Fraser and George Scurfield. The response to these and the purchasing of them proved more promising than we had expected, and I was now committed to the Neo-Romantic cause as entrepreneur, impressario and critic.

At that period I seem to have spent no little time in trying to win over others to the Neo-Romantic colours. I remember walking with Christopher Fry through the small secluded public gardens of Blundellsands, vehemently inveighing against the evils of Social Realism, and discussing how poetry and drama stood in need of a freer, more oxygenated aesthetic. Christopher's poems and the play he was then writing seemed to accord perfectly with the theory of literature I was advancing, but Christopher himself was not a man of theory. Something of a temperamental quietist, he looked askance, I felt, at my controversial plan of attack. I think he disapproved of the unconcealed violent passions

I entertained in this arena of ideas. He was, in every sense, a truer, better pacifist than me. Notwithstanding some possible dismay that I should see art as a sort of bullring, he let me have poems to send to Jack Bayliss for the first two numbers of *New Road*. Wynyard Browne, the future author of such successful postwar plays as *The Holly and the Ivy* and *Dark Summer*, was another I tackled, hoping to recruit him to the Neo-Romantic cause. Wynyard affected great admiration for Christopher's work (Fry was the proudest boast of us all); despite which, I felt, he was not truly on the same wavelength – an intimation I found borne out years later during the Festival of Britain.

The half-Irish son of a Church of Ireland vicar, Wynyard possessed obvious attraction. He was fair, a tall slender straw-blond, compounded of charm and egoism. At that time he had written no plays, but had won an American prize for a novel, *Sheldon's Way*, shortly after coming down from Cambridge. He had gone as assistant editor to Sir John Squire at the *London Mercury*, and would tell amusing stories about the old poet and toper in his decline. Fished out of the gutter in Tottenham Court Road, dead drunk, Saturday night after Saturday night, he was, in the mid-'thirties, no longer the power he had once so obviously been. Nor did he approve the way literature was going or, indeed, had been going for some time. 'Genius is a rare thing,' he would tell Wynyard. 'How many are any good when you really come down to it? Not very many, my boy. Just Shakespeare, you and I.'

Wynyard had a fatal attraction for women. As Mike Hewlett once observed to me: 'Wynyard had more women before he was twenty-one than you and I together will have all our lives.' Mike was a rigorist, and also veracious: I saw no reason to dispute his reckoning. Wynyard would sometimes tell us about one of his early *mignons*. She was a startling and beautiful creature whom he had encountered in Leicester or some other Midland city. As simple as she was ravishing, she found London an astonishing place, and was always marvelling wide-eyed at its sights. Wynyard liked to cart her around, dressed so as to set off her magnificent allure; and had taken her to the Zoo one day wearing a strawberry-coloured dress with a white cartwheel hat. The spectacle of the animals left her spellbound and before the giraffe she stood completely speechless. Seeing this radiant creature, clad in red raiment, staring at the beast, the passers-by stopped in their turn and stared at her. All of which flattered Wynyard's vanity and fed his considerable sense of humour.

He was also a great observer. While Christopher's gaze was often turned inwards, Wynyard's would be turned out to watch and spy. One could see him sometimes seated in the mess or standing on the edge of a group of fatigue-men, silently engaged in taking things in. Fascination, horror, or dawning surprise would cross his features like shadows over corn. 'Could such people really exist?' one almost heard him ask himself. 'How awful! How dreadful! . . . How very fascinating!' He was naturally sceptical; and his intellect was of a scrutinizing order rather than originally constructive. I felt he read the fashionable philosophers – Maritain, Kierkegaard, Berdyaev – to know what they said but not in any way to help change his life. Looking up from the page, over his glasses, as someone noisily entered the Quiet Room of some Forces canteen, he would give the merest glance of faint disapproval before turning back to his reading. One saw in him the fleeting reflection of some Victorian parson with a comfortable living, put out by his wife's intrusion in his study. For myself, I preferred the playboy figure with his scandal, laughter and epigrams.

Despite my obvious failure to explain my Neo-Romantic theories to either Christopher or Wynyard, I did obtain from the former a poem for publication in the first number of *New Road* (1943) which Alex Comfort and Jack Bayliss were then preparing. For the second number he let us have three poems, one of which I give below since these volumes are now exceedingly rare and are priced from £5 to £10 in booksellers' catalogues:

Sea Anemone

In this the rose haunts the unfamiliar
Ways of water. And in this the toad
Uncurls its appetite on to a sick
Shifting air. In one. There is no failure
Here, to unite. The flower picks up the load
Of hunger, and the creature feels the earth

Wholly accepting him. Where through the thick
Tide crept in the fusion of this birth?

Is our blood foreign to this ghost
Of fathoms? Here's the print of the same thumb
On earth and sea. But upon flesh and dust
What sign is carried? Mountains have no doom.
Doom wears us like a flower. Yet deeply here
May lie in wait the small interpreter.

It fell to me to write the introductory essays for these two numbers of *New Road*. In retrospect it seems fairly clear what I was
intending to do, namely to mobilize an allied front of 'goodies'
– Apocalyptics, Surrealists, Neo-Romantics and Anarchists –
against that old popular front of the 'baddies' consisting of Marxists and Social Realists. The Surrealists came in two kinds: those
who, accepting the directions of their leader André Breton, paid
at least lip service to Marxism, though ridiculed and censored by
the C.P.; and those who were freelances and rejected every kind of
orthodoxy, even when it proved to be a fashionable hotchpotch
of Marx and Freud. These latter were prepared to make common
cause with Neo-Romantics and Apocalyptics against the Social
Realists. *New Road* was to represent visual and literary artists who
placed fantasy and 'imagination' as forefront ingredients of the
creative act. For such painters and poets, Herbert Read had
coined the term 'superrealist' – one, he lamented, which did not
catch on. It was to these more 'open' Surrealists, these Romantic
Superrealists, that I addressed a large part of my appeal, seeking to
suggest that the political counterpart of their aesthetic lay in
anarchism, not in Marxism.

But while the Neo-Romantic was fighting on the Social Realist
front, he sometimes found himself attacked by the rigid party man
among the orthodox Surrealists. Toni del Renzio was such a one,
and in the name of ideological purity had not scrupled to criticize
his wife Ithell Colquhoun in his magazine *Arson*. 'Miss Ithell
Colquhoun,' he wrote, 'has finally damned herself publicly with
her admission of endeavouring to do in painting what the "New
Apoplexy" [the New Apocalypse] is doing in literature.' Toni concluded this same 'ardent review' (as its editor termed *Arson*):
'N.B. It will be noted that no poetry is printed in these pages for

the simple reason we do not believe there is a single line approach-
ing the nature of poetry being penned in English.' Sweeping, no
doubt, but engagingly civil compared to what he wrote by way of a
preface to a selection of Surrealist writing edited by him in *New
Road* (1943). A pity that the involution of his prose concealed
rather than spotlighted the targets he strove to rake with fire. To
connoisseurs of critical virulence I commend the following passage
in which Toni certainly pulls out his stops even more whole-
heartedly than do those gentlemen in Moscow talking about bourgeois hyenas :

> We are not afraid to announce with the certainty our lucidity
> gives, that the collaboration of writers in the production of
> pseudo-poetic enterprises under the patronage of those who have
> most to gain and to hide from an assumed leftism and on actual
> defence of the *status quo*, no matter whether 'personalism' or
> some other humbug be invented as a confusionist title for such
> enterprises, we are not afraid to announce that such collabora-
> tion can only be recognized as the hospitality of the earth-
> closet.
>
> To those who can write 'I stand and hesitate. It is so easy to
> fail, so hard to know, so impossible to succeed', we fling back,
> 'Cease your detestable dribbling. Poison yourself with the slime
> that drops from your overworked tongue if your heart and your
> brain are corroded in their inertia.' To those who only now
> understand ruins and visions [reference to a title by Stephen
> Spender] we say 'If you had a life to live, a poetry to write, you
> might then be a person that you might have the courage to be'.[1]

Apart from these pyrotechnic jinks, however, Toni's article was
noteworthy for his discovery of revolutionary monogamy, which
we lesser mortals think of in terms of marriage. He might criticize
Ithell for straying from the narrow aesthetic path, but he was careful, by implication, to show that in marriage she was assisting him
forward on the road to Revolution.

As always, in these dialectical excursions, there were odd in-
consistencies which it requires the humorist rather than the critic
to appreciate. Alex Comfort – 'the heroic toreador of the mad bull

[1] 'The light that will cease to fail', *New Road*, 1943.

1 The Doves public house, Hammersmith, with miscellaneous patrons. This was he Thames-side haunt of the author and his friends in the late 'thirties.

24 Mervyn Peake's drawing of Titus from *Gormenghast*.

of contemporary society'[1] and the ablest polemicist in the Neo-Romantic ranks – happened, in his novels as distinct from his verse, to have adopted the style of the enemy, a Realism of earlier vintage. Wrey Gardiner noted that he 'is still writing in the manner of the nineteenth-century naturalist novel. He is potted Zola watered down for the British nine-and-sixpenny novel-reading bourgeoisie'; and after reading the proofs of Alex's novel *The Power House*, he remarked how the author was suffering from 'a powerful indigestion of long catalogues of the appearances of reality'.[2]

In due time Alex himself looked through the manuscript of the book in which Wrey had confided these thoughts and was, as the latter reports, 'a little nettled by my criticism of his realism, he retorted by saying that I should be accused of escapism, the lovely epithet to hurl at something one doesn't like, a word like fascism'. These storms in a tea-cup did not, however, succeed in rocking the Neo-Romantic boat. Wrey, for one, had no taste for critical disputation. He also had the liveliest respect for Alex. 'All the same,' he concluded, 'he is a genius. He shows the insanity of society . . . he says what should have been said long ago and has not been said by the timid and suckers.'[3]

After more than a year in Liverpool, our Company split up, and I went on a detachment, first to Melbourne in Derbyshire then across the county border to Beaumont in Leicestershire. We were now billeted in Coleorton Hall, the ancestral home of the Beaumonts which they had recently sold to a rich mineowner.

Regency Sir George Beaumont was a great patron of the arts. Reynolds, Scott, Wordsworth, Keats and Constable all stayed at his fine mansion, and a cenotaph to Reynolds was erected in the grounds. This took the form of a stag placed on a stone pedestal surrounded by sombre trees – an odd arboreal vista which Constable commemorated in a crepuscular painting. During the war part of the house was still in private use, while the rest was requisitioned by the Army. About it all, even in the sunshine, there hung an atmosphere of immemorial sadness. What had once been

[1] *The Dark Thorn*, 1946.
[2] *Ibid.*
[3] *Ibid.*

H

the Beaumonts' dining-room was kept now as a reading and writing room for the troops billeted there. Family portraits still hung on the walls, the sensitive or melancholy faces of their subjects glooming down on the lone soldier who chose to pen his letters there. There was something about this apartment which prevented it from being a favourite hideout.

From the reading room to the vast flagged kitchen one passed through the men's mess and then down a long stone-floored passage. Along these cold dark reaches, lit only by two all-too-dim electric bulbs, I would walk last thing at night on the way back to my sleeping quarters. And always behind me, I would feel some gathering source of fear which sped me on.

Coleorton was hung with melancholy as if it lay within some psychic spider's web. I have never seen such forlorn-looking shadows as sprawled beneath its cedars on the lawn or lay in doleful patterns on the floor. Neither its grounds nor its outbuildings were free of this infecting sense of sorrow. Surrounded by trees, a small boating lake, long since gone dry, spread out its trough of leaves. Steps to a strange half-subterranean boat-house were fenced with rusting handrails and overgrown with weeds. Dereliction flowered in the deep banks of nettle.

It was in these surroundings that I received a copy of David Gascoyne's *Poems 1937–42*, along with many other volumes of verse sent me by Wrey Gardiner for the critical work I was writing for him. With its grey-black-and-red Graham Sutherland cover, which suggested nothing so much as a sort of smouldering rubbish-tip in hell, the book seemed somehow to tone in with the countryside surrounding Coleorton. In full summer, the Leicestershire meadows stood basking in the sun, at first glance telling a peaceful pastoral story. This idyllic prospect, however, was no more than one of nature's well-meant lies. The land in wartime is a sad place, worked by women and foreign prisoners while its own tillers are away fighting. Moreover the fields about Coleorton lay on the borders of mining territory, and here disused or unwanted machinery, like satanic black engines of torture, troubled the eye when it strayed to the horizon. Time and place both combined to make my first serious reading of this poet, with the sultry, lowering landscape of his own verse, an unforgettable one.

My personal world also echoed Gascoyne's lugubrious lines. Since meeting her at one of Russell Clarke's parties, when she came dancing up to me swirling her skirts in Spanish style to some record of Albéniz or de Falla, I had been deeply smitten by a certain literary redhead. Her wit, her unillusioned mind and her compact build of a semi-pocket Venus, all helped to captivate me. She was, I think, probably the most intelligent woman I have ever met, and like many highly intelligent women, imaginative, artistic but not intellectual. She was married for a short period to a Latymerian friend of mine, but after she had borne him a fine bouncing boy (whom I remember carrying on a picnic with her and Lia Bayliss on the wartime green of Putney Heath), they separated and were later divorced.

Jean used to write me long letters, humorous and homely by turns, in which she gave me much good advice without appearing to do so. In some ways, I rather intrigued her; but, rightly no doubt, being more mature, she did not take me seriously. I remember her once saying, after reading the introductory essay I wrote for the first number of *New Road*, that she had found it fascinating but felt she had entered in the middle of things. What she correctly implied was how inbred my thinking processes were! This was true enough, but since I was under her spell, could so very seldom get to see her, and was altogether aware of her obvious superiority, depression was what I was feeling.

Shifts in our emotional condition often bring a change in intellectual perspective. My gloom about Jean heralded a period of philosophic gloom. Hitherto I would have described myself as a gay pessimist; but now a gloomier subjectivity began to take hold of me. Leaving Liverpool on detachment, I had lost a number of friends who remained with the main body of our Company. The close fraternity of the group of men's mess orderlies in my charge was dissolved. I had now only one, or at the most two, with whom to work; and the anarchist plan of mutual aid on which we had sought to organize our labours became a thing of the past. The consent of congenial companions is the essence of a cooperative cell, and this I could no longer rely on. In this more isolated position it is not surprising that I turned from reading Kropotkin to delve deeper into Kierkegaard. Loneliness heightens the sense of individuality, and in such situations we may look inside ourselves

to find those answers which previously we have expected to arrive
at in personal or social relationships.

Solitary Sören Kierkegaard had written that 'the communicator
of the truth can only be a single individual. And again the communication of it can only be addressed to the individual; for the
truth consists precisely in the conception of life which is expressed
in the individual.'[1] In another essay he declares that 'the
individual is the category through which, in a religious aspect
this age, all history, the human race as a whole must pass'.[2] 'Truth',
I declared in my first *New Road* introduction, embroidering on
Kierkegaard's theme,

> holds its audience in solitude, and employs its own *decollective
> rhetoric* whose purpose is to make the hearer more aware of his
> individual validity as a moral vehicle, of his separation from
> other men in that the roots of good and bad within him await
> his own virtuous or vicious husbandry before their conversion
> into action.

An introvert who for a number of years had worn the extrovert's
party dress, I was now lapsing back – regressing the psychiatrist
might have said – into my basic state of introversion. But if my
inward condition, and the philosophy which went with it, was
heightening the alienation I experienced (the distance I felt
between myself and my fellows), it was enriching both my reflective and meditative powers – faculties the activist tends to
overlook.

My growing addiction to Kierkegaard did not mean that I was
replacing a political with a religious world picture. For me, in
one sense, Christianity did not come into it, though unlike most on
the side of revolution I did not see it as a necessarily hostile force.
What Kierkegaard was effecting for me at that time was a deepen-
ing of consciousness, a realization that there was, in the dialectics
of inwardness, 'a theory as opposite to policy as well could be
thought of'.

My state of mind was thus favourable to the reception of David
Gascoyne's poetry. Some years later in 1957, reviewing Gascoyne's

[1] *The Point of View*, trans. Walter Lourie, 1939.
[2] *Ibid.*

Night Thoughts in the *Twentieth Century*, Paul Potts described him as 'the poet of man's loneliness'. Certainly he soon became mine. Having written a long study on his work, which later appeared in my book *The Freedom of Poetry*, I mailed it off and asked if I might see him when next on leave.

He was living, in those days, with George Barker off Vauxhall Bridge Road in Bessborough Gardens or Bessborough Place; and I remember making my way there one night, only to be compelled to retreat before the fury of a full-scale air-raid. It so transpired that my first meeting with him was brought about by chance. Scurrying to a milk-bar in Leicester Square one night with Wrey Gardiner, Jack Bayliss and someone I have forgotten, we found the poet seated on a stool at the counter. David was exceedingly pale, 'With a white face which dreams/Have drained of mean-ink',[1] and I thought of him as some large itinerant moth which the glare of the lights had stunned and dazzled. He said little, and after swallowing down a pill with his coffee, very soon got up and left.

With so many people then under stress one did not inquire into someone else's lifeline or placebo. Afterwards, in his strange book of reflections entitled *The Sun at Midnight*, he confessed he was a drug addict at that time, though only of amphetamine compounds. Being for a short time under the unwise control of a refugee doctor, he had taken to exceeding the prescribed dose in an attempt to escape from dispiritedness and the physical lassitude which this produced. David related how, under the influence of the drug, he found himself one Christmas Eve at the gates of Buckingham Palace, believing that he had a great spiritual message to deliver to Their Majesties. Fortunately, as he observes, the policeman on duty at the entrance was a kind understanding man and simply told him that the royal family were away at Sandringham.

In the same work, David confesses how the drug had enabled him to understand the workings of paranoia. Once, at some professedly fancy-dress party, Charles Hamblett had met him standing in a corner, with a length of rope dangling over both shoulders. As he was not otherwise dressed in costume, Charles asked who he was supposed to be. 'Don't you see the rope?' replied David. 'I'm Gerard de Nerval. You know he went mad and hanged him-

[1] David Gascoyne, 'Noctambules', *Poems 1937–42*, 1943.

self.' There was, indeed, always a touch of Dostoievskian extremity about him; and I recollect watching him, once in Chelsea, just after the war, running down the King's Road to catch a bus, wearing a suit of black corduroy or cord. That fleeting spectacle prompted the image of a public executioner, a headsman hurrying to his station at the block. He had lately published a little monograph on Thomas Carlyle whom he found sympathetic (a highly unusual postwar judgement), and probably believed, as Carlyle would have done, that our society merited the axe.

After Eliot, Gascoyne was the leading British poet to delineate the landscape of meaninglessness, to plumb the abyss of emptiness in our time. A passage from a journal he kept in Paris just before the war reveals the emotional raw material of his verse:

> *10.11.38*   Life takes its course, and everything seems all right for a while; then suddenly a rift forms under one's feet, one catches a glimpse of hell: *le monde désert*, a terrible fundamental boredom, a horrible sense of being alone among people who are all alone with themselves and inarticulate, a terrible dry interior sobbing. Night and the rain, and the endless electrically-lighted streets, and the burning, burning. . . . A sense of a world of beings with each one carrying the burden of their own void about with them behind their mask, and who do not know how to communicate their need and suffering.

'A terrible dry interior sobbing . . .' – I heard this verse music in piece after piece of David's volume *Poems 1937–42*. 'They take us,' wrote Cyril Connolly reviewing this book, 'as near the edge of the precipice as a human being is able to go and still turn back', for here, indeed, was a poet driven by a grief which was both private and cosmic, to the borders of madness and sometimes beyond. The answer which David proposed to this *acedia*, this aridity of the spirit, was 'Christ of Revolution and of Poetry'.[1] In the ears of those party members and fellow-travellers who had once been his colleagues this must have sounded a strange solution. Thirty years later, we can reflect, it is the slogan on a holy banner unfurled by Marxist-Catholic priests in Latin America.

Mark Holloway, whom I had known at Cambridge, was one of

[1] 'Ecce Homo', *Poems 1937–42*, 1943.

the few critics to dismiss the poetry along with the spiritual
propaganda. Reviewing David's volume in *Oasis*, he described
it as manifesting the phenomenon of 'Christ in Soho'. This seemed
to me a mistaken judgement. I preferred Paul Potts's description of
him in *Dante Called You Beatrice* (1960) as a 'monseigneur who
has forgotten to be ordained', and while I could not fully go along
with the ultimate Christian view in these poems, I felt that the
negative revelation – the sense of what Heidegger called 'God's
withdrawing' – blazed in them like the writing on the wall of
Nebuchadnezzar's palace. Rather than the poetry of conversion,
Poems 1937–42 was a launching-pad which could transport the
nihilist into the heady ether of faith, always provided that such a
reader was prepared to make Kierkegaard's 'leap in the dark'. It
was not, alas, something I could do myself.

The wear and tear of Army days now began to take its toll of us
sensitive spirits. We moved from Coleorton to King's Newton
near the village of Melbourne in Derbyshire, and here I lost my
good friend Arthur Ford, whose Hampshire yeoman sturdiness
might have been expected to endure better and longer than us of
the sick metropolis. The psyche, however, keeps its own reckoning of how much it can endure. Arthur was discharged, and I was
left without the lieutenant handyman who had done so much to
smooth my own impractical steps through the khaki labyrinth –
for though I could ensure the smooth running of the mess, or
even, at a pinch, march a fire-picket from the orderlies' billet up
to headquarters, the neat laying out of my kit for inspection was
something which defeated me. Such chores, Arthur organized for
me, in return for which I helped him to appreciate the Russian
short-storyists and enjoy the Surrealists' zany paintings. With his
departure, I missed, too, the amusing recital of this graduated
Casanova who was also, strange as it may seem, a member of the
Pentecostal Church. Arthur singing, in his quite tuneless voice,
the words of that Pentecostal hymn –

> I'm going up, up, up,
> Up in God's aeroplane

– made me think of Apollinaire's line about Christ as an aeronaut
in his poem 'Zone'.

For the rest of the war, at least until I left it in the autumn of 1945, our Company moved about in the Midlands round Derby and Nottingham. It was in the latter city that I first encountered the concrete poet Ian Hamilton Finlay, still of tender years and professing himself more a man of paint than ink. Ian had been newly posted to our Company and was very much the Scot, having previously come south, I believe, only on one memorable occasion. That was when, at sixteen or seventeen, he had run away with a girl who was later to become his first wife. Marion was even younger, and when her parents pursued them to their hideout Ian, despite Marion's protestations, found it impossible to resist their demands and both young people were taken back. Only a few years later, with Hugh Macdiarmid as his best man, Ian was married to her, beginning a period of such financial hardship that it left grave marks on him.

When I met him in the summer of 1945 Ian was not yet twenty. My first impression was of some fair-haired and faunlike creature, slender, tall and just a little pitiful. This last quality it was hard to locate, difficult to pin on any specific feature. True, he had a weak chin and what he himself described as large 'poached egg eyes'. He was also somewhat pale. But it was not these physiognomical aspects which constituted his special pathos: this stemmed rather from the look in his eye or from the expression of his features as a whole. It was, however, a transient expression, since, from looking woeful and helpless, his eyes and face would swiftly twitch into wild vivacity and mirth.

Ian's humour was often dry, often self-quizzical. In such moments he would treat what he took to be his weakness of will and his *penchant* for getting into trouble as the substance of a joke to be cherished. Years later, in the 'sixties when my wife and I visited him and his second wife Sue in their croft at Dunsyre in Lanarkshire, I was surprised at how much firmer, how much stronger, his face had become. Some hidden iron had worked to the surface.

At Nottingham Ian and I did not have much opportunity of seeing each other. For the most part, I was still engaged in the mess but sometimes went on a work party which helped to sort letters at an Army post office. The work here went on all round the clock and the Company was divided into sections which took turns on different shifts. Sometimes we would manage a whole evening

together, sometimes just an hour or half-hour before one of us went
on parade. One of our favourite places of refreshment was a pub
in Shakespeare Street, well known as a residential quarter of
prostitutes. The pub, which we patronized early in the evening,
was neat, quiet and homely, with a coal fire burning in the autumn
hearth. At half-past six or seven it was largely deserted, and I enjoyed our long discussions – most of them about poetry, philosophy
and painting – free from the racket of soldiery and bawling
civilians. Sometimes, though, I found it difficult to coax Ian inside.
'What's the good, man?' he would complain, having only half
an hour before going on duty. 'There's no time to get drunk!'
When there was time, often he would make the most of it. On one
occasion he came back to his bunk as loaded as a good Caledonian
could wish and was very soon downstairs again to vomit up his
surplus in the latrines. After a decent time for due unloading had
taken place, I went down to see if all was well. It was a perfect late
summer's night, the sky a deep velvet studded with pearls. Ian
was on his knees in one of the little cubicles, his head hanging over
the pan. Observing that the spasms had passed, I suggested he
return to bed, and attempted to help him to do so. Outside of the
latrines, he collapsed upon the stone-flagged yard. 'Let me die
under the stars,' he beseeched me – a poetic request which, even
in crisis, was not without its undercurrent of self-humour.

Ian would always say that he had received little education. (He
had, in fact, attended an art school but had been expelled for
organizing – unheard of in those days! – a students' revolt, after
which he came back in the role of assistant to help the janitor and
sweep up the floor.) Despite this – could it be because of it? – he
was one of the most stimulating talkers on art and thought I have
ever encountered. At that time he seemed equally drawn to the
abstract concepts of philosophy and the image lore of poetry and
painting. In Glasgow he had mixed with a crowd of artists – the
painters Jankel Adler, Robert Colquhoun and Robert MacBryde
and the poets Hugh Macdiarmid and W. S. Graham – their
company proving a heady yeast to his precocious intelligence.

In 1945 he professed himself a contemporary classicist, influenced in this predilection very largely by Cocteau's brilliantly
informal aphoristic treatise *Recall to Order*. He was fond of quoting, with amused approval, a line from some poem by a friend of

his : 'I have snaps of you with hats on', and in retrospect one can see the essence of concrete poetry existing in embryo in this one line of verse. More frequently, he would recite a passage from Roy Campbell's 'Autumn', which seemed to him to illustrate the classical economy which he prized :

> I love to see, when leaves depart,
> The clear anatomy arrive,
> Winter, this paragon of art,
> That kills all forms of life and feeling
> Save what is pure and will survive.

This I would cap with a stanza from Osbert Sitwell, claiming that it represented romantic economy and proved Lord Bacon's dictum that 'there is no beauty which hath not some strangeness in it' :

> Through his iron glades
> Rides Winter the Huntsman.
> All colour fades
> As his horn is heard singing.[1]

Those who have read Ian's concrete poems or the earlier neo-trad pieces which appeared in his book *The Dancers Inherit the Party* (1960) will have recognized their combination of wit, whimsicality and formal elegance. I am not sure, however, of the many poems by Ian which I admire that I do not prefer 'Postcard from Glenlednoch' which he sent to me in 1946 and which duly appeared in *Poetry Quarterly*. This is how it came to be written. Unlike me, he was still in the Army, having transferred to a combatant regiment. Then, in the mid-summer of 1946, he came to visit me while I was staying in a stable cottage on Ham Common in Surrey. The weather was magnificently blue, the heat intense and the gorse ablaze. 'Maybe it's a bit Mediterranean,' he exclaimed from the centre of a vast surmise. Later, he set down his sense of these antithetical north–south contrasts between the scenery and climate of England and Scotland. There is a whole aesthetic in this poem, and I am only sorry that he withheld permission for me to quote it.

[1] 'Winter the Huntsman', *Collected Satires and Poems*, 1931.

For the serviceman in wartime, there were all too few opportunities of seeing good paintings. When chances offered they were to be seized. Such optical banquets were to be made the most of. The first good show I remember attending was held at Derby and was made up, if I recollect rightly, of the work of contemporary artists. The critic Wilenski was acting impresario, and as I had read his books on modern painting before the war I was eager to see him. The spectacle proved of interest, though hardly in the manner anticipated. Wilenski was revealed as a heavily built Jew, with hair thin on top and thick at the back. He had a comfortable embonpoint and spoke with the combined certitude of an Oxford don and a West End gallery owner. But before he spoke, he fixed his eyes on the little crowd of servicemen and women and culture-starved civilians, and was obviously not impressed with what he saw. As a prelude to his short address, and hardly bothering to raise his hand, he burped loudly in our faces. A fig for your rabble was clearly his feeling.

The second exhibition I attended was shown in the Y.M.C.A. at Nottingham: an excellent collection of Dutch and Flemish painting. I went night after night, taking a notebook with me and briefly analysing the compositions of those pictures which held me most. Time after time I urged Ian to come, but each time he appeared reluctant. At length, I persuaded him, but all he did was to walk cursorily round the four walls, hardly stopping to look at a single picture. This mystified me until he explained that as he had no access to canvas and paints he could hardly bear to be among those which others had created. I have since found much the same reaction on the part of poets no longer able to find publishers for their verse. To open a book of contemporary verse occasions a pain they prefer to forego. Usually, however, they stay faithful to the poets of their prime. Our flirtation with time is narcissistic.

It was at the same show in Nottingham that I met William de Belleroche, who was Honorary Exhibition Organizer for the National Council of the Y.M.C.A. and had produced a little booklet *Art and the Forces*. He was a somewhat pale and dissipated figure with a fine if rather languid manner. This may have been excusable, for he was a Count. His father the Belgian painter Albert de Belleroche painted high-born ladies and nudes in the Impressionist manner of *la belle époque*, while the son was distinguished as a landscape painter. He looked on Brangwyn as his master and, according to William's friend Gordon Anderson, had caught from the Cornish artist his own reclusive hypochondria. William played the Boswell to Brangwyn, publishing three books about him. And only a couple of years ago (1975) in Andy's flat at Brighton, I saw the remarkable collection of the paintings and drawings of master and disciple. Pictures covered every inch of the walls of both the living-room and the bedroom, watched over by a brood of six statuesque cats. It was rather like being inside Oscar Wilde's Art Nouveau poem 'The Sphinx'. Willy is now dead; but Andy's rooms form a fitting archive of his work.

So while Ian mooned aimlessly about the exhibition in Nottingham, fretting every minute to be gone, I planted myself in front of each painting, seeking to puzzle out its compositional essence. Without Ian, who was obviously unhappy among them, I came back every autumn evening while the show remained open with a notebook in which to record the skeleton design of each painting I looked at. In this reiterated act of attention I lost all sense of time and place, and all their attendant distractions, being finally awarded a sort of beatific vision which kept me singing as I made my way back, down leaf-strewn Shakespeare Street and up through the fascinating terraced cemetery, to my billet not far from Nottingham Castle and the famous Trip to Jerusalem.

At one minute past midnight on 8 May 1945, the war against Germany was officially declared ended. In the following August came the atom bomb on Japan who surrendered unconditionally on the 14th.

I have already noted how the 'long-haired boys' of my Company seemed to be breaking up as the war reached its conclusion. Michael Gough, the actor, and Christopher Fry had both been discharged, and I think Wynyard Browne had gone the same way. The only two of us now left were George Painter and myself. George was later to become a leading authority on Marcel Proust and the author of a study of André Gide. At that time, however, he was professing himself a poet. The strange poem sequence published later as 'The Road to Sinodun' had already been written. I remember reading these Housmanesque pieces in a manuscript book which, together with a private journal, he showed me. Sinodun is a small hill on the upper reaches of the Thames and features in William Morris's *News from Nowhere*. As to the content of these poems, they dealt with an unhappy love-affair in which a girl called Ruth had wrought dreadful havoc on the poet. So devastating was her vampirelike conduct that, one by one, George's teeth had fallen out. Or so he claimed in these clipped poems whose mordant humour reminded one of Heine.

In appearance, George was tall and gangling. He had one of those figures not intended to demonstrate a military bearing. Behind his glasses his eyes were puzzled and pained when not lit with intelligence. Having married his golden-haired cousin, he overstayed his leave and returned to trouble. Trouble, as with Ian Finlay, was George's natural element. He had, I conjectured, a special gift for pain, as have had many of the great Romantics. It is possible that he looked on himself as a divinely intended scapegoat. At least, he decided to mark himself out in this fashion by an act of his own. On the day that George was conscripted, he shaved off his moustache and took a vow not to renew it till a free man again.

In the late summer of 1945 my commanding officer noted that I seemed unwell and sent me, after a friendly chat, to the M.O., along with a letter in which he said he wondered if I needed to see a psychiatrist. The M.O. supported this suggestion and before long I spent half an hour discussing Rainer Maria Rilke with a Jewish trick-cyclist who thereupon awarded me my ticket. I was nearer to a nervous breakdown than I realized, and it was only on returning to civvy street that I sensed how maladjusted I had become.

I received my discharge on 20 September 1945. On the morning of the 21st I made my way to Victoria Station, Nottingham, bound for Marylebone and freedom. Beside me through the twilight of deluging rain, the poet Frederic Vanson sympathetically shouldered my kitbag. A Londoner from one of the Hams, Frederic's passion for learning had manifested itself at an early age. I loved the story he used to tell about jolting down to Southend in the 'winkle-picker express' before the war. Still only in his middle teens, he had turned his attention away from his cockney sweetheart in order to read of love in Plato's *Symposium*. 'Now listen to me, Fred Vanson,' shrilled his doll, 'either you shut that ole book, or I'll chuck it out the winder, straight I will.'

Nothing, however, could hinder for long his wide accumulation of knowledge whether concerning church architecture, astronomy, mathematics, or loco-engineering. So here he was on this early sub-aqueous morning, humping my kitbag through the autumn streets, talking of poetry and how he had a place at a teachers' training college waiting for him. I shook hands and thanked him in the lamplit booking-hall.

Thus ended my inglorious war.

Part Three – Post-war

9

'On wid de job'

As with many ex-Servicemen, the war remained with me for a number of years. It stayed on in a pocket at the back of the mind and frequently popped out to occupy the front. One such residue of Army days was the movement I am about to describe, having first encountered it through the magazine *Khaki and Blue* which, though unofficial, circulated among the Forces.

In a basement room in Redcliffe Gardens, Earls Court, an evening of discussion is coming to an end. People still in, or just out of, the Services, aspirant writers and amateur politicians, have been listening to each other's ideas and addresses with 'willing suspension of disbelief'. The gathering exudes goodwill and enthusiasm. Civvy street, at the moment (1946), looks fairer than it is.

A tall, dark young man who appears Italian, with a Ronald Colman moustache, dismisses us with his blessing. His exhortation is spirited. It is also couched in organ-grinder's English. 'On wid de job, and never mind de bloody snobs and de bureaucrats.' This was Peter Ratazzi, General Secretary of the Front Line Generation, a movement to which I belonged up to 1947. 'On wid de job' was our signature tune, a postwar equivalent of Herbert Morrison's wartime 'Get cracking'. We repeated it with glee. Its pidgin lingo appealed to us immensely.

If I had not, while writing this passage, chanced to come across the manifesto of the F.L.G. printed in some little magazine, I should, at this date, have been hard pressed to say what the movement stood for, and would have concluded it was no more than a beginners' alliance against the oldies and the established. I might also say that the Front Line Generation offered umbrella coverage of a most accommodating order, since many of us members were pacifists, non-combatants or civilians who had never been within firing distance of a front line. In offering, then, 'The Ten Points of Front Line Generation', I am dredging up a dodo document which for all its naïveté did summarize, in a very loose fashion, a lot of what many young people then desired. As a résumé of period aspirations, it is sociologically interesting.

1 To preserve and extend the wartime spirit of comradesnip, born in danger and suffering, on all fronts, fields, offices and factories.

2 To maintain an anticapitalist, antitotalitarian platform, and to insist upon the individual's personal responsibility towards the creation of a free society, based upon moral and spiritual values.

3 To fight for the humanization of industry and a more responsible share in its control and development in order to achieve a dignified way of life for the common man.

4 To encourage individual forms of expression, local culture and craftmanship, and to study their relationship to world patterns of thought, belief and behaviour.

5 To oppose restrictive monopolies from financial interests to literary cliques.

6 To combat snobbery, cruelty, exploitation, warmongering, and bureaucracy wherever they are found to exist.

7 To express the need for a complete revolution in the approach to urgent problems of our time (social conditions, reconstruction, economics, culture, education etc.), a change of heart in the individual, and a transformation of social values.

8 To cooperate with all progressive and active thinkers at home and abroad, and to foster this new articulate spirit throughout Britain and Europe.

9 To propagate by books, press, meetings, discussion and social groups the aims of our 'Front Line Generation'.

10 To assist ex-Servicemen and workers in obtaining suitable occupations in which they can best serve the community, and to encourage their participation in local and national government with the ultimate aim of forming a Front Line Generation Government.

'Ouf! But the sigh of relief that I heave at the end of this list', to borrow an exclamation from Max Beerbohm. What, after all this, could be left wanting? And certainly if any of our critics thought that the F.L.G. was a sort of Old Comrades' Club for the long-haired boys out of battledress, they might appear quite justified.

On the other hand, much that I wished for was set down here. The only trouble was that it sounded rather vague. I had a feeling that the movement stood in need of Rossetti's 'fundamental brain-work'. For what my services were worth, the F.L.G. could have them. So for a while I became the Goebbels of the movement, and through magazines controlled by it – *Everyman*, *The Bookshelf*, *New Generation* – I poured out a stream of articles which at least avoided the usual party clichés. The titles of some of these pieces indicate the direction of my thinking: 'The obsolete political mind,' 'Today's unholy trinity' (money, power and war), 'Wanted: a democracy in persona' (direct government by the people rather than government by remote control).

My position was that of the anarchist trying to accommodate thought to the democratic possibilities given. Could we, for instance, achieve a welfare state without a built-in image of governmental dictatorship? In an article entitled 'Bureaucrats or brothers' contributed to Denys Val Baker's magazine *Voices*, I put the matter thus:

'The modern Radical', wrote Kropotkin half a century ago, 'is a centraliser, a State partisan, a Jacobin to the core.' If this observation was possible before the betrayal of the Russian Revolution had bequeathed a model Factory-State as its standing proof of one's own worst fears, how much more clearly is that truth seen today. 'The sin of nearly all Left-wingers', as George Orwell recently remarked, 'from 1933 onwards is that they have wanted to be anti-Fascist without being anti-totalitarian.' In truth, however, this new confiscation of human, in favour of robot politics is not a tendency restricted to the Left. Whenever the Conservative thinker has advanced beyond the old conceptions of toby-jug feudalism or nineteenth-century *laissez faire*, he has arrived at the politics of mass-production, which demand the creation of a mass-produced mind. All over the world, a fresh type of ruling class is in the process of being evolved. The political name such a type will assume is largely an irrelevance: what is of importance is the running programme and immediate methods such a class will employ. These, wherever they are found, will prove strikingly parallel, and justify their users being described as managerial collectivists.

Whether this sounds any more spot-on than the prose of F.L.G.'s manifesto, I must leave it to the reader to decide. What I had in mind, I imagine, was the advent of the ad-men and advertising boys, the 'Go' man of Macmillan's day or the Selsdon image at the time of Heath. I thought of the Front Line Generation as a captive audience, and proceeded to subject them to semi-anarchist saturation bombing. As far as I could make out, the members were little affected.

Peter Ratazzi, our General Secretary, of Dutch–Italian parentage, had once been a member of Hitler's Youth Movement. Falling out of love with Strength through Joy and Truncheon, he had fled to England and immediately asked to enlist in the British Army. This generous gesture was, of course, suspect; and Peter spent the next two months in prison in Manchester, raging equally against Churchill and Hitler. Released, he became a staff sergeant and was soon organizing Service magazines to boost the morale of frustrated Forces tyros. He intrigued me vastly, though I never got to know him well. He was such a mixture of idealism and self-interest; so thrusting and dynamic, whether on behalf of himself or some cause. I thought, too, that he often failed to create the best impression because he made me think of Machiavelli. Ending some Gladstonian oration, as highminded as but vaguer than that Grand Old Man, he would take his seat to respectful applause, only to be noticed a moment later tugging his moustaches and smirking like a Cheshire cat who had pulled one on the mouse.

One thing Peter certainly had: a flair for publicity. At the start of the movement he had complained of lack of coverage in the press. His way of remedying this was brilliant, and I was soon to read, on the front page of a Sunday paper, of the efficacy of his gambit. A concert at the Albert Hall had been seriously disturbed one Saturday afternoon by the insistent ringing of an alarm clock. This clock, it transpired, belonged to Peter – a new purchase just made by him and safely deposited in his suitcase. Asked afterwards by reporters why he had not switched off the alarm, he replied that he had been too scared; and that, anyway, he had mislaid the key to his suitcase. 'It was all very alarming,' he told them, 'but then it is later than we think.' I can just see his underground smirk emerging after that last remark.

Peter even turned his girl-friends to account. I remember inquiring about one such, and being told that she was a pin-up, 'a Forces' glamour-puss – that sort of thing.' As a reward for being good, she was put on the cover of *New Generation* from which vantage point she glamour-pussed out, bringing more male recruits to F.L.G.

Peter overdid these futurist tactics. For a movement like Vorticism, they were just right, but our General Secretary was no Wyndham Lewis. F.L.G. had the punch all right but lacked intellectual toughness. As a mutual aid platform for younger writers, it was an encouraging gesture. As a 'social-literary movement', it lacked coherence.

I remember, for example, an open forum which we held one evening at Earls Court ('the F.L.G. Secretariat', as Peter liked to call the Redcliffe Gardens address). Peter had invited two speakers from the new firm of Falcon Press to present their views: Roland Gant who was Marxist, and Peter Baker, a Conservative M.P. for Norfolk. There was not much point in his choice of speakers. Neither had anything fresh to say, since both spoke from their party line; and, of course, there was no chance of reconciling their opposite approaches. But ideas to Peter were insubstantial things: they were slogans, captions, ad-men's dressing, never ordered units in a sequence of thought. Personalities alone were real to him: of their publicity value he was never in doubt. Perhaps it was his

German background which made him so misty in his intellectual
bearings with regard to British politics, literature and culture. Or
was it Hitler's fake ideology – an ad-man's politics if ever there
were such – which gave Peter's intellectual performance so spurious
an air?

On the evening in question, I was acting as chairman to the
meeting. We had advertised it widely, and one or two Tory M.P.s
were coming. We had a packed house, and I remember Major
Legge-Bourke, carrying his top-hat fresh from the House, perplexed
and annoyed that there appeared to be no chair awaiting him. I
must admit I sympathized. What beer-cellar politicians were these,
the Major must have asked himself. Clearly not a gentleman's
concern. But the fiasco of the evening was provided by the speeches
of Peter Baker and Roland Gant. Roland was competent enough,
but Communistic explanations were platitudes now to all of us.
Peter Baker, on the other hand, had the politics of a jolly public
school boy. It was all so hearty and terribly old-hat that I wondered
how he could use such clichés without being covered from head to
toe with blushes. I recognize now that such predigested pap is
approved by all parties. Life is very largely a matter of lowering
one's sights on all occasions. Feeling such scant respect for the
viewpoints I knew our speakers represented, I had lapsed somewhat from chairmanly decorum by introducing both of them with
ironic words. I saw Mrs Baker, in a Royal Enclosure hat, regarding
me with evident hatred. I doubt if she grasped what I was saying,
but sensed I was laughing at her darling son.

After this meeting, my interest in the F.L.G. rapidly declined.
Que diable allais-je faire dans cette galère? There was clearly no
satisfactory answer.

Poor Peter Baker turned out to be Wrey Gardiner's evil genius,
though when the Grey Walls Press and Peter's firm of Falcon
Press combined there were no intimations of any sad end. With the
termination of wartime conditions, Wrey's publishing enterprise
needed more money, and this was something that Peter had in
plenty, his father being associated with the flourishing film studios
at Ealing.

Peter and Wrey were not perhaps the most natural partners in a
literary venture. Peter appeared the bustling extrovert. He was

young, and had come direct from the Army, having obtained some decoration for dash or daring during action. 'With his brown, confident, hilarious eyes,' he infected the older more meditative man with a sense of animation. In the early days of the amalgamation, Wrey's verdict was favourable. 'Peter Baker, my vigorous partner,' he wrote, 'is suave and well-dressed and full of a rather attractive laughter, dark-eyed and explosive, slipping from floor to floor like a flash of quick businesslike comedy.'[1] The disintegrating effects of that explosiveness were still far off.

For my part, I found Peter something of a bore. He was cheerful rather than genial, and appeared fundamentally to be a philistine, though he himself sometimes wrote poetry of a sort. I thought he would have been more at home as a sales director in some thrusting City firm, and especially good at selling cars. His ragging fifth-form behaviour I felt to be tedious. One had had enough of that in the Army, and in its high-spirited fashion it had often helped to pass the time or to punctuate long stretches of depression. With the war ended, one expected to put some of this rollicking stuff aside. I had had a bellyful of jolly laughing cobbers, and wanted a regimen of quiet in which to think. Perhaps in 1948 I was a shade too much of a young sobersides.

Peter, however, loved a scrimmage. I remember standing talking with Wrey in his editorial room in Crown Passage. Peter came bursting in at the door, shouting like any pissed-up subaltern, 'Let's debag Stanford'. Since resistance was necessary, Peter and I were soon tussling on the floor, while Wrey, as the owner of this large unruly dog, stood by grinning and nonplussed. In those days I very much sported a cap. Peter seized this and threw it out of the window into Crown Passage. This was quickly followed by his tie which I managed to wrench off him. Regarding these items below, Peter shouted at a passing workman: 'Hi! I say, just bring those up, would you?' the man looked more puzzled than annoyed, but he came puffing up the stairs with the two errant items of clothing. Whether he was rewarded, I cannot say.

All this hearty romping was innocuous enough, though a little wearing. But Peter could reveal himself as quite manic and badly lacking in responsibility. Wrey recalls him, after a good lunch at the Gargoyle, driving 'away impatiently along the pavements of

[1] *The Flowering Moment*, 1949.

Soho back to the office, fifty miles an hour down Shaftesbury
Avenue the wrong side of the road, twisting the wheel among the
traffic of Piccadilly Circus, making people in the road jump for
their lives'.[1] No doubt he thought he was still in his jeep, roaring
into Germany. As the postwar years went by, he began to give less
attention to his publishing and more to politics and the bottle. The
outward and visible sign of this inward condition of his was when
the packer in the firm's basement, in addition to parcelling up books,
began to sell whisky. Peter was now in the liquor business – on an
under-the-counter basis.

Through his father's money and his own gift of the gab, he now
had a seat in Parliament; and, with the bally-hoo of 'a second
Elizabethan Age', began to weave dreams of a noble export drive
which should do the country and himself some good. Not without
a flair for the salesworthy phrase, he coined the notion of a 'League
of Merchant Venturers'. To launch this scheme to the nation, he
hired the Albert Hall. Bigwigs from all walks of life were invited
for the occasion; and there were even one or two bishops with
attendant actresses.

It was a Saturday afternoon and Peter, of course, was to be the
chief speaker. All things boded fair, but a few of his myrmidons
were worried. If Peter could be kept from the bar he would
probably acquit himself well. Steps were therefore taken, and the
bar used by performers was shut until the meeting finished. Peter's
soldierly tactics now combined with his slyness as an alcoholic.
Giving his well-wishing guards the slip, he got himself down to a
bar used by electricians and maintenance men in the very bowels
of the building, and when run to earth was abundantly tanked up.
Churchill's oratorical powers could withstand considerable intake;
but Peter, sadly, was no Winston. The address he gave insured
that the League of Merchant Venturers issued forth stillborn into
public life.

From this point onwards, things went fast down hill. His
marriage had not been happy, it being said that he had changed
horses when half way to the altar. For both the lady and himself this
had not proved auspicious. More and more, drink became his only
standby. The end came when he signed a cheque for some £10,000,
I believe, with the name of Bernard Docker. His parliamentary

[1] *Ibid.*

and publishing career in ruins, Peter was now deprived of his seat and went to prison for several years. From time to time I would send him a postcard, remembering his mad frolics. His family stuck fast to him; but, on his release, he never made a comeback. A mere shell of his ebullient self, he was now a gravely sick man and died before the end of the 'sixties.

But more was lost than Peter's reputation and a large amount of money. As a fellow-director of the firm, Wrey Gardiner was worried that he might be liable in the ensuing bankruptcy of Falcon Press, and ultimately came to lose his house in Vicarage Gate, Kensington.

Others of us who had basked in the warmth of Good King Charles Wrey Gardiner's golden days, now counted our losses. I had published two books through the Gardiner–Baker nexus: *The Freedom of Poetry* (critical essays) with Falcon Press, and an edition of Thackeray's *English Humorists*, appearing with the Grey Walls Press imprint. These, as non-best-selling titles, inevitably became remainders, though the first now appears in the catalogues of secondhand booksellers at £4 or £5 a copy. In addition, I had a contract to edit a selection of George Darley's poems which I had prepared for press, plus a promise that when this was published it should be followed by a similar selection from Beddoes, both to appear in that attractive series known as the Crown Classics. I was also to have put together a volume of Beddoes's letters which I regarded as some of the most striking correspondence written by a poet. All these toys of time have been swept away, I fear, for good; but my loss was nowhere near so bad as that of many others; or of Wrey himself, the chief living survivor of that shipwreck.

One day before the Falcon–Grey Walls empire crumbled, I had met the artist Cecil Collins on the stairs to Wrey's office in Crown Passage, and had been as impressed by his appearance as I had already been by his painting. Wrey had paid £22 for Collins's 'Three Fools in a Storm' some time in 1943 or 1944 and had then proceeded to identify the figures with Nick Moore, Fred Marnau and himself. As if to prove the strange durability of foolhood – the survivalship of the outsider – this picture came through the bombing of Wrey's tiny town cottage in Red Lion Street with no

damage done to it at all. A little later, at the end of the war, Grey
Walls Press had issued a small illustrated album of these paintings
entitled *The Book of Fools*, prefaced with an introductory essay by
Collins.

With their tall dunce's caps, their slender bodies and sad, gentle,
dreaming faces, the image of these figures appealed to me greatly.
I saw the Fool as one type of the Romantic, the uncommitted
contemplative man, horrifically alien in a world of action, and wrote
a poem on this theme. The piece appeared in Herman Peschmann's
anthology *The Voice of Poetry 1930–1950* but since it does not
appear in either of my two collections and has not been reprinted,
I give it here:

Poem for a Picture by Cecil Collins

The Primitive, the Child, and the Poet are of imagination
all compact. . . . They are fools, of course.   PETER GOFFIN.

> The golden bodkins of the sun
> transpierce the dimpled green
> of the dale's bright bosom.
> Blossoms festooned along each lilting bough
> explode in jets of cotton wool and steam:
> and here – where noon assays
> its consummation –
> pillowed upon a shady hump of grass,
> in pointed cap, the Fool achieves perfection:
> asleep upon the daisy-shackled earth.
>
> Above, in the sky's
> clematis-coloured lake
> a stalkless tulip floats in molten fire.
> Under the clustered awning of an oak-tree
> a woman sits
> with dove-calm lips and eyes.
> Two dreaming hands
> within her lap lie folded,
> and fate's quiet needle-work
> seems laid aside.
>
> Her smile is like a clock
> that stopped in sunlight.

With thread of stillness
she has stitched the hours
into a flower-shaped sampler of the present,
and rests content
in unforeseeing peace.

Midsummer silence –
mood of the heart's high season!
Which, then, is an illusion;
which is real:
this world where time's green well
remains unruffled,
or that where fools
must wait their turn to sleep?

It is easy enough for me now to fault the poem for wilful Romantic *luxuria*, overindulgence in picturesque diction, but at the time I felt it somewhat conveyed the timeless, almost spaceless, world of the Fool; as well as asking the (answerless?) question: how is reality known and tested – by action or by contemplation?

Cecil Collins, along with John Craxton and Lucien Freud, seemed to me the most interesting manifestation in English painting since Wyndham Lewis and William Roberts before and after the First World War. I saw them as having much in common with two older men, Stanley Spencer and Graham Sutherland, who belonged more to the English world of Blake and Palmer than the deracinated international scene dominated by Picasso.

It was Ian Finlay who introduced me to three painters of note, who have all since come to an unfortunate end, dying by suicide or what looked like self-destruction: Robert MacBryde, Robert Colquhoun and John Minton. The two Roberts were possessed of a prodigious reputation in the war years and just after: reputation in the singular, because they were always reckoned together as if they were one unit rather in the manner of Chester-Belloc. This unity of reference sprang from their relationship rather than from their painting styles, similar as these sometimes were. They were, in fact, homosexuals ('I didn't count them as queers,' Paul Potts had once remarked to me. 'They're just like any old married couple.')

When they came to London, Colquhoun and MacBryde had been

taken up by Wyndham Lewis, who lived in Notting Hill where they also came to settle. Mention of Wyndham Lewis leads me to digress with the following short incident. I had been told that the artist was to be found, during drinking hours, in the buffet of Notting Hill Gate station. On one of my leaves, I discovered him there, seated on a stool at the counter and wearing a black patch over one eye. Having published an essay about him in *The Fortune Anthology*, I shyly approached to make myself known. But when I addressed him with the words: 'Mr Wyndham Lewis, I believe', he swung round, denying that the appellation fitted. 'You're mistaken,' he insisted, referring to himself as 'Captain Brown'. Some time after this event, I mentioned it to Roy Campbell, who had known him quite well when they were young. Campbell capped my experience with one of his own. Once, years before, they had been dining at some restaurant when Lewis had leaned forward and told him they must talk more quietly. 'There's a man at a table behind listening to everything we say.' Campbell had looked around the restaurant on all sides. There was no one within six tables of them. 'He thought he was being persecuted,' he explained. 'The syph he had in 1914, when he tried to cure himself, had touched his brain.'

Back to Colquhoun and MacBryde. The former I did not like at all when I attended, with Ian Finlay, a party given by the two Roberts. It was a New Year occasion, and the hospitality was lavish. They were both the type of Scot who makes his money in England but remains formidably anglophobe. Both liked making gestures of defiance; but whereas MacBryde expressed his nationalism cogently enough, it was normally contained within the framework of his natural courtesy. Paul Potts, who revered him, has left a loving portrait in *Dante Called You Beatrice* (1960):

> I once saw him iron a shirt with a spoon. He was a Celt, a King and a radical. He had a Latin love of life and a Scots sense of simplicity. He could turn a cup of tea into a feast. He loved children, dancing, singing and giving away money. . . . He hated bad art, the Hanoverian dynasty and Lyons tea-shops; loved Turkish baths, patrons and cooking. He had probably more love in his nature than anybody since St Francis of Assisi or Spinoza. He could hate well, too.

More than Colquhoun, he was addicted to wearing the kilt in Kensington or Soho; and would execute many a sword dance on the pavement. Less ebullient than MacBryde, Colquhoun I found gloweringly offensive. Perhaps we struck the wrong chord in each other; perhaps he intuited I did not much care for his painting. I remember one mould-brown canvas of a sort of mangy cubist cat, and another ('Girl with Circus Goat') which had little left to it when the ingredients of Picasso and Klee were subtracted. Maclaren Ross received the same impression of Colquhoun as I did, and in his *Memoirs of the Forties* (1965) depicted him as 'wolfishly lean and sullen [with] something of the handsome hell-fire preacher' about him, 'as if he might at any moment call down the wrath of the Lord on Sodom and Gomorrah that surrounded him'.

Another factor that did not much endear the two Roberts to me was the inarticulate sounds they would make during their pub crawls in Soho. I suppose if one caught them early in the evening, before the point of no return had been reached, one might expect, and receive, conversation. Later than nine it was my luck to hear them reply to questions or greetings with grunts, growls or unintelligible mutter. Perhaps I was wrong in asking for speech from artists whose medium was not that of words.

Johnny Minton, who sometimes shared a studio with the two Roberts, was a very different cup of tea. Horsefaced and Byronic, a man of wit, sensitivity and tact, he was one of the few people I have known whom the possession of wealth became (he belonged to the family famous for its china). He had none of the wealthy person's all too frequent petty meanness; he gave away a fortune, pound note by pound note, as others would hand out betting slips. On the other hand, it is arguable that his life might have been more self-disciplined had he not possessed, like E. M. Forster, the inheritor's store of 'golden guineas'.

Preparing a risotto for Ian Finlay and myself one day, a dish which we ate with a downpour of red pepper, he asked me if I knew George Barker. I replied that I knew his poetry.

'Well, if you haven't heard George performing at the Windsor Castle on Saturday night,' said Johnny, 'I doubt if you know what poetry is. Odes and elegies by the dozen. They sweep them up after closing time.'

'What is the secret of this? What is George's favourite drink?'

'They're all his favourites. He's a good Catholic; a good bad Catholic, that is. As for the secret, George is a good poet. So is his little benzedrine spray.'

There must be many who blessed Johnny for his easy kindness right up to his death. When Ian was living in a Highland croft, painting away at starvation level and opening the door to the snow on winter mornings in the hope of popping a hare into the pot, he was many times succoured by Johnny's fivers. The best verbal portrait of him occurs in Maclaren Ross's *Memoirs of the Forties* (1965) where he describes Minton as 'tall, bony and attenuate, his face swarthy and elongated [with] white front protruding teeth which caused the mouth to remain open in a slightly awkward oval'. He notes, too, Minton's 'Spanish quality', remarking that 'had he been an actor he'd have been a natural for the role of Don Quixote'.

It was at a New Year party given by the two Roberts that I met George Barker and his friend Dylan Thomas. Dylan was clearly intoxicated (as I also was somewhat on that occasion) and, along with some other party-goers, was treading out the measure of a slow impromptu dance. The dancers all faced inwards and, standing on the periphery, I greeted him by name as his shuffling form came revolving past. Hearing himself called – though he didn't know me from Adam – he turned, and with an old-world gesture, bowed and bade me a very good evening.

Dylan already had the girth of a Silenus (in a group of friends discussing war work, he once said he would go as a tank), but had not become that mountain of corruption which he sometimes looked in his last days. Artificial light suited him best; but I remember seeing him five years later; walking down the Strand, a putty-faced ghost, wearing vibrant Augustus John colours (including a magenta roll-collar sweater) which threw into relief his ghostly paleness. He then looked like the apparition of that 'transcendental tinplate worker' who had so impressed the young Keith Brace when an undergratduate at Oxford. Maclaren Ross recalls that in 1943, when he first met Dylan, the poet no longer resembled 'that much reproduced early photograph of him' which the original would contemptuously refer to as 'the Fucking Cherub'.

I never knew Dylan well enough to exchange anything but

random pub greetings and had not much regard for his work till I
was won over to a larger measure of appreciation round about 1949.
Following his death I wrote a book about his poetry, and, in the
course of composing it, collected quite a few stories about him.
Here is one not included in my book which was told me by Wrenne
Jarman, a Richmond poet and literary hostess.

On one occasion she had arranged with Dylan for him to come
and read his verse to some local poetry-lovers. These maidenly or
matronly fanciers of Apollo were gathered together under her roof
on the evening in question, waiting for the poet. Seven o'clock, and
Dylan wasn't there. The hands crept on, and still no Dylan. Half
an hour passed . . . three-quarters of an hour . . . a whole hour late
and still no sign of him. People had started to mutter and complain.
Two had actually bade their adieux, when suddenly, a ring . . .
Dylan was on the mat, apologizing, smiling, and woefully drunk.
By a superhuman effort, he controlled himself, and read to the
scandalized audience one of his best and newly written poems.
Annoyance and boredom were conjured away by the spell of his
magnificent voice. Royally, the poem drew to a close; and as the
listeners broke into applause, Dylan turned his back on them and
proceeded to retch and vomit in the hearth.

Wrenne took rather a dim view of Dylan. She narrated his
behaviour at a Poets' Club dinner at which, drunk as usual, he had
smoked throughout. 'Don't you think the writing of poetry ought
to be limited to gentlemen, Derek?' I agreed that would be an
ideal condition, but doubted whether her proviso would produce
the best verse.

I was at first not much interested in Dylan's work, and as late as
1947 wrote that the poetry of Thomas and Barker seemed not to
belong to the English tradition (Barker's mother – 'as huge as Asia,
seismic with laughter'[1] – was Irish). It represented, I pontificated,
'a Gongorism of the modern Celt'. There is nothing like the
evocation of tradition for dealing with what is not our cup of tea.
Somewhere about 1949 Muriel Spark made me see sense by
reading 'Fern Hill' to me. From that time I was a convert to Dylan
– to the tune of about a dozen poems. When I wrote my book on
his work, I suggested his status as a poet would place him alongside Thomas Gray, like Dylan, no over-producer. G. S. Fraser

[1] 'To my Mother', *Eros in Dogma*, 1944.

thought this somewhat too high, and substituted the name of
William Collins as a more suitable analogy. Which of us was right,
I wonder? If only there wasn't that inconvenient 'Elegy Written in
a Country Churchyard', Dylan would obviously be Gray's peer.

To return to George Barker, who was David Gascoyne's friend
(they dedicated poems to each other). Someone once said that
Barker's poems were those of a hoodlum angel. The phrase
certainly described the poet. There was a smiling gigolo allure, a
sweet *diablerie* about the man. How well I recall him wearing his
famous brown leather raincoat which MacNeice had given him in
Birmingham; or hearing him read, in his magnificent black velvet
voice, the ballad of 'Tam Lin' at a poetry gathering in Bayswater:

> O I forbid you maidens a',
> That wear gowd in your hair,
> To come or gae by Carterhaugh,
> For young Tam Lin is there.

George had the same sexual charisma as the demon lover Tam Lin;
and has well described the male braggadocio which fuelled his early
and middle years in a poem from his book *In Memory of David
Archer* (1973):

> Heavenly events of those Venetian evenings when
> with such well washed sexual pride we stalked up and down
> those Chirico esplanades, shirts open to the belt, an erection
> like a Guinness bottle in the trouser pocket, and a supreme
> confidence like a Canaletto illuminating all
> that we said and did.

In the immediate postwar days, I had my head full of
Kierkegaard, Martin Buber and other gurus. This sometimes made
me unreasonably solemn when potations were being circulated.
I remember one Soho evening, when I might have been more
exegetically tedious than usual, George saying to me: 'You need
to go on the Big Wheel at Battersea.' What he was recommending
was an immersion in crude excitement. Vulgar action was what I
needed to blow away the cobwebs of philosophic introspection.

George Barker, Dylan Thomas and David Gascoyne were the
leading luminaries among the Parton Street poets who, in the later

'thirties, had spearheaded an alternative movement to Social Realism. They preceded the Apocalyptic poets published by the Fortune Press, and were thus in one sense the forerunners or founding fathers of the Neo-Romantic trend, though they never employed this epithet in speaking of themselves. Recently, however, in an interview, George Barker declared 'that I was the first chap who had the gumption to use the word "apocalypse" ' and he described it as an 'absolutely Rome/Bernini word'.[1] If we take it to refer to the Revelations of St John, with its story of the passing away of an old heaven and an old earth to be followed by the coming of the new, and then recall that Barker employed the word two years before the war, then his nonchalant claim is validated. More to the point, these Parton Street poets were, at their best, superior writers to all but a handful of the Neo-Romantics proper.

When something like a full history of twentieth-century English poetry is compiled, the colourful origins and associations of this group will merit fuller attention. So far, little has been written on it as a collective manifestation, though Rosalind Wade published an essay on some of its communal features, entitled 'The Parton Street poets' in *Poetry Review* (Winter 1963–4), and Maurice Carpenter has written of them in his reminiscences *A Rebel in the Thirties* (1975).

The name of the group derived from a bookshop run by David Archer in Parton Street off Red Lion Square, Holborn. The Parton Bookshop was the equivalent, in the late 'thirties, of Harold Monro's Poetry Bookshop of earlier date. Like Monro's experiment, the bookshop also housed the editorial offices of a small publishing firm, the Parton Press, as well as a sort of rudimentary dormitory where poets, not living in central London, could stay overnight. Just across the narrow street lay the Parton Café which served to quench the poets' thirst with innumerable cups of coffee after they had talked themselves hoarse. It also provided more solid victuals.

All this was the work of David Archer, a man whose orthodox exterior gave no clue to his being the patron and impresario of a motley band of younger poets (including the young John Pudney) who were gipsy and bohemian in their behaviour. David Archer's

---

[1] 'An interview with George Barker', *Contemporary Literature*, vol. 12, no. 4, 1971.

K

background – a west of England military family – was impeccable, as was the cut of his suits. Neat, well groomed but not a dandy, he answered absolutely to Lionel Johnson's dictum on dress that in his clothes a gentleman should be perfectly unexceptional. One thing which put David among the outcasts and poets was his homo-sexuality, something much harder to get round before the war. George Barker, in his book *In Memory of David Archer* (1973), speaks of his cruising through Soho for sailors. But he also cele-brates his affection and generosity:

> the enormous gold
> urn of your heart
> in which lie the ashes of your friends.

From being a rich man who had used so much of his money to promote the poets who were his personal friends, David's last days, before his death in the 'sixties, were impecunious.

Gascoyne, Barker and Thomas were usually grouped together like the Englishman, Irishman and Welshman in a joke. There was also a Scotsman who completed the quartet: W. S. Graham, whom we called Willie or Sydney without distinction, and whom I found the most congenial of the lot.

Sydney was sometimes described as the Scots Dylan Thomas, but though he chose words for their suggestive and non-rational value, his poems were often without that torrid proliferation of adolescent imagery which cluttered so much of Dylan's early verse. Some of his poems seemed to be erected out of blocks of sounds in which the auditory content was far in advance of the semantic one:

> By this loud night traded into evidence
> Of a dark chord of voices at hand
> I lie, work of the gruff sea's innocence
> And lie,[1]

I first encountered Sydney at a poets' weekend held by Denys Val Baker at his bungalow, the Wood House, some way out of Tring. There were so many there that some of us had to sleep in a caravan parked in a field half a mile away. I was one of those who

[1] 'Night's fall'.

slept in the wheeled contraption, made the more uncomfortable that September night by a number of mosquitoes who were holding a house-party there. My somewhat oddly titled poem 'The Unicorns take Sugar with their Tea', refers to our morning walk from the caravan back to the Wood House for breakfast. I thought of the poets as unicorns – noble and mythical beasts.

Sydney was seen at his best on this occasion, though the fact that he and Ian Finlay had marked down the same girl as companion for the night did entail some confused comings and goings. Sydney had worked as a riveter in the shipbuilding yards on the Clyde, but his fresh complexion and rolling eye reminded me of Robert Burns. Like that dionysian ploughboy, Sydney enjoyed his potations – 'big drinks' was a favourite phrase of his. He was also the soul of generosity. When he won an Atlantic Award a couple of years after the war, he did not possess the proverbial two pennies. No sooner had he his £200 cheque than he insisted on buying us all doubles, even unto the third time of asking. One night's drinking with some friends cost him about £8. No wonder he had to be rescued by Vivienne Koch, the American critic, and shipped to the United States a few months later.

One of my first recollections of him is of his singing, in his fine soaring voice, the words of that lovely song 'The Lark Ascending'. He also had then a beautiful girl-friend with the douce name of Nessie Dunsmuir. Nessie, coming from a country where knowledge is respected, had more to recommend her than the mere in-and-out statistics of her starlet sisters. Daughter of a miner, she had sharpened her native Scots sense with extramural philosophy lectures. Sydney had sung her praises in a number of poems:

> O gentle queen of the afternoon
> Wave the last orient of tears.
> No daylight comet ever breaks
> On so sweet an archipelago
> As love on love.[1]

For all his modernism, Sydney's muse had a folksong suggestion about it. He possessed the common touch and was a great success with the young. Ian Finlay told me how he had taught some children

[1] 'Poem', *Cage without Grievances*, 1942.

from the poorer tenements in Greenock to sing a refrain from a poem he had made:

> Excepting Nessie Dunsmuir
> The fairest of them all.

When Nessie appeared in the street, she was duly greeted by this salutation.

Nessie had written verse herself. Here is a piece characteristic of her – the natural expression of her warm radiant nature:

> I would have chosen children,
> the breathing hearth. And made my own.
> ritual in winter, birth and bone.
> Not this wordy ferment in the fingers,
> this sailing hunger capsized in the breast.
> I would have chosen children,
> and roofed with rose of fire their early east.

Nessie had long ruled supreme over Sydney's heart, but at one point they parted. This must have heralded in the regime of Vivienne Koch whose brunette qualities were in contrast to Nessie's blonde glory. A clever Jewish academic, Vivienne had the poise of a women of the world, though based, perhaps, upon the habits of American society (with its open explicit appreciation) rather than our own where praise and recognition are less overtly stressed.

I remember how a few of us were staying with Wrey Gardiner at Grey Walls in Essex. Although not the ancestral home, it was hung with portraits of Wrey's forebears, eighteenth-century soldiers and sailors – a house with a past but no future. Vivienne was of the party; and as some of us stood by the hearth, talking and drinking before lunch, we became aware of a presence outside our small semicircle by the fire. Turning our eyes away from the flames which flickered cheerfully in the grate, we perceived Vivienne poised momentarily in the doorway. She had gone upstairs to change (though no one else observed this nice distinction) and, coming down 'tarted up to the nines', had no intention of letting the impression made by her be lost upon us. Determined, therefore, on an effective entry, she remained in the doorway until we broke off our chatter and directed the batteries of attention upon her. An academic oracle (her book on Yeats's later poems was not written to be overlooked), she sought also to appropriate the image of both butterfly and *très grande dame*. And where better than in a house which could boast its own ghost and in which some of Old Noll's redcoat troopers had been billeted? Vivienne was a fine conversationalist, though her bent was rather for solo performance. This I registered all too well on the journey back from Billericay to Liverpool Street. No male chauvinist pig, I trust, I was none the less glad to bid adieu to this attractive and dynamic (but also unremitting) talk-machine.

Shortly after one of Sydney's visits to America to lecture and read his poems, I heard he was laid up in hospital. The cause of his illness was not single, but one of the factors was unusual. He suffered from sauce mania. When I first knew him, he would shake up the bottle as if he were preparing himself a cocktail. And if there was nothing to go with it, he would spread the ketchup on bread and butter. His search for piquancy reminded me of Keats sprinkling pepper on his tongue the better to appreciate a peach's cooling juice. Both poets were connoisseurs of the senses, savourers of experience. Only too often there was little to go with the O.K. or H.P. sauce. For days at a time Sydney would live without a proper coating of food to his stomach. He once told me about plucking turnips in the field and eating these in an uncooked state. Without digestive shock-absorbers, spoonfuls of tomato ketchup or pints bought him by his friends proved to be duodenal blockbusters. Sydney was admitted to hospital and given the milk-drip treatment.

The last of the non-Sassenach painters and poets whom I met through Ian Finlay was Paul Potts, in some ways the oddest of the lot. Paul was an Irish Canadian, whom I once mistook for Jewish (more about this anon); and I am sure he will forgive me if, in an Irishism, I describe him as a true 'English eccentric'. (He was, after all, born in Berkshire and educated at Stonyhurst, while his paternal grandfather was a small East Anglian landowner.)

According to his own reckoning, Paul was a failed poet. With this statement I would not entirely concur. Woodenness of statement and lack of rhythm marred most of the small amount of poetry he published, but there was a small percentage of it which by its economy and simplicity overcame the poet's technical awkwardness. Such pieces, it seemed to me, had the wholeness of home-baked bread. Here is one (from *The Faber Book of Twentieth-Century Verse*, 1956) which I very much like:

Prayer to Our Lady

Mary Cohen get for me.
Those things you had yourself.
You wrote a poem
Had a son
Lived a proper life.

All points in this brief poem are telling: the Christ-child spelt with a small 's'; the Magnificat spoken of as a poem; the rough and colloquial verbs ('get' for 'obtain', 'had' for 'experienced'); and the longing for normality ('lived a proper life').

The title of Paul's volume *Instead of a Sonnet*, published by Tambimuttu, is indicative. Because his verse was 'no good at all', he had to express the evident poet in him through some other medium. 'I try to write prose,' he admitted, 'as charged with intensity as true poetry', and there are pages in *Dante Called You Beatrice* and its follow-up, *To Keep a Promise* (for all the book's disfiguring sentimentality), which are among the finest passages written in prose since the war.

Through being *manqué* as a poet in print, Paul became all the more a poet in his living. His excited talk was often poetic in its intensity, and his vision of Socialism so poetic that he became a party of one, removed alike from the pedestrian prosing of Labour after the war and the arid theoretical legalism of the Communists. His contemporary hero in this field was Orwell, a man whose old-fashioned forthrightness the New Left find it hard to stomach.

Readers of his book *Invitation to a Sacrament* will remember how he tells us that had his chosen woman wanted his love, 'she would have had to share it with all the poor and each of the lonely', and the force of his feelings for her, when at length his hopes were confounded, only served to confirm and strengthen his own quite individual politics of charity and his ethics of compassion. T. E. Hulme once described Romanticism as 'spilt religion', and perhaps it could be said that Paul's Romantic politics (as opposed to *Realpolitik*) were a sort of spilt sexual love. Hence the aura of his perfervid devotion to the small nations, Ireland and Israel, whom he frequently features as attractive women molested and assaulted by bullies. His *Dante Called You Beatrice* is the story of an unhappy love-affair whose scars are deep. Yet it seems to me it would be a mistake to regard Paul's disappointment as an unmitigated disaster. Perhaps it was 'not a bad fate' after all. To adapt the remark of a writer on Novalis, 'his affections were not for purely personal use'. Cheated of their natural goal, they have been employed by Paul Quixote Potts to help defend causes which have not proved Everyone's Sweetheart.

But all this is to anticipate our first meeting, when Ian Finlay took me to call on him in a street off High Street, Kensington, in 1946 or 1947. All I knew of him at that time was his little volume *Instead of a Sonnet* published in 1944, and his general reputation as 'the People's Poet' – an oddly legendary being who had lived in Red Lion Square and hawked his own ballad-sheets through Soho. Since poetry was not at that date in London the flourishing light industry it has now become, Paul's peddling of his poems seemed to me a right and courageous gesture.

Predisposed as I was in favour of Paul, the feeling was not reciprocated. After a tea of bread-and-honey, we sat talking for a while in the darkish den of a basement room, and then retired to a nearby pub for drinks. I had just bought him a pint when the storm broke. Roland Gant, I related, had mimicked the authors who climbed the stairs at Crown Passage to see Wrey Gardiner in his office: David Gascoyne, Paul, myself and many others. At this, Paul took violent offence, directing his anger at me. He picked up his pint from the green painted table, where we stood talking in the pub yard and hurled it to the stone-paved ground, where it broke into a thousand splinters. I had thought that Roland's act was a perfectly harmless one: we were, after all, equally mimicked. For some reason, Paul seemed to think that he was being mocked exclusively; and this, in conjunction with the fact that he quite erroneously believed me to be the recipient of a private income, filled him with exasperation. It was no doubt the latter error that led him to describe me (an attested anarchist in those days) as 'a bloody little bourgeois'.

Not having any special respect for what was, or is, called the working class (I have certainly put in a good many more working man-hours than dear Paul), I was not mortally offended by the term. For the record, however, I sought to put things straight. I explained that all of us had suffered equally at the block of Roland's humour (what more could the egalitarian demand?); and that, much as I regretted it, I had only my gratuity and what I could earn from writing to support me. Later, I understood what had caused Paul to blow his top. Although he had kept his liberty, the circumstances of his life had been hard. Nor was his temper of the gentlest. He had once, someone told me, visited a publisher to collect a cheque which was overdue. Having been fobbed off again and again, and still meeting with no redress, he had picked up a typewriter from a desk and hurled it across the room. On which my comment is : Good for him!

Misunderstandings removed, I came more and more to enjoy Paul's not over-frequent excursions into print. Essays he wrote on Walt Whitman, Ignazio Silone and George Orwell seemed to make most critical prose so much grey-mottled academic fudge. Then came his book *Dante Called You Beatrice* which I reviewed enthusiastically in *Time and Tide* in 1960, following up with an article in the *Meanjin Quarterly* in which I spoke of his work along with that of George Barker, David Gascoyne and W. S. Graham.

Once more, it appeared, I was in trouble – to explain which I will quote the letter he wrote to the editor of the magazine in question :

Dear C. B. Christesen,
    I would like to correct a serious factual error about me in Derek Stanford's article *David Gascoyne and the Unacademics* in your last number. However, before I do so, I would like to make it quite clear that the essay as a whole was of real import-ance and his treatment of my work was a triumph, at least it was a triumph for me. It was the first or almost the first time that my work was treated so seriously, certainly in such distinguished company. But Mr Stanford insists that I am Jewish because I am so pro-Jewish. I believe that this comes about because anti-semitism is unconsciously so deeply rooted in people that they can't believe one can be so permanently pro-Jewish unless one

is oneself a Jew, or half or quarter Jewish. That is why I have gone to all the trouble to write to you across the whole world about this. I am not a Jew, and have no Jewish ancestors, although I am very proud to relate that I went to Jerusalem to join the army of Israel in the hill country of Judea during the country's War of Independence.

In one instance, Mr Stanford really did cheat, which is quite frightfully extraordinary in such a good critic. He says that I wrote to thank him (for a beautifully intelligent review of my book) in Yiddish. Whereas what I did do was to write to him *in English*, and say 'For this, I write to thank you, twice in Yiddish, once in Hebrew'.

It was not, as Paul suggested, any unconscious antisemitism that had led me to ascribe a partially Jewish strain to his make-up. My own goodwill to the Jewish people has never been in doubt. My reason, rather, for attributing it to him was the generous sprinkling of Yiddish locution assisted by Jewish gesticulations, which Paul evinced in conversation. What I did not realize was that his love of the Jewish nation extended both to Yiddish and Hebrew speech. If ever there was, in Wyndham Lewis's phrase, an honorary 'pukka Kosher', then Paul was one such.

Seeing that the tone of his letter signified a correspondent as least as gratified as annoyed, I was surprised to come upon him in Piccadilly some months afterwards and hear him explode once more in wrath. I had just passed the Royal Academy and was about to cross Bond Street when he confronted me shouting that, in my essay, I had made nonsense of his life work by attributing Jewish blood to him. Dismay and amusement led me to dangerous jay-walking, all the way to Green Park, while Paul ranted and I attempted to damp down the flames with honest explanation.

Wrey Gardiner once described him as one of 'the grand *pitres,* Christs with a sense of humour'.[1] The hardest test of humour is when its object is the self; and I cannot say that it was much in evidence in Paul that afternoon. I believe I was forgiven, however, which I should emphatically wish to be, since I would rather remain in Paul's good books than in those kept by many a more bruited author.

[1] *The Flowering Moment,* 1949.

Should anyone ever ask me to name the finest memorial essay penned by anyone since the war, I should be tempted to refer them to Paul's essay on Orwell, 'Don Quixote on a Bicycle'. If I could write on anyone whom I have both loved and respected as well as Paul wrote on Orwell, there would be good reason for me to feel proud.

10

A Girl of Slender Means

It must have been about 1948 that I went round, cap in hand, to see Muriel Spark at Portman Square, where she edited *The Poetry Review* from the London headquarters of the Poetry Society. 'Cap in hand' is a metaphor descriptive of the state of mind in which one approaches an editor when asking for review work. As a literal definition of my headwear, it was inaccurate, for by then I was affecting a black, soft, somewhat furry hat which gave me the appearance of an undertaker's man afflicted with bohemian leanings. Fred Marnau had worn a similiar model which conferred the look upon him of some anarchist friend of an archduke. With me, the impression was less aristocratic. I called it, in fact, my suicide hat.

By this time I had published one volume of critical essays and a volume and a half of verse. This half is to be accounted for by a book of poems which Jack Bayliss and I shared. *A Romantic Miscellany* contained twenty-three pieces by Jack and eighteen by myself, and although we dated its defiant Preface '29th October 1944' it did not appear till two years later. Jack had already published an earlier volume, *The White Knight* (1944), which had won him many golden opinions from many critics, including Walter de la Mare and Osbert Sitwell, who were later instrumental in getting him a Hodder and Stoughton bursary. Jack would also relate how Robert Nichols had waxed enthusiastic about the book, only to die a fortnight after those fair words had been spoken. He remarked that this did not seem to augur well.

My own first book was *Music for Statues* (1948), one of the last titles which Herbert Read accepted for the Broadway House Poetry series published by Routledge and Kegan Paul when the wartime boom in poetry began to abate. Various people who have been kind enough to read the poems in it have asked me, somewhat puzzled, the meaning of the title. I have told them that the statues are all those many persons with ears, like the statues of bronze or stone who cannot hear the music of the spheres. Perhaps this ironically worded forecasting was needlessly glum, as a number of these pieces appeared afterwards in anthologies, Geoffrey Grigson choosing eight of my poems for his anthology *Poetry of the Present.*

I envisaged that such small status as might come to me would probably result from my critical writing, and my first volume of prose *The Freedom of Poetry* (published in 1948 and not in 1947 as the printer's date proclaims) had received a promising press. I had tried in the Introduction to these essays to sketch in a tentative anarchist aesthetic, something I should now repudiate on political and philosophical grounds. Five years later John Heath-Stubbs described it as a work of existential criticism – an honourable attribution in those days but not one I had intended. Best of all comments on the book was one which my old friend Robert Armstrong made while introducing me as a speaker at the Poetry Society when he referred to me as the author of *The Freedom from Poetry.* Of course, I knew how destructive of individual poets critics often are, but the notion that I might have succeeded in eliminating the art form as a whole certainly came as news to me.

In 1948, however, my name was a reasonable one. Reginald Moore had described me as 'one of our rising young critics' especially commending to the subscribers to *Modern Reading* my wartime essays in *New Road*, while Herbert Palmer in *The Fortnightly* declared that 'Derek Stanford is a gloomy, adventurous and rather flat symbolist but he seems the most promising of our young poet-critics'.

When I entered the portals of Portman Square, I was not, one might say, without *cartes de visite* – credentials, at any rate, of a minimum order. Even so, I had not the easiest of manners, having spent the first six months out of khaki theoretically considering the case of suicide; and my black hat heightened the mortality aura.

But if I was tense and anxious, I found that Muriel Spark also exhibited nervousness. This put me more at my ease, her own diminutive stature adding to my confidence. Since I have already described my first meeting with her (*Muriel Spark: a biographical and critical study*, 1963), I will merely say here that I became a regular contributor to *The Poetry Review* and the editor's friend and *confidant*.

Muriel had a clever manner and a quick mind, added to which there were the attractions of her person, themselves of no mean order. First as the Secretary of the Poetry Society and then as both Secretary and Editor of *The Poetry Review* she had her own backers among the male officers of the Society and among the men and women who made up the General Council. Always, however, she was aware of the opposition element out to get her. The old gang did not take at all kindly to her introduction of much new work by younger poets, and though she invariably showed respect for the formal well-made poem and what we used to speak of as 'tradition', she little favoured the conventional composition which so many less well read readers tended to confuse with it.

Then, too, there were those male officers among the top brass of the Society, who thought that their support of her and her programme should be repaid in favours. I remember her telling me of the trouble that one of them, in particular, had given. At all times he had a merry look in his eye, and the suggestions he made to the Society's blonde and glamorous Secretary were of a more than merry order. Apparently, he had some plan of rooting out that old poet, the Chevalier Galloway Kyle who had a flat at the top of the Society's premises, and installing her in his place. As she was then living at the Helena Club in Lancaster Gate (the original of the May of Teck Club in her novel *The Girls of Slender Means*), the project was not without its attractions. Galloway Kyle, the sitting tenant, however, proved unshiftable, and this may have saved Muriel from entering into a state of full siege. As it was, she literally had to fight off these amorous solicitations. Painting a rosy dream of the Portman Square pent-house, he had assured her, on more than one occasion, that he would carnally possess her in every room. This generous assurance was not at all to her liking; and once she had only escaped his pressing suit by a fight in which she lost a front tooth.

Muriel was said to be 'all in favour of the younger poets', and most of them reciprocated the sentiments. Some were in love with her platonically, a few in a more aspiring fashion, and the rest wooed her with compliments and courtesies out of enlightened self-interest. Nor was her phalanx of admirers without the more prosperous middle-aged head. I would say there was some quality in her which caused others to ignite quickly. On one occasion, in a pub at Marble Arch, she introduced me to a new conquest who, I gathered, was about to pop the question. He and Muriel drove off in a taxi; and she rang me next morning to tell me she had become engaged to him before they stepped out. This was followed in another hour's time by news that the engagement was off. It was, seemingly, a romance on wheels not really adaptable to pedestrian level.

One of the most embarrassing scenes in Muriel's amatory annals occurred when I was drinking with her and my friend Ted Toeman, editor of the magazine *Prospect*. Conversation happened to come round to the name of a poet known to us all. Ted remarked he had seen him a day or so before, and that he had reported he was shortly to marry again. Apparently the lucky woman was a young school-teacher whose name Ted could not remember.

'I'm sure you've got this wrong,' Muriel interjected; but Ted, in his firm slow fashion, indicative of his later role as a measured and sober legal eagle, asserted that, No, that was what he had been told.

Muriel arose in an irate flurry, very cross with Ted for knowing something which she did not know herself.

'X is marrying me,' she proclaimed. 'I must ring him immediately.'

Such was the tempo of commitments in Muriel's ambience in those days. It was not, I think, that she was by nature a quick-change artist in the emotions, though she had, like most pretty girls, a tendency to fairly harmless flirtation in which she exercised and gratified her power to captivate the male. Having made one unhappy marriage (her first husband shot her through the leg while they were out in Africa, an incident reflected in her brilliant short story 'Bang Bang You're Dead'), I think her deepest wish was for stability. In her own private scale of values, loyalty to her own person stood first. About this, she was both tremendously susceptible and enormously demanding. The faith and security she never found among either her early men or women friends, she later discovered in the Church of Rome, though here, as before, there were stormy passages when she thought the faithful guilty of some extraordinary presumptuousness. I am not certain that G. S. Fraser didn't put his finger on the growth of her personality at that time, as well as on her poetry, which was what he was talking about when he described her as 'a distracted classic'. It was just that she was very far from having found herself, and this lack of certainty about her nature led to a turmoil beneath the surface and a tendency to adapt to each new change in the hope that it might possibly lead to a situation of self-recognition. As her personality structure was considerably less plastic and ductile than it might have appeared, there were a number of false starts which she would write off with a fine angry retrospective dismissal.

Muriel's inability to locate her own image led her to assume roles which were sometimes contradictory. I have seen her, with her face and fingers all stained with ink, as she put to bed some new issue of *The Poetry Review*. She was then the editorial professional woman; and very competently she performed this office, as she later did editorial tasks at Grey Walls Press or at Peter Owen's.

Then there was the inspired writer persona – large-eyed, vague-looking, very much a feminine Shelley. When this fit was upon her she would convince herself and others that she was completely impractical, lived solely for her art, and found the world too much in every way. She once told me that her mother had refrained from teaching her, as little girls are generally instructed, any of the skills of housewifery, since she had wished her daughter to have something better. Another of her convictions was that her hands (she did have diminutive hands) were too small to allow her to make the bed. Practice and ingenuity, it seemed, had triumphed over this incapacity.

Her third self-image was that of the young-woman-about-town. Long after she had served her apprenticeship as an editor, biographer and reviewer, and was already beginning to make a name for herself as a short-story writer following the publication of her winning tale in the 1951 *Observer* Christmas competition, she liked from time to time to think of herself as not a writer but a young woman of fashion. Muriel, of course, was far too intelligent to subscribe seriously to the precepts which her character Selina had obtained from 'the Chief Instructress of the Poise Course'.[1] None the less, she did believe, as all sensible women must, that 'elegant dress, immaculate grooming and perfect deportment all contribute to the attainment of self-confidence'.[2] I have no doubt that when she wore her flared black tent coat, with which she sported a small black hat becoming to her petite blonde figure, she seemed at least a half-sister of the shrewd, glamorous, empty-headed Selina.

When I first knew Muriel she assessed males in terms of a descending hierarchy of values: intelligence, first; charm, second; with good looks alone, an honoured third. She was too much of an elitist to promote number three to a higher place. There is an amusing story about her subscribing to the school of charm. One of her beaux at that time was a young-middle-aged Scots laird, a very pleasant and personable fellow who lightly dismissed the Duke of Edinburgh as being rather like 'a man-servant of good appearance'. His patronizing tone towards royalty tickled Muriel's fancy. It appealed to her sense of the comedy of manners. This laird invited Muriel and me to his castle where he thought there were documents relating to Mary Queen of Scots, a selection of whose letters we were contemplating editing. Perhaps the reason that we did not take up this invitation was that Muriel feared it might prove a fiasco. Some time earlier, the laird had asked her to join him in a party to Ascot. She had duly turned up to find the grey-hatted men with their morning coats and much be-ribboned women seated in a motor-coach in some West End side street. She thought it seemed just like a jaunt to Southend, and had made her excuses and hurried away. Perhaps the castle muniments room might offer some similar incongruity.

It must have been about a year and a half after I first met Muriel that she was thrown out of the Poetry Society at a stormy Annual General Meeting. When she first became its Secretary, the Society was as full of literary reactionaries as it is now of uncompromising (and undiscriminating) experimentalists. In fact, it was rather

[1] *The Girls of Slender Means*, 1963.
[2] *Ibid.*

like an old folks' home for retired Georgian poets. There were also
a number of prosperous patrons of decidedly amateur status
chinking together their last golden sovereigns from the palmy
prewar era of private incomes. These last lived for a while in the
hope that they could manipulate Muriel as editor of *The Poetry
Review*, not realizing that behind her Dizzy Blonde front, she
had her own obstinacy and integrity.

One of her misdemeanours, it seems, in the eyes of the Old
Guard was that during her regime the funds of the Society had
diminished considerably. The reason for this was that she had
paid for all the work contributed to the magazine, and at a higher
rate than had previously been the practice in those cases where
payment *had* been made. Muriel's defence was that if the review
were to carry good verse and prose, it must pay for it in a manner
that would attract professional writers. This, of course, meant
younger members of the Society itself, whose poetaster *rentier*
ranks did not take kindly to this innovation. They on their
part were glad enough to have their names published without
payment, and in some instances would indeed have been prepared to pay to have them made public.

The Poetry Society then contained a number of middle-aged or
older women who prinked and paraded about its premises, assuming the role of Lady Bountiful or of *très grande dame*. These were
frankly envious of Muriel, her youth, her talent and the band of
poets who acted as her special body of house-carls.

What with one faction and another, that Annual General Meeting was a tempestuous affair. One of those affronted female
dragons was none other than Marie Stopes who, for all her
gynaecological specialization, seemed seriously to doubt whether
Lord Alfred Douglas was fundamentally homosexual, and who
also adhered to the heresy that it was Wilde who corrupted him.
In those days her ample blowzy figure, in conjunction with the
clothes with which she chose to cover it, gave the impression of a
silk-clad sow. Her hat was certainly an extraordinary phenomenon,
reminding one of nothing so much as some highly inventive con-
traceptive device she had dreamed up in partnership with Heath
Robinson. As a poet, the great Marie was hardly a starter, while
as a sexologist, she was much challenged. I have heard Muriel
say that the Stopesian contribution to twentieth-century domestic

L

living was to have rendered hundreds of women, satisfied with their husbands until they had read her books, a restless tiresome sisterhood full of grievance.

On this occasion, Marie Stopes had become infuriated with Tambimuttu, who had just delivered an animated speech on Muriel's behalf and was engaged in interrupting a veteran representative of the Society's extensive bumbledom. So incensed did she become that she shook her umbrella many times above his head, threatening to strike him if he did not desist. Tambi's defence of Muriel was one of the high-spots of that exceedingly bad-tempered meeting. While most attackers and supporters alike were growing red-faced or tensely thin-lipped, he put over a performance which was both humorous and relevant. Whether he intended it as humorous it would be difficult to say. It was not that Tambi was without his own vein of mirth, but rather that he had only to present his own attitude freely and humour, most likely, would be the result.

Tambi once unashamedly admitted that he did not possess a Western sense of time. Neither did he possess a Western sense of money, as demonstrated by his defence of how Muriel had diminished the Society's funds. He began by saying that he had heard that during Mrs Spark's editorship the resources of the Society had fallen gravely. That was very good; that was how things should be. A poetry society ought to be for poets, not shopkeepers or stockbrokers. Poets needed money, very badly indeed. Shopkeepers and stockbrokers did *not* need money. They had plenty of it already. If you paid your poets well, your funds would sink. That was a proof you were doing your job. A good poetry editor would certainly endanger the publisher. He, Tambi, had endangered publishers on more than one occasion. The real test of a good poetry editor was perhaps that he should make his publisher bankrupt. Such behaviour would show true devotion to the Muse.

Of all the literary characters of the 'forties none was so colourful as Tambi – J. Meary Tambimuttu, to give him his more formal address. And this colour was the more evident in that it was all on the surface: one did not need to dig down for it. Indeed, I suspect that this vivid pigmentation of personality grew the less panchromatic the deeper into Tambi one delved. What lay at the centre who could say?

On the top, however, one was in for bright surprises; though it was the dressing he gave to his attitudes and opinions that made them remarkable. Tambi was not an original thinker, but the manner in which he took over our English bohemian ideas and approaches and strained them through his Tamil make-up resulted in something which appeared both novel and very exotic.

I do not in any way mean to deprecate his contribution to the poetry scene of the war and postwar. As an editor he had a distinctive flair, all the more unusual since he was not bound by a narrow coterie taste in selecting the poems for *Poetry London.* Neither was his interest confined, by what was to be called the generation gap, to the pages of his magazine containing the work of three generations of poets. (Even so, one must discount the report of that lady, Kitty of Bloomsbury – as described by Maclaren Ross, who maintained he did not need to read a writer to know whether he was worth publishing. Even Tambi's intuitions had their limits.)

Because his nature was not a deep one and his mind was un-inhibited and uncomplicated, he proved a useful publicist for some of the opinions then in circulation. I would hazard that the personal letters which he wrote by way of editorials to various issues of *Poetry London* did more to popularize the New Romanticism than the critical and philosophic lucubrations of Henry Treece and J. F. Hendry. Like all good publicists, Tambi simplified his material; and just as T. E. Hume assimilated and related the philosophic and aesthetic ideas of 1910 to produce a useful workshop version of them, ready to hand for the new Imagist poets, so Tambi concocted his own *Poetry London* pot-pourri from the thoughts of more independent scribes.

Notwithstanding his contribution, the impression made by Tambi in person exceeded that of Tambi in print. Maclaren Ross, who wrote brilliantly of him in his *Memoirs of the Forties*, said there was something of the snake-charmer about him. He also spoke ironically of his 'Holy Fakir of Poetry side' for which, he declared, he personally had no use.

Tambi's romantic appearance no doubt helped to sell the idea of him as an embodiment of all that was poetical, just as Richard Le

Gallienne's inspired coiffure had done for the poetry reader in the 'nineties. Regarding him, one could not but think of the damsel with the dulcimer in *Kubla Khan*, whose music led Coleridge to issue his warning:

> And all should cry Beware! Beware!
> His flashing eyes, his floating hair!

Whether or not Tambi had drunk 'the milk of Paradise' or some other liquor, he was an unforgettable phenomenon.

Some, of course, look to a poetry editor for a due quota of bohemian glamour: others prefer a staider image. (Ever since Eliot's bank suits and stiff collars, sartorial formality has been acceptable.) When, at the age of twenty-four, I met Wrey Gardiner wearing a lounge suit and carrying an attaché case, I was disappointed. Conversely, my friend Robert Greacen, used to the businessmen's ways of Belfast, had come in for something of a shock when he first clapped eyes on Tambi. Although Robert had already edited one or two selections of Ulster prose and verse, he was still unused to the Bloomsbury–Soho climate, and expected a poetry editor (at least with a good-sized firm behind him) to approximate in external appearance to any other middle-class professional: a doctor, a lawyer, a teacher, etc. Robert's first sight of Tambi, and the revelation of his *modus vivendi*, filled him with astonishment. Was this a species of indigenous deviation or was it to be counted a Ceylonese import?

Robert remembered visiting him on one of his forays from Ireland. At midday, Tambi was still in bed, with drawn curtains in a darkened room. Lighting a candle, he slowly dressed. Then he fumbled around in some papers and showed Robert a letter from T. S. Eliot wherein the venerable Possum opined that Tambi should return to his homeland. After this, they went out for beer and sandwiches, for which, necessarily, Robert paid.

'Do you know who I was with last night?' Tambi asked him.

Robert wondered which stars of the poetic firmament Tambi had spent his evening with. Perhaps it was Spender, or Louis MacNeice, or Dylan Thomas or some bard back on leave.

'Burglars,' Tambi told him, occasioning another shock.

Other surprising discoveries might be made in Tambi's flat.

Wrey Gardiner told me how he had once attended the great man's levée and come upon a new poem by Dylan Thomas in a most unlikely place. Tambi, with bedclothes swathed around him, had been saying how Dylan had just given him this new composition . . . a first-rate piece, but where the Devil was it? Directed by Tambi, Wrey hunted high and low.

'Look under the bed,' Tambi instructed, and in the process of this Wrey dislodged a brimming chamber-pot, causing its contents to spill upon the floor. Wrey then reported a sheet of paper floating on the surface of the utensil, and observed that it looked like a poem.

'That must be where I put it,' exclaimed Tambi. 'I was wondering where it could have got to.'

I have spoken of Tambi's unconscious humour and also of humour intended by him. This latter was generally of a satirical or fantastic order. One day, in the Wheatsheaf, Wrey had been showing him the proofs of my book *The Freedom of Poetry*, which had just been printed in Holland. Discussing the spirit of partisan ideology which, it seemed to me, then permeated not only political writing but creative and critical literature as well, I had spoken of the latter, rather foolishly, as 'lay art and literature', and Tambi went off into such cackles that I thought he would lay a golden egg. 'I see, Charles,' he told Wrey, handing back the proofs, 'that the Grey Walls Press isn't just a nest of singing birds. You keep bloody battery hens there as well.'

Recalling Tambi's erotic proclivities, I thought there might be another reason why my phrase 'lay art and literature' had triggered off such cachinnations. Indeed, anything concerning sex led Tambi to expressive utterance, whether of fact or fantasy. I went to his office in Manchester Square one afternoon after attending an exhibition of modern paintings at the Tate, and was enthusing to him about the little figures like tiny toys and homunculi in the canvases of Kandinsky, Miro and Klee.

'They look,' I said, 'like miniature gifts of little counters shaken out of a dice box.' They reminded me, too, of those old-fashioned sweets which used to be called Hundreds and Thousands. No, replied Tambi, I had got it wrong. They were little drops of sperm spouted out of a penis. Tambi always held to what one might call a urino-genitary theory of art.

Despite such shortcomings, I felt sorry when he finally left these shores. Would the ceremonial elephants really bow down, I wondered, as Tambi told me they would do when he returned to his native village? However, it was not his homeland but that city which Lorca saw as the megapolis of chaos – New York – which was to be his headquarters for so many years to come. When he returned to London in the 'seventies and hoped the Beatles would finance him, things were not propitious for a restart. He republished some of his old titles; brought out one or two new ones; and started a series of microdot books which likewise seem to have fizzled out.

Perhaps it would have been better had he succumbed to the dread disease of Sohoitis about which he used to speak to Maclaren Ross. Apparently, this fell infection could only be caught in that part of the area north of Oxford Street. Its final or tertiary phase was that one stagnated, paralysed of movement, in that section of W.1. Maclaren thought Tambi a terminal victim.

About this, he was wrong. The address of the Lyrebird Press today is 14 Cornwall Gardens, S.W.7, from which he issued, in 1972, a birthday book for Katherine Fally Bennett who had been associate editor of *Poetry London–New York* and 'the chief mover behind the rebirth of Editions Poetry London and the Lyrebird Press'. Needless to say, Tambi's relaxed and oriental sense of duration prevented the publication from celebrating the nativity on time. Even so, *Festschrift for K.F.B.* remains an attractive small volume in which many ghosts from the past keep curious company with prodigies of the present. Nostalgia and trendiness walk there hand in hand.

I I

Collaboration in Kensington

It was after the time of Muriel Spark's dismissal from the Poetry Society that I began to know her rather better. I had been a member of the Society's executive committee during her reign at Portman Square, and this position I now resigned. Others of her supporters, including Jack Bayliss and Hugo Manning, did likewise, though there was no pressure on us to do so.

Muriel, like a woman scorned, angrily shook the dust of the West End from her heels and took refuge in the house of Christmas Humphreys in St John's Wood. A legal luminary like his father the old judge, he was a man of wide interests, poetry being one of them. Here his insights were not always of the most perceptive order, one of them leading him to become the titular head of the Shakespearian Authorship Society which peddles that most snobbish of all heresies : that the writer of the plays was the Earl of Oxford (an exceedingly minor Elizabethan poet who has left us a few slight, not unpleasing lyrics).

Philosophically, Christmas Humphreys was a man of firmer mould. He had founded the Buddhist Society in London as far back as 1924, and published a number of books on the subject. He inclined to the Zen system, but believed this to be a matter of personal affinity, and thought that Buddhism for Western consumption required a combination of all the schools before the full grandeur of its nature could be comprehended.

He was, in all senses, a compassionate person, and since his wife (who called him 'Puck') felt it added to his well-being to have one or two young people in the house (students, refugees, protégés), 58 Marlborough Place, N.W.8 was a pleasant and interesting *ménage* to visit.

One such invitation I particularly recall. There had been some talk of forming a splinter movement among the Poetry Society poets who looked on themselves as Muriel's friends. John Waller, Ian Fletcher (who wrote his Christian name in those days with the difficult spelling 'Iain'), Herbert Palmer, Howard Sergeant, Erik de Marnay, Jack Bayliss, Stefan Schimanski (literary editor of *World Review* and co-editor with Henry Treece of the Personalist anthology *Transformation*), Derek Patmore (whose mother Bridgit had been Richard Aldington's mistress) and myself, had all been summoned to witness what was hoped would prove the birth of a new literary group.

Schimanski, whom I met on the doorstep, wanted to know whether there would be a manifesto, his central European background making it seem inconceivable that anything new could be done without one. As it turned out, the meeting was a failure. The necessary spadework had not been undertaken, and the reluctance of the English literary mind to think in terms of collective issues or express itself in articulate generalizations ensured that any result would be stillborn. After some desultory conversation in which the old poet Herbert Palmer objected of one of his coevals that 'he knew nothing about Symbolism' and Ian Fletcher riposted with 'which of us did?' the poets settled down to reading their own poems while flashbulbs exploded to right and left. As a synod of poets convened to frame some fresh statement, the meeting was a fiasco. Otherwise considered, it made a pleasant evening. Muriel's honour, at least, seemed satisfied. Something had been done to prove she still had friends. Perhaps, too, I was somewhat mollified that she thought the likeness of me, in the agency photographs when they arrived, very suggestive of a scholar of the 'nineties who had left his hansom at the door and come to listen to some half-hour's literary chatter. It was an image I liked to foster.

Muriel was soon busied, keeping her end up in another fashion. She had started the little magazine *Forum* which published verse and prose, mostly by known names whether young or old. She asked me to become her co-editor; the second, and final, number was the brainchild of us both.

I had already tried my hand at one such publication, the social-literary magazine *Resistance* which I had edited with my friend David West, just out of the Intelligence Corps. Among its miscellaneous contents were pieces by C. S. Lewis, Alex Comfort, Apollinaire and Baudelaire. It carried a top-heavy editorial which promised 'qualified support' for the then Labour government and proclaimed itself to be 'a forum for that small body of religious independents, revolutionary humanists and rationalists with a sense of the mysterious who are all, in their several fashions, united to stem the tides of materialism'. The first number appeared in October 1946, and then I left the editorship to David, who thereupon combined with Edward Toeman, amalgamating *Resistance* with the latter's *Prospect*. A full history of the period's little magazines would reveal many curious alliances and quarrels.

Muriel handed over the prose contents of *Forum* to me, keeping the verse for herself. I have always liked a programmatic approach to editing, and duly declared in an editorial that *Forum* would now seek to encourage three forms of writing then neglected: the prose-poem, the confessional or autobiographical sketch, and the critical dialogue. Henry Treece let us have an article on the prose-poem as a specific form of writing, and Dannie Abse provided an amusing account of his Jewish boyhood in South Wales. I was also concerned to set down in black and white the perennial debate between Romanticism and Classicism as it appeared at that moment, and invited G. S. Fraser to kick off on the subject. He contributed an excellent dialogue which I hoped would be followed up, feeling that the time had come for reconciliation between the two camps, based on a clear statement of their respective claims. In an editorial, I looked forward to a phase of art in which the Romantic's dynamic imagery would be combined with the Classicist's feeling for over-all form.

Forum, at least, was not to manifest this. Its second number was its last. With its primrose covers designed by Dorothy Childs, it bloomed for a short space on the bookstalls of Kensington. We carried copies round to Bernard Stone whose little shop in Church Walk, Kensington, at the back of the church of St Mary Abbots, had not yet reached the dignity of becoming the headquarters of the

Turret Press. Bernard beamed behind his thick glasses and displayed *Forum* in his window as well as on his counter. A month later, half the copies had sold; but, with printing costs mounting, we could not proceed without a patron. There were several benefactors who wished us well, but, alas, their largesse was limited. The most curious offer of help we received came from a poet who said he would pay a handsome small sum on the understanding that we printed his poems and published a full-page photograph of him. He also declared he was ready to purchase some fifty copies of the issue containing his apotheosis. Unfortunately his verse was less attractive than his undeniably dishy appearance, so we sadly declined his proposition and *Forum* paid the price of our probity.

Our experience of editing *Forum* together convinced us that we worked well as collaborators. Money, as at most times, was generally short; so soon we were knocking on publishers' doors, ringing them up and writing them letters (postal rates then encouraged correspondence).

The first fish we landed was a commission to edit the complete works of Anne Brontë in one large omnibus volume; namely, her two novels and a small harvest of verse. Lindsay Drummond the publisher asked for full introductions; Muriel tackled the biographical and I the critical presentation. Then, among the first of the postwar calamities, the firm was declared bankrupt and the liquidators wrote to us in the hope of reclaiming the advances which had been paid to us. What a hope, indeed! We wrote saying that they could have the book but were getting no cash. In all, I have had five publishers who, like Lindsay Drummond, ceased upon the midnight but not without some pain.

Our second venture was a symposium to commemorate the centenary of Wordsworth's death. It had been to fourteen publishers before Alan Wingate accepted it. There we met debonair Anthony Gibbs, long-shanked son of Philip, the successful novelist. A visit to Wingate's in Beauchamp Place always left us considerably cheered. Anthony, with eye-glass and elegant tweeds, made publishing appear a gentleman's concern. Muriel would absorb his smile, his voice, his laugh, while I would stare with wonder at his shoes, his cuffs, his tie. Our jaunts to the Knightsbridge address were always decorative occasions. Certainly, they were different from our interview with some other publisher – the name I can no longer recall – whose editor was a rawboned American with a crew-cut, who sat facing us with feet up on the desk. His contribution to the Atlantic Alliance was to pronounce unreservedly on the decadence of the British literary scene. In those days Muriel possessed an umbrella with a long silver filigree handle. Sometimes when we went visiting together, I would carry this exquisite instrument while she would sport a pink-and-white parasol which I had given her. Even to an ex-G.I. rough-head, the vision of Muriel in her green 'new look' costume and frilled white blouse, with her parasol suggestive of Renoir's 'Les Parapluies', cannot have been proof of a deep degeneration. But her escort toying with the black tassels of a woman's brolly . . . ! I felt his glance upon the chased silver handle and gave it a few more provocative twiddles.

Tribute to Wordsworth was the first of a number of joint efforts. It was mostly written in Vicarage Gate where Muriel had a small bed-sitter off Church Street, W.8. Cats fought ferociously and miaowingly made love in the deep well-like yard beneath her window. We were seeking to compose a general introduction to be followed by separate statements prefacing a selection of opinion on Wordsworth by his contemporaries and a further body of essays by present day writers. I was responsible for the former and Muriel for the latter sections of the book; but the general introduction had to be a combined operation. To compose a sentence, or part of a sentence, turn by turn is no easy matter. Authors have their different ways with words, their innate speech and prose rhythms. Good will, patience, enormous enthusiasm and, when these inclined to fail, a bottle of Beaujolais saw us through our task.

Kensington was then rife with poets, and we had asked four of them to contribute to our symposium. John Heath-Stubbs had a flat in John Waller's family house in Cheniston Gardens, behind Barker's. Robert Greacen, fresh from Ireland, was set up with his wife Patricia Hutchins in a handsome flat in Palace Gardens Terrace. George Woodcock, the anarchist poet and critic, lived in a dolls' house studio at the end of a little cobbled yard close to a famous Church Street *pâtisserie*. Down in Beaufort Street, Chelsea, dwelt George and Paddy Fraser – George also contributing to our *Wordsworth*. Nor must I forget Roy Campbell, a man in bigger mould than all these figures, whom we often met parading down Church Street, and who would stop when he came upon us, one

foot on the kerb, one foot in the gutter, his broad-brimmed hat
removed from his head and held in his hand while we talked.
Roy's old-fashioned Spanish courtesy in the presence of a woman
could surprise those who looked on him as some sort of dangerous
beast from the veldt. His chivalry is attested for by Percy
Wyndham Lewis in his collection of W.8 and W.11 sketches,
Rotting Hill (1951). He observed Roy, one day, complete with his
'large coffee-coloured hat' walking down Church Street, as if the
ground was 'paved with eggs, putting down his feet with measured
care' (the result of a war-wound which imposed on him this gait
of 'a legendary hidalgo'). He was making for the Catherine Wheel
when:

> As he was about to enter there was an incident. A small old lady
> in a bonnet appeared suddenly, shooting out of the Jug & Bottle,
> seemed to get her ankles entangled, and fell. She was clutching
> something bright, I believe a new half-crown. Campbell stooped
> with the grandiose stiffness of a lay-figure, and lifted the dis-
> reputable marionette to her feet. Saluting her majestically with
> lifted headpiece, he proceeded on his way into the tavern.

Of all these poets it was John Heath-Stubbs who most impressed
me then as now. The authority of his learning and the inborn
dignity of his mind influenced me the more strongly because he
himself made no effort to do so. In 1947 I still called myself an
anarchist. I had contributed to George Woodcock's anarchist
magazine *Now*, and very much respected George with his quiet
gentle manners. Like me, he had worked on the land at Cambridge
in the early years of the war, and had then, with amazing industry,
turned out one pamphlet after another in which he set forth the
anarchist programme: on railways, on agriculture, on factories,
etc. These were not the rabble-rousing statements which the public
mind associates with his brand of politics, but reasoned and reflective arguments, fed with a full sufficiency of facts. It always seemed
to me that George and not the more dynamic Alex Comfort was the
rightful lineal descendant of Herbert Read, about whom he was to
produce an excellent book in 1972. Muriel also liked and admired
George. She had met him regularly as a reviewer in her days at *The
Poetry Review*, and used to say that he and his wife must be very

much in love for him to be able to write so much in the cramped quarters of their tiny abode without their strangling each other. When George went as an academic to teach in a Canadian university – since when he has remained in Canada – the English literary scene lost a lot. Nobody who knew him in his English days, unless they had been informed, would have recognized that he was Canadian-born.

It was not George's departure from these shores, however, which led me to question my anarchist faith. I had already begun to have doubts, starting from the days when I commenced to read such philosophers as Kierkegaard and Unamuno. Now, it is possible to hold a 'tragic view of life', as I suppose did George Sorel, and still support a revolutionary programme which looks towards some future unlikely 'good society'. A tragic point-of-view more generally inclines one to a pessimistic attitude, to one which stresses man's limitations, his tendency to moral deviation. This was how I had now largely come to look upon the anarchist blueprint. In itself it seemed to me the plan or preview of a just society. It was not, I felt, the blueprint which was wanting but the power and ability of those who were to implement it. In other words, the anarchists were not up to anarchism, simply because the state of anarchism demands of man more than he possesses. The anarchist posits, as the essence of his political psychology, something which might be called Original Virtue; whereas, it appeared to me that Original Sin – however one regards it, whether in a spiritual or secular sense – is much more in evidence. It was thus that I ceased to profess adherence to the anarchist cause. I still respected the spirit of the movement, and believed that the image of a free society was something one should hold before one – a model for all time unattainable yet exerting, none the less, a majestic noble pull. Anarchism was the true democrat's dream – democracy to the nth power; a vision possibly the purer since it could never be realized.

Meeting John Heath-Stubbs, I derived from him a notion of a traditional society. Hitherto, I had imagined that only a revolutionary perspective was intellectually respectable. John, while retaining his scholarly poise, had heard C. S. Lewis lecturing at Oxford, and had been imaginatively influenced by other members of the 'Inklets' – Charles Williams and Professor Tolkien – that informal group of esoteric Tory and Christian thinkers. Essential to the traditional

society, at least in Europe as I now saw it, was the religious element
which, for the purposes of Christendom, meant one aspect or
another of Christian orthodoxy. Without this spiritual historical
leaven, the hierarchical society today would amount to little more
than Conservative materialism. I had not seceded from my
anarchist faith to give my blessing to the plutocratic rat-race.

Provisional adoption of this new rough draft of the universe did
not mean that I now called myself a Tory in any way consonant
with the usage of that word by Central Office. Nor did it imply I
was to be counted a true son of Mother Church. I have never been
confirmed; and if anyone today asks me where my religious sym-
pathies lie, I can only tell them that I am an anti-papal pro-
Catholic Anglican agnostic.

During the war years I had believed that Romanticism implied
a revolutionary politic. It was only when I began to look at certain
nineteenth-century German aspects of this, as represented by, say,
the Schlegels, that I saw that it could also be associated with a
traditionalist attitude. In the essay he contributed to our *Wordsworth* symposium, John Heath-Stubbs considered the poet in the
light of tradition, an approach which came as a revelation to me.

John's own poetry belonged to a different wing of the Neo-
Romantic Movement from that of the wild and woolly boys who,
without Dylan Thomas's talents, followed in his chaotic footsteps. It
was disciplined, ironic and formal, though with no shortage of
vivid imagery or of rhetorical *élan*:

> Orthodox in beliefs as following the English Church
> Barring some heresies he would have for recreation
> Yet too often left these sound principles (as I am told) in
>   the lurch
> Being troubled with idleness, lechery, pride and dissipation.[1]

With a quizzical eye on the inveterate pigeon-holing of critics, he
had spoken of composing verse 'In a classical romantic manner
which was pastoral.'[2] Even this wry formula met with my approval,
as it answered to the synthesis of these two warring schools which I
had called for in *Forum*. I liked the inclusion of the 'pastoral' touch

[1] 'Epitaph', *Selected Poems*, 1965.
[2] *Ibid.*

also. The retention of certain notes from descriptive nature poetry preserved our sense of the organic world in a poem chiefly dealing with urban or industrial landscape. (My wartime friend Ian Finlay once said my Muse would end up in a haunted barn complete with Georgian bats and modernistic lighting.)

Another impressive thing about John was his orotund recitation. I can think of no contemporary poet who read his own verse so well: employing neither the throw-away manner, nor the liturgical Yeatsian chant, nor the 'organ voluntary' style with all stops dramatically pulled out. (Magnificent as he was as a reader, George Barker by comparison seemed a bit of a barnstormer.) John's everyday speech was measured, emphatic, clear; and when speaking from the platform, his voice had the resonance of some cathedral bell. Because of his sonorous declamation I christened him the Rector of Modern Verse. The curate, fluty and a little mournful, was John Busby Smith, now plain John Smith, who was for a number of years in the 'sixties editor of *The Poetry Review*.

When I think of John Heath-Stubbs today my memory often returns to one specific image. At the bottom of Church Street, Kensington, around the year 1950, there stood a restaurant with swing-doors adjacent to the premises of an undertaker. Beside the doors, in an urn on the pavement, an immense truncated column of candle, a sort of monstrous dark red phallus, burned night and day under a striped red-and-white awning which screened it somewhat from the elements. Walking up Church Street with Muriel Spark one sultry afternoon in summer, I saw John standing beside the guttering candle, reflectively using a toothpick. Placed between these two symbols of sex and death, the candle and the funeral parlour, he looked so haggard and pale that Muriel, turning to me, said 'I don't think John will live much longer.' This was twenty-five years ago, and was one of those occasions when feminine intuition proved mistaken. Yet I well understood her remark; and it is that obscurely sacrificial image which explains the poet to me, though he remains alive and well.

The traditional figure of the blind poet, from the Greek Homer to the Irish Raftery, is one known to many cultures. Milton was blind for some twenty-odd years; John has endured a condition of damaged sight, increasing to near or total blindness for most of his life. Sometimes, as in his case, a deprivation can imply a dedication; and when the Queen's Gold Medal for Poetry was conferred on him in March 1974 such dedication was publicly recognized. In the days when he used to wear a black shield over one eye, he bore the appearance of a scholarly gaunt-faced pirate chief. But whatever the role, whatever the persona, it is one he would fill with dignity.

About this there was nothing assuming; no trace of pomposity whatever. On one occasion, when I had arranged a reading of Chatterton's poems at a house in Battersea, I had brought a complement of poets (including John) along with me, and we were each taking our turn to read 'The Bristowe Tragedy', a longish narrative poem written in archaic manner. Some of the poets and their accompanying girl-friends were very young and somewhat unread in English idiom before 'The Waste Land'. To them the medievalism of thought and diction occasioned some small mirth. This display of giggles and titters was, to John, *lèse-majesté* to the Muse. When the volume from which we were all reading arrived before him, he quietly opted out, passing it on to the next reader. Any more open criticism, in somebody else's house, would have seemed to him socially inadmissible. The dignity, which is part of him, hardly derives from personal assumptions. It is just that he regards himself as Poetry's liegeman: he has a duty and honour to protect her.

John's landlord at Cheniston Gardens was John Waller, another figure associated with *Eight Oxford Poets*, a selection of university wartime wits. He had started the literary quarterly *Kingdom Come* (which he claimed to be the first magazine of the war generation) while still at Worcester College, and in Egypt, when in the R.A.S.C., had mixed with the contributors to *Middle East Anthology* and *Personal Landmarks: an anthology of exile*: Lawrence Durrell, Terence Tiller, G. S. Fraser, Bernard Spencer and a whole host of other names including John Gawsworth, like him a founder member of the Salamanders, a society of poets who first met in Cairo in 1942.

In those early postwar days, Waller had not yet inherited his baronetcy, but was still very much the golden boy, wearing a belted teddy-bear overcoat like some actor-manager and knight of the stage. With his Oscar-down-from-Oxford manner, he appeared to have tailored his personality with such fine economy that only a silhouette of anecdote and gossip remained. I never heard him speak a serious word, nor do I recall him uttering a dull one. He presented a front of comprehensive worldliness, and sometimes struck me as the sort of man who might feel obscurely ashamed to be known as the performer of kindly actions. (That he *had* performed such, I knew to be true and just before Peter Baker died – a sick man and an alcoholic, completely broken by his prison sentence – John had him to stay at his house over Christmas, at a time when few others wished to see him.)

John made a great thing about food and drink, especially if it was to be obtained free. He would relate how he had attended such and such a lunch or dinner and recite the menu he had worked through.

'And there was old William,' he would say, 'and he didn't want his smoked salmon so I ate it for him. Five shillings extra!'

He also had a nose for the presence of wine. One evening when Muriel Spark was living in Sussex Mansions, Old Brompton Road, John and a bevy of poets called unexpectedly. Muriel set to, making them coffee, having stowed away a bottle of claret that we had intended drinking later. It was hidden behind a pile of books under the table at which we sat, but it is just possible the cork could be seen. At least, it was not long before John had dislodged the books with his foot to reveal the bottle which he insisted on our drinking.

If his generosity in calling for drinks at a bar was a little slow in dawning, his hospitality as a host was in no way wanting. He was always ready with invitations, and the actor and raconteur in his make-up invariably provided lively entertainment. At one party at Cheniston Gardens he executed a festive dance while carrying a feather-duster with which he chucked his guests lightly under the chin, prodded their middles or dotted them on the head. This was many years before Ken Dodd popularized his act with the aid of his famous tickle-stick.

Once John took Muriel to show her his study, proudly boasting how he had every mechanical device on his desk to facilitate composition. Everything was present – save the will to work. As he gaily confessed, he was lazy. I believe he might have done more literary work if there had been greater inducement. Muriel always maintained that he was a born journalist of a gifted order. I myself

M

can envisage a John Waller column on the lines of the Earl of
Arran in the *Evening News* – something which seems easy until
one tries it. His ambiguity of being was perhaps best expressed in
his witty poem 'Oscar Wilde and Aubrey Beardsley' in which he
both describes and criticizes the ethos of the 'nineties :

> The jaunty adventure was emotionally ending,
> Decked out with china and farthing victories,
> When Beardsley painted the plush and pomegranate perils
> And no one could see the devil for all the pear trees.[1]

One might have expected John to have succumbed to this cult of
'delicate perverted pastures',[2] but the wordliness which entraps a
man in the tastes and fashions of his own day no doubt led him to
write off the period as old hat, or as something which had
misfired :

> This was an age which might have proved so famous
> With wealth to spend and actors who were able,
> But somehow it blazed quite out in a swirl of tinsel
> With naphtha lights and scandalous talk at table.[3]

There is more than a little truth in this, but could our 'forties claim
to have minted so distinct an image, it would have had much to
boast of.

Around the corner from Vicarage Court, just two minutes away in
Palace Gardens Terrace, lived the poet Robert Greacen and his wife
Patricia, who published her two books on Joyce and Pound under
her maiden name of Hutchins. Robert was as carnivorous as they
come and devoted to his pork chop but Patricia was a vegetarian,
and sometimes there would come a plop on the mat at Vicarage
Gate when, ever-mindful of the meat-eater's plight in those days
of shortage, she popped her bacon ration (duly wrapped) through
the letterbox for Muriel.

[1] *The Kiss of Stars*, 1948.
[2] *Ibid.*
[3] *Ibid.*

While still in the Forces, I had reviewed Robert's first book of verse *One Recent Evening* (1944) and his second volume *The Undying Day* (1948) had just appeared from the Grey Walls Press. For a short spell during the war, Robert had been a Communist, preferring the discipline of that party to anarchism's philosophic individualism. By 1949 he had put the C.P. a long way behind him but was still committed to a sort of socialistic United Front. He became the Secretary of the Writers' Peace Appeal, which included such figures as Christopher Fry and L. A. G. Strong. Christopher was, of course, a pacifist and Strong very much a Marxist. In fact, here as elsewhere, the Communists were seeking to use the name of causes that were respectable as a cover for their own activities. With half Europe locked away behind the Iron Curtain (and the all-too-soon-to-be-built Berlin Wall), the Soviet Union wanted a pause in which to consolidate its new depredations. What better slogan than that of Peace? Accordingly, when asked to become a signatory, I declined. Robert told me, years later, how I had proved right in maintaining that the Communists were seeking to dominate it and its policy for their own purposes. He said that they had sent a party propagandist to try to get them to amend a proposal they had drafted. He lectured them severely for over an hour and Robert and a few others, annoyed at his hectoring obstinacy, had opposed him again and again. Finally he had swung off in a great huff. Like all non-democratic people, Communists are bad losers.

To anticipate the cat-call of 'Fascist hyena' with which my verbally inventive Marxist friends will, no doubt, salute the above passage, I will now relate another small incident in the history of literary canvassing. In the late 'forties, moves were afoot to petition for the release of Ezra Pound from St Elizabeth's Hospital, Washington, where the American authorities had incarcerated him to avoid putting him on trial for treason. I was approached and asked to sign; and again refused.

A man's opinions are his own, but do they justify treason? Pound had lived in Italy for some twenty years, identifying himself with Mussolini's corporate state while still retaining American nationality. William Joyce, on the other hand, had gone to Germany before the war and renounced his Allied nationality in order to become a German citizen. This did not prevent him from being put on trial and executed after the Allies had captured him at the end of the war. About the Joyce verdict of 'Guilty', I wrote a long letter to Jack Bayliss (who completely disagreed with me on this matter) while we were both in the Services :

Having met Joyce and hating his politics, I am still quite sure there is a miscarriage of justice. Since he became a German subject, his position is clearly that of any other enemy subject. By all means let him be treated as a War Criminal, but as a traitor : No. I am all against the Law currying favour in the eyes of the populace by acting as an instrument of popular revenge.

After all, the prime duty of the Law is to counteract the element of accident; to judge of affairs with even partiality; and to restore by an act of conscious will, the essence of equality lacking in society.

Now Joyce's birth as a member of the Allied nations [he was an American *not* a British subject] was an act of accident. By an act of naturalization; that is, by resort to the law of equity, he is given the chance of deciding his status for himself. He contracts with the society he chooses, and this act of choice should be more respected than the random windfall of birth.

If society fails to retain the adherence of any member's respect, there should be no obstacle to his transferring – by legal contract – his allegiance elsewhere. This Joyce did; and now our society – eager to fake up scapegoats – finds a good opportunity to execute Joyce. . . . If I was out of the Army, I would write a pamphlet on this, and try to organize some troublesome petitions.

There are certain easy and high-handed assumptions about the nature of law, equality and society which remind me, now, that this was written in the September of 1945 when my anarchist principles still naïvely shrouded me from reality's painful *status quo*. Even so I would, substantially, stand by the argument today; namely, that a man should be able to renounce his citizenship of one nation and take on (if that state is willing) the citizenship of another. I would say this was not an anarchist claim but rather a democratic way of reasoning which respects the individual's right of choice.

Pound's case was entirely different. While doing the Duce's

work for him, he posed as a good American who knew what was best for the rest of his countrymen. His curious synoptic gospel, which impressed such a founding father of the American constitution as Jefferson into service alongside such a figure as the German economist Gessell, made his propaganda all the more insidious. One knows what to make of a man who proclaims himself one's country's enemy, but there was 'ole Uncle Ez' posing as the friend of America while, at the same time, threatening American and European Jews with all sorts of nasty eventualities. For myself, I saw no reason to wish the decision of the U.S. authorities reversed in his case. He was lucky to escape with his life.

There are those who regard the poet as a sacrosanct individual. With this attitude, I do not agree. Even so, I honour Paul Potts – among those petitioners who did not impress me – for having written in defence of Pound. Paul, with his great cult of Israel, had better reasons than many for refusing to raise his voice in a plea for mercy. That he did so is proof of the wholly independent imaginative compassion in his nature. Yet, after Pound's release in 1958, Paul had this to say of him :

I waited to ask you this
I could not ask you in prison
I waited until you were free.

But why, why did you let them use
Your name and your greatness
As so many pennies to put
Into the meters of their gas machines.
You know what they did with their gas
Your gas, Ezra Pound.
The crime was too big.
There are no extenuating circumstances.
You should have known better.[1]

To return to Robert and Patricia, it was at their Palace Gardens Terrace flat that I heard one of those remarks that make one's evening. There were several literary people round there, including

[1] *Dante Called You Beatrice*, 1960.

Leslie Gillespie, Robert's old friend from school and Queen's University, Belfast. Leslie had been a bit of a poet, but since his visit to the Café de Flore in Paris, where he heard apocryphal tales about the number of women pulled from under Sartre each night, he became convinced that existential fiction was now the all-important thing. On this particular evening, however, it was not the great status of Camus and Sartre which we were collectively discussing but the claims and achievements of Surrealism. Leslie, raising his glass, declared that Breton's unspoken commandment, reversing Sir Philip Sidney's famous dictum, must surely have been: 'Heart, look into thy fool and write.' Leslie may have spoken *in vino veritas*, but his aphorism certainly expresses the spirit – and inanity – of what one might call 'Dylanism' or the wild-and-woolly-bear aspects of Neo-Romanticism.

After a spell at Palace Gardens Terrace, Robert and his wife moved to the Boltons; then back again to High Street, Kensington, to Number Ten, Church Walk, a house in which Ezra Pound had lived, led to that address because Patricia was writing a book dealing with his Kensington associations. The house stood in a little flagged courtyard, almost immediately opposite the churchyard of St Mary Abbot's a corner offering quiet respite, and one which for me today is full of ghosts. I like to think of the bearded poet to-and-fro-ing there some fifty years ago. At Number Ten he had cursed the bells of St Mary Abbots breaking so rudely into his Sunday slumber. I like to recall Richard Aldington's poem describing church-going before the Great War, even though I think it a little hard on the average member of the congregation:

> Their clothes are black, their faces peaked and mean;
> Their legs are withered
> Like dried bean pods.
> Their eyes are stupid as frogs.[1]

Aldington, too, had lived in the district. A step or so away, in Holland Street, one could still (until three years ago) drink tea and nibble macaroons at the café which, so Aldington claimed, saw the Imagist Movement projected over coffee. (The site is now occupied by Cassidy's Restaurant, 'Home of the Heavenly Ham-

[1] 'Church Walk. Sunday Morning'. *Images*, 1909.

burger', though its propinquity to the publishers of Academy Books may be thought to commemorate its past connection with the arts.)

In this neighbourhood the hauntings are of a more personal nature. I remember Robert, as he was some twenty-five years ago, with fair reddish hair and sensuous lips; Patricia, tall, slender and dark; and their daughter Arethusa who inherited her father's colouring and whom, when she was two, I once carried in my arms the length of Church Street and back. But it is a small public garden, beloved of old ladies in gloves and black straw hats, which most surely evokes this period for me. This little close, with its wooden seats and rose-plots, is securely hedged in by municipal wire fences. At the end of the 'forties, there was no fence there. The ground was unlevelled, with rough grassy hummocks, beneath which lay the parish's ancient dead. Three or four tombstones, with time-worn lettering, rode at anchor, half-submerged in the grass. Seldom do I pass this spot today without recalling its original condition.

12

Polishing the Church Silver

It is summer in the old garden at St Mary Abbots, and the grass is bleached and dry. There sits a neat diminutive figure with the head of a beautiful blonde bulldog – a human bulldog with Bette Davis eyes. Her gaze is 'away and somewhere else'; her strong chin betokens determination. This is Muriel Spark, *circa* 1949, sunning herself and wrestling with a poem. Her 'Elegy in a Kensington Churchyard' takes this setting for its theme.

Oh, yes, Muriel was very much the poet, though for a thousand readers who know her novels, perhaps not one is aware of that volume of her *Collected Poems* published by Macmillan in 1967, wherein the early flowers of her career – the small book *The Fanfarlo* (1952) and other later pieces – are brought together.

Both of us, then, professing the Muse, it was natural that poets rather than novelists should have been the company in which we chiefly found ourselves.

At the end of the 'forties, the verse-plays of Christopher Fry, with their outspread peacock's tail of speech, offered the romantic alternative to Eliot's West End classicism, *The Cocktail Party* rather suggesting Noël Coward steeped in Original Sin. In 1950 I had obtained a commission to write a book on Christopher Fry; accordingly, in early June, I took Muriel down to visit him where he and his wife Phyllis were living in a cottage in Shipton-under-Wychwood, a remote Cotswold village about twenty miles from Oxford.

Christopher and Phyl had come to the cottage, which they rented from a local farmer, shortly before he was called up. It was attractively situated on a hill above the village, which lay in a valley but was also somewhat primitive. However, it suited them at the time, being not too far away from the Oxford Playhouse with which Christopher was connected. It was also cheap: a necessity at that time.

The war over, and *A Phoenix too Frequent* as well as *The Lady's not for Burning* eminently successful on the stage, Christopher and Phyl thought they could improve on the austerities of their dwelling and run to the amenities of bathroom and indoor lavatory. Then the farmer-landlord came to call on them. He explained that he had been happy to let them have the cottage cheaply during the war, but that now their rent would have to be increased. He did hope they would understand this. Christopher's credit was satisfactory by this time, but who knew what sum the farmer had in mind?

'I was thinking, Mr Fry, of another two and sixpence.' This brought it up from five shillings to seven and sixpence weekly (or some other such terrifying increase), which Christopher felt he could afford! Apart from this, the cottage remained largely as it was when they first took it over, but certain ornamental touches bespoke the presence of romantic residents.

On a large grand piano, which took up half the living-room, stood a massive twin-armed silver candlestick such as one might expect to see in some old manor house or baronial hall. For Christopher this served as his torch of inspiration, since he felt that night was the best time for writing. It was, however, by the soft glow of a more homely oil lamp that he continued, usually in an adjoining shed which he had converted into a study.

The first day we visited Christopher's cottage, his wife came gaily in at teatime with a bronze eagle which she had unearthed in some antique shop in Burford (where his brother now keeps an emporium of fascinating old-fashioned treasures). Christopher was delighted with this new discovery, for although he was not a connoisseur or collector in the ordinary sense, he took enormous pleasure in certain objects combining the appeal of age and fancy. On the mantelpiece of another room there ticked a clock curiously adorned with birds on branches, a waterfall and frogs, spanned by a dome of glass. Christopher wound a small spring, and we waited. The birds opened and closed their wings, one dipping its beak into a stream, while from tiny boulders, the waterfall emitted a tubular glassy current. How gravely, almost, he listened to the delicate cadenzas of mechanical sound accompanying this clock-work pastoral performance! With its source concealed and un-detected, this frail subtle concert of mimic bird-song temporarily bewitched him. It was as though the ghosts of finches chirped and piped within it.

Christopher's vein of fantasy contained a streak of provocative playfulness. On the wall of the living-room he pointed out to me a painting which hung there in mellow glory. In passing, he re-ferred to it as 'a portrait of my grandfather'. In fact, he presently added, the picture had been found in an Oxford secondhand shop. The weird thing was that, some days after the purchase, he re-ceived an early snapshot of his grandfather (whom he had never seen in the flesh) which bore a strong resemblance to the portrait. The painting thereupon received the titular description 'Portrait of Grandfather'.

My book *Christopher Fry: an appreciation* (1951) appeared within the year, to be followed by a theatrical volume *Christopher Fry Album* (1952) in which I supplemented the illustrations with a brief biography and account of his career. Meanwhile Christopher had written his most controversial play, at least as to form and meaning: the pacifist expressionist drama *A Sleep of Prisoners*. Its premier was to be given at the Church of St Mary the Virgin in Oxford as part of the Religious Drama Festival then being held throughout England.

I was covering it for *The Spectator*, so down I went with Muriel to the church of silver-tongued John Henry Newman, to see what Christopher had prepared for us. The play was powerful in the extreme, a tense and violent situation (four soldiers during war-time taking shelter for the night in a church in enemy territory) combined with a rhetorical urgency of language which, how-ever, did not exclude humour. Even so there were certain critics – particularly those who did not know their Bible – puzzled by refer-ences in the play here and there. I thought the clue to the drama's fuller import lay in the story of the Three Men in the Fiery Fur-nace. The dreams of the soldiers also point to further scriptural incidents: Cain's murder of Abel, Joab's assassination of

Absalom, and Abraham's near-sacrifice of his son Isaac. In all, one might say, a bit of a handful for an infidel intelligentsia more primed with Marx and Freud than with the text of an earlier Word. But whether or not the play's meaning was apparent at every point, its dynamism was never in question; and when the curtain fell it received good applause.

After the performance we repaired to the Playhouse, where Christopher was giving a sherry party. There we met our old army friend Wynyard Brown with his lovely actress wife, and fell to talking about the play. The poet, playing attentive host, was absent when Wynyard, lowering his voice, said to his wife, to Muriel and me, 'How can we possibly tell Christopher?' Was it a trace of Irish mischief or a touch of jealousy which made him speak thus? The dark glasses which Wynyard wore against the light that sunny evening seemed to me symbolic at that moment. 'Eyes they have and they see not.'

A poet whom I associate more essentially with Muriel, since it was she who introduced him, was the old veteran Herbert Palmer.

He was nearly seventy when I met him for the first time, and I had never envisaged any understanding or affinity between us. Indeed, I had just written a scornful notice of his book of verse *A Sword in the Desert* (1946). This volume contained, by way of foreword, a blast of the trumpet against the monstrous army of modernists. With my finicking devotion to Rilke and Alberti, I felt myself under the ban, and replied without respect for the poet's age in the brash cocky way of enlightened young men. 'These thunders from Sinai,' I declared in *Poetry Quarterly*, 'are a case of grandpa with a bad attack of the tantrums. Excalibur had better go back into the desert.'

The review had gone to press but had not yet been published when I was first invited to meet him. The occasion was a Brains Trust, arranged by Muriel, which was to be held at the Poetry Society. She had bruited the matter in the paper, and Palmer and I were billed as gladiators in the cultural arena. He was to put the case against modern verse and I was to present a defence of it. Muriel was to take the chair; Jack Bayliss, Howard Sergeant and William Kean Seymour were also on the panel.

The best description of Palmer that I know is that of the ancient poet Percy Mannering in Muriel's novel *Memento Mori*. (This was published in 1959; incidentally, it very much hurt Palmer and his wife from whom Muriel had many times received hospitality.) Percy, of course, is a caricature figure; even so, it gives a good idea of Palmer's gleeful, wolfish but generous nature. What, perhaps, it does not include is a sense of his stature, his curious old-fashioned spiritual integrity, apparent right to the end, in his last book published when over eighty, the perfervid apocalyptic *The Ride from Hell* (1958).

The first impression I received of Palmer was one of fierceness and frailty. He was old, he was poor, he was terribly proud. He looked like a kind of scarecrow hidalgo, his white scanty hair suggesting a patch of thistleheads in seed. On our first meeting he wore a black suit, black tie and soft black hat, every inch a veteran poet of respectable Edwardian vintage. Later, in St Albans (where he lived), I was to see him in patched and mended clothes, under constant care from the needle of Hettie his wife. Behind his steel-rimmed glasses, his eyes burned fiercely blue. He made me think of some Viking skald. His glance and gaze were challenging. When I employ the phrase 'scarecrow hidalgo' of my first sighting of him, it does not refer to any sartorial unkemptness (which he never revealed in public), but rather to a certain ravaged Quixotic air as of a man who has spent a lifetime undauntedly tilting at windmills. The windmills had won, their victory being pyrrhic, however, since Palmer's spirit remained unsubdued. His white locks, always a little dishevelled, always a little resistant to the authority of brush and comb, and being frequently further disarranged by the hand which he ran through his hair, added to the picture of a harassed nobleman (a Saxon thane after the Conquest) who has had his quota of adversity.

Strangely enough, with all our respective prejudices, we fell in love with each other's personalities. Palmer could rant and rave like a lion and I would hiss and bite like a snake. As it was, we hardly ever turned our invective on one another. We were saved from this by our sense of humour; or, more accurately maybe, by our sense of fun. For a number of Palmer's poems, as I came to know them, I felt much admiration. Some handful of his pieces – 'The Wounded Hawk', 'Cats of the Sky', 'Autumn: an ode',

'Rock Pilgrim' and 'The Fiddler and the Girl' – I would count among the worthwhile poems of our age. But it was the man rather than the poet who, primarily, delighted me; the reason being that the man *was* the poet. He made no attempt to conceal or disguise the vatic and creative Ishmaelite in him. When other men *spoke*, Palmer *held forth*. Much as he relished a titbit of gossip, he had no time for ordinary small talk. His speech was couched in audacious overtones for the most part absent from conversation. To say that he possessed a fulminating mind coupled with a simple rejoicing heart might serve to indicate a little of his nature. 'Damn braces, bless relaxes', as William Blake shrewdly remarked; but Palmer so mixed anathema and praise that both his Yea and his Nay acted as stimulants.

'Stimulating' was, indeed, the word for him. There was something so bardic and positive about him that it would have seemed unnatural not to listen. Like the music hall stars of the 'nineties, Palmer felt that he and his public were one. Poetry was an emotional entertainment exciting and immediate as the can-can or a turn on the trapeze. His reading of his own poetry to what is now termed a live audience was certainly very much of a turn. His delivery reminded me of nothing so much as the Metro-Goldwyn lion. He opened wide his jaws and roared the words. The earth appeared to shake, and spittle descended in showers. (Those who went to hear him read did well to sit back in the third or fourth row.)

Muriel and I would sometimes visit him at his house on the outskirts of St Albans. We liked our jaunt out to the great Norman Abbey, its once monastic lake now white with civic swans. Palmer lived in Batchwood View, part of an estate of neat council houses overlooking a golf course set on woody downs. (Although he had a small Civil List pension, he had been terribly poor since the war, with his work being taken in fewer places.) Number 41 had acacias by the front door, their overhanging branches darkening the porch. Our knocking or ringing would be followed by a pause, then Palmer would come padding down the hall to greet us.

'Come in! Come in! Did you see my latest letter?'

He would soon be launched on some minute hard issue in the literary wars, his latest skirmish in the long campaign for lost causes. Some critic had spoken ill of him and must suitably be taught a lesson. 'Did you see my reply in the *T.L.S.?*', or 'I put him in his place in *Poetry Review*.'

Between the Georgians (whom he largely despised) and T. S. Eliot (whom he hated and reviled), Palmer led a lonely existence as a poet. He had once been given an advance and contract to write a book on Eliot, but on reading him further had returned both, convinced that what he wrote might constitute a libel. He did, however, publish his long poem 'Cinder Thursday', a gritty rather than witty comment on Eliot's 'Ash Wednesday'. Of the two of us, Muriel and myself, he considered me the better poet and Muriel the better critic. His reasons for this were largely partisan. Muriel had written an excellent book on Masefield, a writer Palmer very much preferred to the younger poets I had espoused. When I published my study of Dylan Thomas, Palmer told me I had sold my soul to the Devil. 'If Dylan Thomas was in heaven,' he once shouted, 'I'd rather go to hell!'

Argument and anecdote were what he most liked by way of conversation. Religious arguments we had a-plenty – arguments both serious and playful. Palmer had a strong vein of imaginative mischief in his nature, and often enjoyed stirring things up. By the middle 'fifties, Muriel had become a Roman Catholic, and we all found plenty in her conversation to set our tongues wagging and flip logic flying. Palmer and his wife Hettie were both Methodists and children of a manse (an account of his own early days being given in his book *The Mistletoe Child*, 1935). Hettie remained faithful to the liberal and progressive faith of her fore-bears, but her husband dallied imaginatively with other creeds for the sake of his Muse. He had read and admired Swedenborg, and had written a play on the life of Villon in which the praises of Our Lady were sung. Hettie was sorry that Muriel had made her submission to Rome. Herbert, on the other hand – chiefly, I suspect, to vex his wife – would sometimes say that Rome was, in one sense, probably still the True Church. To add fuel to the fire, I would invariably take Hettie's part. All of us, save this worthy old lady, partly spoke tongue-in-cheek. A good, if noisy, time was had by the four of us.

Talk of Muriel's conversion takes me back to the start of the story – at least to that earlier part of it where I made my own entrance.

A word or two first though, on Muriel's background, since such factors have their relevance.

Her parents lived in Edinburgh; her father (a Levite or scribe) was a professing Jew, a good, simple, sincere man in no way intolerant. Her mother, a more sophisticated person, looked on religion as something which offered social intercourse and entertainment. She was as much at home in an Episcopalian or Presbyterian church as she was in a synagogue, provided only that some friends of hers were there or that some interesting proceeding – a marriage, a birth, a death – was the occasion of the service.

Muriel's grandma on her mother's side was very much a character. Before 1914 she had kept a little sweet and paper shop in Watford, and had married a younger man of affluent family. His people were not at all pleased with the match so he had not brought his money with him. He was, however, most personable, and though his labours never extended beyond tending his roses or cutting buttonholes or a posy for the ladies, his wife was well satisfied to have so handsome and elegant a husband.

Muriel always maintained that her Watford grandmother had gipsy blood in her; and her own mother exhibited a flamboyant superstitious streak which might well have derived from such a source. But along with her provincial and homely wisdom, the grandma (original of Louisa Jepp in *The Comforters*), evinced certain progressive traits which made her, in the world of Watford before the First World War, a woman of consequence. She was a leading member of a number of local societies which looked towards a more emancipated future as a surely dawning goal. She joined the Suffragette Movement (much to the amusement of her husband, who used to refer to their leader, quite without malice, as 'Mrs Spankarse') and recalled walking up and down a lawn with the anarchist thinker Prince Kropotkin. In the days when I too worshipped at that shrine, these stories from the past intrigued me.

Thinking of Muriel's forebears, I have often wondered whether she inherited her religious instinct from her father, her fascination with the arts and her flair for them from her mother (who at one time had hoped to be a pianist), and her attraction to Socialist politics from her grandmother. At least, when I first knew her she proclaimed herself in sympathy with anarchist principles; and when I called myself a 'medieval Tory' or 'sceptic Conservative', she said that if she did not vote for the Labour Party, she could not bring herself to support its opponent. All that, of course, was more than twenty years ago, and some of us have changed our coats more than once. I recall that Muriel made a statement favourable to the Liberals some two years ago, but have never heard of her reneging on her old anti-Tory stand. This seems to me a matter of some interest. The working-class cradle Catholic in England is usually a Labour vote: the intellectual convert, a potential Conservative. Muriel, in those days, was an exception – part, perhaps, of the inheritance from her Watford grandmamma whom, in her childhood, she had loved deeply.

So much for politics: now for religion. Muriel, when I first met her, blithely called herself a pagan. The epithet I used to describe myself was 'an Anglican agnostic'. The interest I had in religion slowly infected her. With a father who worshipped at the synagogue and an education at a Presbyterian school in Edinburgh, it took her some time to work out where she belonged theologically. (There is, of course, much of her schooldays in *The Prime of Miss Jean Brodie*, and I well remember being introduced to the original of that audacious teacher by Muriel at the Poetry Society. That good lady, now deceased, was hardly like her fictional counterpart: Muriel excelled at caricature, not copy.)

If I was, in some small measure, Muriel's instructor in certain Christian mysteries, it was not long before the disciple was far outpacing the master. My interest in Christian thought was tied up with religious journalism; and from about 1950 onwards I contributed to both Anglican and Catholic papers besides reviewing religious books in general in the pages of the magazine *Truth*. One of my friends, the Reverend C. O. Rhodes, was editor of *The Church of England Newspaper*. The journal had an evangelical past which Rhodes was busily transforming into a species of 'social Christianity'. He was also Secretary of the Modern Churchman's Union, on whose committee I came to sit.

Rhodes, as editor, was a proper firebrand. One week his paper would come out with a scorching attack on the Supreme Pontiff (this was in bad Pope Pius's day); the next week it would be Dr Fisher of Canterbury who felt the impact of his broadside. Rhodes was the most quoted cleric in Fleet Street, and his combativeness often worried the evangelical directors of the paper as much almost as the sociological Christianity that he propagated. This tension between editor and backers left Rhodes dangerously frustrated; and with Muriel and me – whom he had first invited to lunch at the Cheshire Cheese – he was able to let off steam. On working days he wore no dog-collar and had always a sprawling freedom of posture. He said that his family were somehow connected with Oliver Cromwell, and his own high-powered intransigence possibly proclaimed him kin.

Rhodes was a no-nonsense cleric. He was not out to lure souls into his net, but ready enough to bid them welcome if their own spiritual metabolism had directed them towards him. 'When are you going to be sprinkled?' he asked Muriel one day before she joined the English Church. 'I can always do you – do you here for that matter [in the offices of his newspaper]. All we need is a dog's bowl, or a flower vase full of water.'

Having been born in a Jewish household, though educated at a Presbyterian school, the Christian rite of baptism was one which had eluded her. Self-declared pagan as she was when we first met, Muriel had impressed me with her wide reading of the Scriptures. To the Bible, which she continued to read for its poetry, its stories, its anagogic meaning, were added the writings of John Henry Newman, probably the most potent intellectual influence in her conversion. At length she felt the time for 'sprinkling' had come; so one November afternoon, with mist and sunlight goldenly competing, Rhodes baptized her in the Church of St Bride, off Fleet Street, and the two of us set off for St Albans.

We were always jaunting there in those days, and would strike out beyond the Roman ramparts, striding up through the fields to Great Furzefield Wood. On the far side of this, some mile and a half away, there lay a snug but isolated pub which went by the name of the Holly Bush. Here, after an afternoon's blackberrying, we would call for pints in the silent bar.

Muriel always felt at home in Hertfordshire. The little shop her grandmother had kept still existed at the old end of thronging Watford town. Sometimes we would visit an uncle and aunt on her mother's side who continued to live there. To talk to these two in their fruit-tree-gardened house was to savour a peculiar provincial peace. The uncle kept pigeons in much the same way as Louisa Jepp in *The Comforters*.

N

We liked, when returning from these country rambles, to come into St Albans through the old monastic gateway, hard by the fine and ancient Grammar School where Herbert Palmer had once taught English. This was a massive structure which had held at bay Wat Tyler's armed peasantry. Over on our right beyond the grass sward, the vast bulk of the great Abbey seemed, on late autumn afternoons, like a battleship at anchor. The history of St Albans, its outlying land cultivated for centuries, always impressed us happily. Ithell Colquhoun, the painter, once told me that – according to occult reckoning – the city lay at the bisecting point of two esoteric lines of influence. This, she said, made it an auspicious spot. My sense of affinity with the place was commemorated by Muriel when she gave me a book entitled *The Monastic Chronicles of St Albans*. On the fly-leaf she wrote: 'To Derek, of St Alban's Company on the Feast of St Margaret, 1953.' The style of this inscription is indicative. The Feast of St Margaret is not one of those set down to be observed in the Church of England, but is to be found in the English Missal, a book which certain Anglo-Catholics employ based closely upon the Roman model. Such was the direction in which her thoughts had tended, following in the steps of her beloved Newman.

So having been baptized by a modernist churchman, she was now confirmed by a 'spiky' prelate, the Anglo-Catholic Bishop of Kensington. On this we did not see eye to eye. For myself, I venerated the image of Our Lady (a term which seemed to me a more likely description than that of the Blessed Virgin Mary). The saying of George Santayanna, 'There is no God and Mary is his Mother' appealed to my paradoxical nature. A committee member of the Modern Churchman's Union professing a devotion to Our Lady was, of course, an odd phenomenon.

But though I might say a Hail Mary, I did not take kindly to the Anglo-Catholic way. Precariously, sometimes confusedly, poised between Canterbury and Rome, its believers too often seemed to me 'neither fish, flesh, fowl nor good red herring'. I objected to their intellectual position, which appeared both historically and logically shaky. I would not be thought, in any way, to impugn the good and holy lives which many Anglo-Catholics, both of the laity and clerisy, led; nor question the attractiveness of many features in their church worship. For example, I always remember a

Maundy Thursday occasion at the church in Gloucester Road which
T. S. Eliot used to attend. I had gone there with Muriel for a late
night service, in which the whole of the Christian story from
Genesis to the Crucifixion was read in a series of lessons. The
ending of this anabasis was appropriately dramatic. St Matthew
tells us how

> Jesus, when he had cried again with a loud voice, yielded up
> the ghost.
> And, behold, the veil of the temple was rent in twain from
> the top to the bottom, and the earth did quake and the rocks
> rent;
> And the graves were opened; and many bodies of the saints
> which slept arose,
> And came out of the graves after his resurrection, and went
> into the holy city, and appeared unto many.
> Now when the centurion, and they that were with him,
> watching Jesus, saw the earthquake, and those things that
> were done, they feared greatly, saying, Truly this was the Son of
> God.

When this passage had been read, the lights were extinguished
one by one in the church, and benches were thrown about in the
vestry to simulate the noise of storm and earthquake, which seemed
to me a 'happening' of impressive poetic efficacy. Then, when the
lights came on again, the congregation queued for Holy Communion; and there was Eliot at the back of the line looking like a
jaundiced ancient eagle. (This was before he married his
secretary and began to appear more spruce and cheerful.)
The ingrown church life which many of these ultra Anglo-
Catholics lived seemed psychologically poverty-stricken. Indeed,
I used to twit Muriel on the limited company she kept at this time.
'We A.C.'s don't mix much,' a saintly silver-haired old vicar had
told her. This led her to spend certain hours with a homosexual
verger, helping him to polish the church silver. Seeking in this
etiolated arena to perform works of mercy, she visited, at the
vicar's suggestion, an old lady who lived a lonely existence. This
woman had done a fair amount of water-colour paintings, a number of which had been exhibited. Unless Muriel was close to a person, or faced with talent of a distinctive order she found it difficult

to be interested, her awareness of her own gifts coming immediately in between. In the end, I visited the old lady twice; but since I was not myself of the faithful, this was not quite the charity required. It was sensible of Muriel to learn quite early that this kind of neighbourly compassion was not to be her own contribution to the Faith.

During this period she once remarked to me that she could not decide which most truly represented Christ: the Roman Catholic Church or the Society of Friends. Perhaps it was significant that she could make this statement yet never once attended a Quaker meeting.

Of course, it was not for me, in any way, to seek to influence Muriel's choice. As an agnostic who said his prayers but remained uncertain of God's existence, I was in no position to do so. I could only point, when issues arose, to a number of historical or logical difficulties in what seemed to me the Anglo-Catholic argument. At that period both Muriel and I enjoyed the kind help of a patron, the poet Iris Bertwistle, who came of a family of considerable means. Iris was a Roman and looked with some amusement upon Muriel's Anglo-Catholicism. One weekend, Muriel was invited to stay with her, and came back distraught and angry. Apparently, Iris had subjected her to theological cross-examination that had both annoyed and upset her. She asked me to call Iris off this sport – a sport I regarded as eminently natural, and one in which Muriel ought to have been able to hold her own.

When finally she left the half-way house – as so many of its residents find it – and became a fully fledged Roman, not a few of her friends were relieved. It is true she did not dawdle on her Anglican bed in the tiresome manner of her hero Newman but, even so, vexations of spirit were not to be avoided.

13

Ordeals and Comforters

While she was being instructed in the Roman Faith by a kindly Benedictine Father at Ealing Priory, Muriel began to experience a number of hallucinations. She believed that T. S. Eliot had broken into her flat and taken items from her food cupboard; that there was a Greek text underlying Eliot's plays, to be arrived at only by some special phonetic pronunciation of the lines in English; and that the blurb in certain of Faber's children's books contained a personal message from the wily Possum to herself. In actual fact, she was suffering from the same condition as Evelyn Waugh had experienced when writing *The Ordeal of Gilbert Pinfold*, a book which came out in the same year (1957) as her first novel *The Comforters*. Both of them were taking pills, prescribed medically, but possibly not according to the doctor's strict instructions. In Muriel's case it was no more than a simple slimming remedy, the trouble probably starting from the fact that she was neglecting herself at the time, eating very little and living largely on excessive potations of tea and coffee.

When she told me of her suppositions concerning Eliot, not knowing of the dosage of pills she was taking, I could only conclude that she was ill and urged her to see a doctor. Sometimes, as we walked up Church Street or Old Brompton Road or Gloucester Road, she would urge me to speak lower, believing that what I said might be overheard by somebody surreptitiously trailing her. She took to wearing dark glasses, as if to disguise herself or so that she should not recognize her own ill-wishers.

Frank Sheed had commissioned her to write a book on Job, whose own incommunicable position she readily identified with, and about whom she held some interesting theories. She had gone to live in Queen's Gate Terrace, and I recall the evening she read me a draft of the introduction to her book on Job. Our thought processes had always been very different, but I had invariably been able to follow the course of her thinking, finding it stimulating to move in the purer ether of her imagination. Now, confronted with her thoughts on Job, I could no longer keep track of them. Her brain seemed to be furiously free-wheeling; and, listening to her words, I felt I was travelling at great speed in a car through a darkened countryside into which would come, every so often, a blinding patch of illumination: the moon on some lake, a building festively ablaze with lights, a well lit road junction; then, again, sweeping blackness. When I questioned her about points in the passage, she seemed uncertain. She said that it was only a very rough draft, but it also appeared as if she herself hardly recognized what she had written or how she had come to set it down.

I now came to the conclusion that she was badly disorientated, and that, somehow, something must be done about it. There were two difficulties here: one, to persuade Muriel that she stood in need of attention and treatment; and, two, to find the money for her living expenses during the period when she was ill. Living as we both did by our pen, from month to month, it was not often that either of us had much of a reserve to draw on.

In seeking to convince Muriel that her hallucinations were due to sickness and were not the work of daemonic powers, I met some opposition. During this period when her thoughts were disordered, she behaved with great gentleness, but to say that she proved docile would not be correct. I felt, too, that Muriel's Catholic friends – people whom I liked and generally respected – were not exactly helpful in this matter. Whether out of misplaced kindness or discretion, or because they thought her experiences attested to a colourful supernaturalism, they would not come out positively with advice that she should seek medical aid, but engaged in a kind of running chorus, making sympathetic noises on the touchline. Those I am referring to were ordinary lay persons. Father Aegius of Ealing Priory, the Benedictine who was instructing her, acted in a shrewder, more pragmatic fashion. He sensed she was half-starving herself, and used to have her served with warm milk and biscuits in a little parlour before they had their meetings. And when she told him some of her fantasies, he did not rebut them but said he thought she was not at all well and should visit a doctor.

So a sort of 'Save Muriel' fund was instituted and a number of distinguished people made their contributions. Due to Muriel's obsessive theory that the late plays of T. S. Eliot contained a concealed code of meaning, I wrote to him asking if he would help with her living expenses. The correspondence I received revealed him, anew, as the subtle precise-minded Possum, master of the great conditional. First, I had a letter from his secretary, saying that if I would acquaint Mr Eliot more fully with Mrs Spark's position, it was possible that he might be able to offer some assistance in the region of £100. I did as I was told, writing him a letter of three closely typed pages. Upon this, he wrote to say that he could only help her if her father-confessor agreed to her receiving psychotherapy from some psychiatrist the latter recommended. Eliot did not know that Muriel was removing herself to the Roman fold and believed she was still an Anglo-Catholic, so all his splendid conditions remained a charitable thought without deed.

Very different was the response I had from Graham Greene. He was due to go away when my letter arrived, and sent me a telegram asking if I would ring him straightaway. Could I spare the time to see him at his chambers in Albany? I told my story to that quiet modest man over a sherry, and he asked me why I had thought of him in connection with Muriel's troubles. Because, I replied, he seemed to be a writer all of whose work revealed a sense of compassion with no strings attached. I can only say how wonderfully he lived up to this impromptu description, helping Muriel most generously for over a year. Other leading benefactors were Frank Sheed, A. J. Cronin and David Astor to whose *Observer* Muriel had been contributing spritely reviews. Astor made his offer of help on the understanding that Muriel must receive therapy, and since his assistance was on far more princely lines than that proposed by Eliot, no conflict of charities was involved.

I rather think, too, that Father Philip Caraman, for whose magazine *The Month* I had written for some years, was among those who sent helpful cheques. It was certainly he who received her

into the Roman faith in the Jesuit Church at Farm Street. Some
while before her reception, after she had acquainted her mother
with her resolve to become an R.C., Muriel heard from a Jewish
uncle who ran a chain of stores in South London. Uncle Solly (I
believe his name was) represented that prosperity which so many
Jewish families of limited means can boast. He said he would like
to take her out to lunch, and she inquired if she could bring a close
friend. The uncle said: By all means. The more the merrier. So
there we were, the three of us – a Jew, an agnostic, an embryo
Catholic – seated round a table at the Strand Palace or the
Cumberland, I forget which, to discuss Muriel's spiritual destination over our melon, soup and steak.

Uncle Solly, who was cheerful and expansive, was not a man to
waste his time on theological niceties. He rather thought that
money or a job must have something to do with it. If he could be
useful in any way, Muriel had just to mention it. . . . Learning that
I was not a Catholic, he asked what I thought of the matter. I said
everyone must choose for themselves, but I personally preferred
the religion of Jesus Christ to that of the Vatican. At this, he seemed a bit uncertain, and when it became clear I was referring to the
Jewish faith, he was even more mystified. No doubt he wrote me
off as a *meshuggha*, or plain bloody mad.

Uncle Solly's mission having failed and Muriel being now within
the True Church, she agreed to receive supporting therapy from
a Rosminian priest who was Rector of the Church of St Ethel-
dreda's, the oldest church now Catholic property in London and
which had once been the site of the town house of the Bishop of
Ely. As with Lincoln's Inn, it possessed its own beadle who, in
green coat and top hat, regulated its traffic. In the pub behind the
church, where Muriel, I and the good Father would sometimes take
a snifter, there was a vine planted in the time of the last Catholic
Bishop of Ely growing through the wall, still very much alive.

All these idiosyncrasies of place took Muriel's fancy and
augured well for her progress at Father O'Malley's hands. A big
exuberant fellow with a core of concealed sensitivity, he
practised a Jungian mode of healing. He had been a sculpture
student in Rome but ill health had led to his abandoning art for
the priesthood. All in all, he proved the man for the job, and about

six months later, when he felt she was quite better, he helped, through his cousin Teresa – a nursing sister and health visitor in Camberwell – to secure her accommodation at 13, Baldwin Crescent, S.E.5. *Memento Mori*, Muriel's cruelly brilliant geriatric novel, is dedicated to this cousin.

After Father O'Malley had seen her two or three times, he suggested she might like to live in the country and come up to see him once a week: it would be both quieter and cheaper for her. I think it was Frank Sheed who suggested Aylesford Priory, a Carmelite house in Kent where, both at the Priory and Allington Castle (an adjacent property), there were guest rooms for visitors and those in retreat.

Muriel was soon installed there. Nor was it long before she demonstrated a lack of that docility usually expected of converts. She was certainly not one of those 'faithful little famuli' whom the Jesuit priest speaks of in Thackeray's *Henry Esmond*. While prepared to listen to priestly counsels, she had little patience with the prying surveillance of all those lay myrmidons in which retreat houses always abound. The amiably or otherwise proffered advice from *bien pensant* hangers-on – usually women – irritated her extremely; the more so since she contended their suggestions were frequently based on misunderstood doctrine: the product not of dogma but hearsay. When these *dévots* came sidling up with hints as to 'the proper Catholic way of doing things', they were met in silence, offhandedly, or with a sharp tongue which Muriel could employ on occasion. This type of monastic female camp-follower who proved such a trial to her has been immortalized in the character of Mrs Hogg in *The Comforters*.

Even the Prior was not exempt from her outbursts of contemptuous anger. Father Malacchi Lynch had all the qualities necessary to make him a cult figure down at Aylesford. He was a large man with silver locks and a rubicund complexion – a Carmelite Santa Claus, one might say. He was also very much the Irishman, the blarneying, soft-spoken stage-Irishman almost. That he was a good man I had no doubt, but the paternal regime which he sought to establish over the surrounding laity all too often revealed his slenderness of culture and intellectual powers. Like many of the Roman priesthood, he was much happier with T. S. Eliot's *Four Quartets* than the literary Jansenism of Graham

Greene, whose subtle charity of heart was something beyond his understanding. He certainly paid lip-service to the contemporary Muse by having one of the cloister walls at Aylesford engraved with the words from *Little Gidding*:

> You are here to kneel
> Where prayer has been valid. And prayer is more
> Than an order of words, the conscious occupation
> Of the praying mind, or the sound of the voice praying.

This went down exceedingly well with the charabancs of pilgrims who came to see the shrine of St Simon Stock in the grounds of the Priory, and also with visiting theatricals among whom Father Malacchi was able to claim a number of converts. Indeed, he was on a much surer footing with professional Thespians than with writers or intellectuals, being something of an actor himself. The palpable worship with which he was surrounded was not perhaps good for him, but it is the situation in which men of parts so often find themselves. One of the harmless silly tales told about the Prior by his fans took the form of the following joke:

Two Irishmen were in Rome at the time of some religious procession. 'Who's that fine big man,' asks Paddy, 'him as looks like a full-blown saint?'

'Oh, by Jesus,' replies Mike, 'that's Father Malacchi, Prior of Aylesford.'

'Indeed, now,' says Paddy, 'and who would be that scrawny wee fellow that looks half-starved?'

'Ah, that's the Pope, the poor man,' answers Mike.

Clearly a pre-Johanine story.

One can imagine, then, the consternation caused among the 'uncou' guid' when Muriel, in a sudden tantrum of annoyance, enquired as to the whereabouts of 'that bloody Prior', demanding to see him instantly. She had small respect for those cosy circles of unofficial canonizers. To Father Malacchi's credit, he did not hold it against her. He was, I think, both amused and fascinated by the small stormy petrel in their midst.

These lay faithful of longer standing must have found Muriel's assertive convert Catholicism far from their liking; and the fact that she was more intelligent and better read than most of them

would have heightened the impression of arrogance. I remember
that Father Caraman, with fine Jesuitical tact, had once bidden her
to heed the watchword 'Discretion'. At Aylesford, certainly, there
was need of it.

But the Priory and its circle by no means constituted the
intellectual desert my account may have suggested. First and foremost, there was the Librarian, Father Brocard Sewell. He was a
smallish ruddy-faced man who had been in an Anglican order as
well as the R.A.F. (which makes another, if you incline to T. E.
Lawrence's brand of asceticism). He had a great interest in comparative religion, particularly in Zen Buddhism, and published the
hip American poets in the pages of *The Aylesford Review* which
he edited, all of which caused the Prior to have the gravest mis-
givings. Since he was later to be suspended for a period (wrongly,
as he told me recently) from administering the sacraments and
from preaching, in consequence of a letter to *The Times*
criticizing the nature and exercise of papal power, Father
Malacchi's doubts were not without substance. As a supporter of
the Conciliar Movement, which had sought in the Middle Ages
to replace papal authority with government of the Church by a
council (a sort of constitutional monarchy in ecclesiastical affairs),
I could only commend his courageous protest; but since I was an
outsider in affairs of the faith, my feelings were irrelevant. It was,
I mean, none of my business.

Whatever Father Brocard's superiors made of his praise of the
Orthodox Church and his rebuke of Latin Christianity, he was one
of those priests well versed in the common language of ideas. His
spiritual home seemed to be the Reading Room of the British
Museum as well as the priory of his own Order. The men of the
'nineties fascinated him, and he did valuable work on the poet
John Gray, wrongly (but how plausibly!) taken to be the original
of Dorian Gray, in Wilde's famous novel; also on Baron Corvo,
Montagu Summers and others. His latest monograph on Olive
Custance, wife of Lord Alfred Douglas, appeared in a new series
Makers of the Nineties, as I was writing these recollections.

The second intellectual solace at Aylesford was Alan Barnsley, a
Maidstone doctor who wrote under the name of Gabriel Fielding
and was later to win the £1,000 W. H. Smith Award for his novel

The Birthday King. Tall and lithe with lean witch-dark features –
such was my first impression of him. I had gone to Allington
Castle where Muriel was beginning to write her first novel, *The
Comforters*, which reproduced, in fictional dress, some of the
symptoms of her breakdown. Allington Castle, the Reformation
home of the poet and courtier Sir Thomas Wyatt, had again become Catholic property, providing both a mother house for a number of Carmelite tertiaries and a guest house for those seeking
respite and quiet.

Allington was all grey stone and winter peace. A frozen blue
twilight hung over its battlements, its hushed Italian garden and
tree-lined river. Electric heating did its best to compete with the
siege-resisting stone of the walls but seemed to burn with a disenchanted glow in the halls and chambers used to roaring open
hearths.

I recall sitting at tea with Muriel as we talked of her novel and
explored the spartan resistance of the rock-cakes on our plates. It
seemed the cold had got into them too; and I drank my tea with my
overcoat on. Into this polar Kentish scene there burst, like a sudden
grenade of heat, the mercurial author of *Brotherly Love*. John Blaydon, hero of several novels, was still unknown to the reading
public; but hearing Alan read from his typescript that night, I understood how ardent was his search into the unsifted substance of
his youth. Through the character of John Blaydon, he was trying to
understand himself; to seize, with a sense of exact location, the
moods and masks of his boyhood years. Into this search he put all
the concentration, the warmth of affection, the depth of insight, the
colour and humour of his vivid disposition. Some personalities
burn steadily like candles in a room undisturbed by draughts.
Alan, on the other hand, was like magnesium. For the first few
minutes one was startled, astonished, for the next two hours ex-
hilarated, and after that exhausted, quite used up. Besides having a
private practice, he officiated as prison doctor at Maidstone Gaol.
He was very popular with the prisoners, drawing freely upon them
for 'copy' as readers of his *Gentlemen in Their Season* will
recognize.

Part of his charm and volatile emotions might well have derived
from his reputed Welsh blood. His love of tall stories, his spell-
binding talk, the range and richness of his rhetoric, all these helped

to make one feel in the presence of a first-rate conjuror. But this mobility of penetration, of registering your wavelength and then tapping it, was not without its attendant dangers. Because he won one's confidence, one might find oneself, along with others, giving a vivid colloquial report of all one's bowel movements throughout the week; and then suddenly be taken with doubts concerning the nature of this narration. Then, too, while generous in his praise of one's own work, he was a great reader of his own writings. He liked to try out his chapters in progress and demand a full-hearted response from his audience. Since the content was dramatic and the reading powerful, I very much relished these sessions, however extensive in duration.

Muriel, though, often found them exhausting. Her idea of the novel was something quite different, and the extraordinary human richness of his themes and the excitement of his drama was largely lost on her. Since, with whatever material, however sinister or kinky, she wished to build a doll's house, Alan's more expansive emotional realism was not to her taste at all. Once, when we were hearing from him a section out of *In the Time of Greenbloom*, she surreptitiously inserted cotton-wool in her ears.

Alan, for his part, was quite fascinated by her. He admired her work tremendously and sought to encourage her in every way. Both, however, were demanding as friends – demanding in quite different fashions – and when Muriel left the small dwelling she had taken at Allington (named by her St Jude's Cottage, since St Jude, as she said, was the saint of hopeless cases) and took a flat in Camberwell, periods of mutual appreciation were followed by periods of coldness.

Even so, I remember many occasions when we were all happy together. (Muriel was fond of quoting St Thomas More's words to his executioners: I trust we shall all be happy in heaven.) I recall dashing with Alan in his Jaguar (he was always changing cars) through the pitchblack windings of Kentish lanes while Muriel sat rigid on the back seat clutching her rosary and hoping for the best. I always felt when going out with Alan that we were carrying our lives in our hands. That was part of the excitement which yielded a more substantial bonus when one was safely back home.

I think of his sudden, disconcerting practical jokes. Once on a

night of thick fog in the depth of the countryside, he announced
to a car-full of us that we had run out of petrol. He had with him,
on this occasion, his uncle 'Doggo', a sweet and frail Anglican
cleric. I and Doggo, Alan suggested, should try to find a petrol
station.

'Look after Doggo, Derek,' he added. 'There's a bridge with
practically no parapet to it about fifty yards up the road. Doggo's
not too steady on his pins, you know. With this fog, he can't even
see his own boots.'

We set forth with a sort of fearful courage, only to hear Alan
recall us when we had ventured some twenty murky yards.

'Derek, Doggo, come back. The feed must have choked. All's
right after all.'

It was a good thing that Alan could take a joke. We scared the
daylight out of him one morning after he had returned from his
rounds, by telling him the Prison Governor had telephoned for
him urgently. An ex-murderer, one of Alan's patients, had apparently committed suicide by swallowing some ointment which
he had prescribed for a rash. Alan was off to the phone like a shot.

'Don't worry,' we told him, 'the feed must have choked.'

Alan was a generous host, and his wife Dina a splendid Ceres
figure. She was always being called upon to mother some lame
duck of a poet, some irritable author chafing with genius. I do not
think this was her chosen role: she told us once of a schoolgirl
fantasy in which she went round in a long cloak, reading Shelley's
more vaporous poems and thinking how romantic it must be to die
of consumption from pure high-mindedness. I have no doubt that
she could have refined on this image had circumstances permitted.
As it was, however reluctantly, she played Candida to perfection.
Dina's Shelleyan aspirations when young caused Muriel much
secret amusement since, looking on her ample figure, she found
herself quite unable to visualize her other than a sturdy strapping
hockey-girl who might have inspired Sir John Betjeman. Muriel
herself, though short in stature, was quite a plump little dumpling.

I much enjoyed parties at Alan's. I recall one in the middle
'fifties, a blue and burning Whitsun during a rail strike. I had managed, by initiative and good fortune, to get as far as Chatham.
There I was met, in the bar on the platform, by Muriel, Alan,
the critic Neville Braybrooke and his wife June, who wrote fiction

under the name of Isobel English and was to win the Katherine
Mansfield Award for her stories in 1974. Muriel and June had
brought their cats with them, Muriel's a blue-grey Persian which
went by the name of 'Bluebell' and June's a tawny Siamese. These
pussies were both very young, and to see them disporting themselves on the marble-topped counter of the buffet, among the beer
handles, was a beautiful sight. It was no doubt an affluent order
of double gins and double whiskies which had guaranteed them
so unusual a playground.

Neville Braybrooke was a liberal-minded Catholic. As a schoolboy at Ampleforth, he had founded the magazine *The Wind and
the Rain* when only sixteen years old, the first English journal to
publish the work of Simone Weil. The maestro who excited him
most was Teilhard de Chardin, some of whose work he published
in an Easter anthology. In his own devotions, Neville was ex-
emplary and practical. Every morning, before breakfast, he would
be off to early Mass. In return for this assiduousness, he felt himself justified in asking Our Lady to help him win the football pools.

As to appearance, he seemed perpetually young. A touch of the
public school beau – hands in trouser pockets, gracefully loung-
ing – always hung a little bit about him. With a Panatella between
his lips and the ghost of a lisp adorning his speech, he invited one
to dream of refreshment marquees, blazers and white flannels.
But though he evoked for me the image of a prewar houseboat at
Henley, there was not the slightest doubt he was of his own time.
One of the evidences of this was his plan to edit a symposium of
essays for T. S. Eliot's seventieth birthday. He asked me on what
theme I would like to write, and, picking on the subject of an un-
reprinted piece from the first edition of *For Lancelot Andrewes*
(1928), I said I would call my piece 'Mr Eliot and Machiavelli'.
When the proposed list of contributors was submitted to the
worthy Possum, he demurred at my particular act of homage.
Having written some tart things about him in my time, I could
hardly complain about his slighting my offering.

Neville and June were not entirely comfortable in Alan's company. The dynamic unpredictable nature of his aura did not always
promote relaxation. On this weekend in question, Alan and Muriel
were having one of their famous misunderstandings, and, as if to
symbolize his sense of apprehension, Neville fell through the

Barnsleys' garden hammock. The Whitsun day was bright as
polished sapphire, and he had been idly rocking himself when the
weather-worn strands gave way depositing his considerable weight
into some flaring flowerbed. A nice means by which to remember
one's birthday (which it was).

June and Neville lived in Gardnor Road, Hampstead; and
Muriel and I would visit there, and from time to time she would
stay the night. She got on well with them, since she did not inter-
pret their atmosphere as a competitive one, which she had inclined
to do in the case of Alan. This was largely due to June who was
too sensitive and good-mannered to parade her own writings as
Alan did his. For this non-assumption of rivalry, she was rewarded
by Muriel finding her a title for her second novel *Every Eye*, taken
from a quotation by Auden which serves as the book's epitaph:

> Every eye must weep alone
> Till I will be overthrown.[1]

Such are the rights and generosities of friendship.

The Braybrookes were connoisseurs of the odd, and June said
that they acted as magnets instinctively drawing what was strange
towards them. Its arrival sometimes proved a disconcerting matter.

Massive Hugo Manning – who painted spirit portraits and
wrote poems which I. A. Richards praised – was one of their
Hampstead neighbours. Now Hugo had the reputation of being a
species of guru; so when he spoke of a young man he had met as
looking like the Archangel Gabriel, recommending him as a suitable lodger for the Braybrookes' basement flat, necessarily they
took his word. The young man was duly installed, the more welcome since he was editing a magazine in whose pages, he said, he
hoped both June and Neville would appear. And appear they did;
though when it came to payment, the editor chose to settle for
their contributions in an unexpected fashion. He asked if they had
accounts outstanding at local shops, and then called in with small
cheques at the newsagent's and the grocer's. It was said he had access
to riches.

One night June and Neville were disturbed in their bedroom by
the sudden irruption of this beautiful young man wearing only his

[1] *Another Time*, 1940.

pyjama trousers, in which semi-nudity he no doubt looked even more like the Archangel Gabriel. Apparently, in the course of some editorial altercation, a friend of his who shared the basement with him had flung a lighted paraffin stove at him. He reported that this had set fire to the carpet, an item which June happened to treasure. So the Archangel had to go, later ensconcing himself in Fitzroy Square, at which address I called three times before obtaining payment for an article on Christopher Fry I had contributed to his paper. A threefold application for payment when dealing with editors is not, of course, to be thought excessive, and in the world of little magazine publication must not be viewed too censoriously.

Muriel loved to hear stories of this order. She once described herself as being a sucker for anyone who could tell a good tale; and the strange verbal and literary humour with which the Braybrookes adorned their house in Gardnor Road was completely to her taste.

These were some of Muriel's first Catholic friends, to whom must be added the novelist Jerzy Peterkiewicz – a Polish Adonis, famed in his country as a poet before he was twenty years old – and the scholar and novelist Christine Brooke-Rose to whom he was then married. Jerzy fascinated Muriel with his angelology, folk lore and humour. He was one of the most charming men I ever met.

Two final names to be mentioned here: Paul Allen, a modern language graduate from Trinity College, Dublin, who became literary editor of *Courier* and the *London Mystery Magazine*, and his friend Igor Chroustchoff whose father had married Peter Warlock's mistress some time before she committed suicide. Igor celebrates his birthday on Keats's nativity, to which 'season of mists and mellow fruitfulness' he attributed his elegiac nature. Igor remained an agnostic though he had submitted himself for instruction at Farm Street. Muriel said she had these two friends in mind when she wrote *The Bachelors*, and had told them they should be featured in the dedication, but when the book appeared it was Jerzy and Christine who received that honour.

Muriel's most interesting non-Catholic friend at that period was Rayner Heppenstall, a literary all-rounder who set a personal stamp on everything he wrote. He had come her way in his

o

capacity as a Third Programme producer, having suggested to her
that she write some playscripts for radio. These 'ear-pieces', as she
used to call them, were later collected, along with some short
stories, in her volume *Voices at Play* (1961).

Heppenstall himself I found of interest. He had transformed
prejudice into a system of thought all his own. I loved to hear him
fulminate against the South as being compact of snobbery, simony
and sodomy. The best of England, according to him, lay North of
the Wash (Heppenstall was born in Huddersfield). The natural
religion of the English people – as opposed to the Establishment –
was to be found in non-conformist chapels, or in the faith of old
Yorkshire and Lancashire families. He liked to parade this point of
view, though he himself was a rationalist agnostic.

There was certainly something un-Londonish about him.
Climbing the stairs to his flat in Holland Park one looked out of a
landing window over to the distant heights of Richmond and the
hills of Surrey. On the sill, stood a number of large laboratory-like
bottles. These contained varieties of home-made wine which
Rayner had prepared himself. They tasted delicious and were
potent in effect. Drinking them, I thought of my maternal grandmother who came from Warwickshire and made her own wines.

It was at Rayner's that I met Father D'Arcy to speak to, though
I had first set eyes upon him at the Newman Society. Tall,
saturnine and very distinguished, this ex-Master of Campion Hall
rose to sum up the evening's discussion and to thank the speaker,
Dr Straus, for his paper on psychiatry and faith. Orations of this
order were often fulsome, fiddly with detail or inane with idle
praise. Father D'Arcy, however, took such ceremonial words and
lifted them into a higher sphere. Touched by some lucid clemency,
niggling objections became harmonized. Diverse and untidy comments from the floor were gathered together and clarified.
Criticism grew to reconciliation; variety changed to a luminous
whole.

Father D'Arcy's dialectic was only matched by his rhetoric and
grace. I have seldom met a thinker whose strong powers of thought
were so takingly linked with felicity and charm. All his words were
notes cast in favour of civilized values. Later, at Rayner's dinner-
table, this public impression was confirmed in private. His long
lean frame and Spanish-style features, his burning eyes and darkly

marked skin gave him something of the look of an El Greco dia-
bolist. Jung had declared how close he felt to be the attributes of
Godhead and the Devil. Father D'Arcy was no satanist, of course,
but his vast liberal intelligence and sensitive nervous system were
perceptive enough to apprehend the dark side of the spirit's moon.

His continued friendship with Rayner proved him no compul-
sive hawker of salvation, since the latter had slipped through
Father D'Arcy's net some time in the 'thirties. From thence forward it seemed apparent that no chance would be given of getting
him within the Church. Since Rayner has told the story of his
abortive love-affair with the faith in his autobiography *The
Intellectual Part* (1963), I shall not repeat the facts here.
Sufficient to say that the much-prized convert *manqué* who, at the
last moment, had avoided his clutches at Campion Hall, on the
convenient completion of a long religious poem *Sebastian* (1937)
written under conditions of free board and lodging, still retained
Father D'Arcy's interest and goodwill. It was typical of Rayner's
abrasive humour that he should have greeted his guest by asking
how many duchesses he had been chatting up lately.

Sometimes I felt with Rayner that he was one of those men who
wished to be more amiable than his temperament permitted. I
have spent several afternoons and evenings at Rayner's drinking
tea, cider or home-made wine with no verbal *contretemps* or ugly
exchanges; but I recall an occasion when Muriel, he and I met for
supper at some Notting Hill restaurant. All went well till at one
point Rayner attacked me abusively. He did not like what I was
saying and told me so in singularly discourteous terms. 'A man
like you ought to be keeping pigs, not writing.' I replied that had
I followed such a calling no doubt I would be better breeched and
we would all be eating a more expensive meal. I said something,
too, about not having an objection to pig-keeping but a strong dislike of eating with hogs. Rayner was shouting and I was laughing
and shouting when Muriel, both amused and apprehensive, stood
up and called us to order, saying if there was any more bloody
nonsense she would get up and leave straightaway. I wondered
afterwards what had precipitated this outburst. I was not even engaged in fierce argument with Rayner at the time.

The last book on which Muriel and I worked together was a
selection of correspondence *Letters of John Henry Newman*,
which appeared in 1957. Muriel had been responsible for choosing
from the letters he had written as a Catholic while I had picked
mine from his Anglican period. To these we added separate
introductions.

Everything about this book satisfied my ambiguous religious
sense. It had obtained the *Nihil obstat* and an *Imprimatur* from
the diocese of Westminster and was reviewed enthusiastically in a
number of Catholic papers. At the same time, Katherine Nott, a
scientific humanist, noticed it sympathetically in *The Observer*.
Part of my own introduction, dealing with the psychology of
Newman, had already appeared in *The Humanist*, organ of the
Rationalist Association. So both the Catholic and the agnostic
press were pleased with the book. It was only the Anglo-Catholics
who disliked it – which was just as I had intended. After all, they
could hardly have been expected to endorse my interpretation of
the Oxford Movement as a trade union for inbred and out-of-date
ecclesiastics.

There was something fitting, as well, that this work on Newman
should mark the end of the partnership between myself and
Muriel. It was I who introduced her to his writings in whose steps
she had followed. Attracted by his style and his gifts as a thinker,
I did not go along with his conclusions. Nor did I admire his
personality (the combination of a masculine intellect with a
feminine temperament). Newman, it seemed to me, believed he
had *thought himself through* from Anglicanism to the Roman
Church; whereas, I felt, his personality had prospectively
chosen that destination. *Anima naturaliter Catholica* – as an
Anglican, he had been a Catholic without recognizing it. In going
over to Rome, he found what he was looking for – what, indeed,
he *was* – though without liking it when he got there. Perhaps the
same, in some sort of fashion, might have been said of Muriel. At
any rate, she accepted Newman whole and some years later made
and published a selection of his Catholic sermons.

With the appearance of her first novel *The Comforters* (1957),
she was launched on that creative path down which she was to
parade herself with so nice and astringent a grace. I was in at the

gestation, though not the parturition of her second novel *Robinson* (1958) which – to those who can read aright – contains the swansong of the earlier Muriel, she who was a girl 'of slender means'.

To say that Muriel regarded her gifts with expectant fondness would not be in any way an overstatement. I remember, when she lived in the Old Brompton Road, discovering her in the act of shredding a disused manuscript into tiny pieces. I asked the reason for this great precaution, and was told it was to protect the copyright of her vision against marauding poets who might come visiting her dustbin for verbal tip-offs. Was this a fantasy or a joke?

One further remark by her returns to mind. We were walking on a cold late autumn day in 1957 in Kensington Gardens, a month or so prior to the appearance of *The Comforters*. 'If only people knew how famous we were!' she observed with a sly innocent-eyed laugh. I could only bow at her kind inclusion.

14

On my right, Roy Campbell . . .

When the history of British poetry in the 'forties and 'fifties comes
to be written, the part played by the Ethical Church in Bayswater
in promoting verse-readings will merit a footnote. This organiz-
ation did not represent the credal commitments of the poets themselves. I doubt if more than one out of a hundred poets reading
there could call himself an Ethical Churchman. It was just that a
band of Ethical Society members formed what they called the
Progressive League, which included among its activities a Contemporary Music and Poetry Circle whose meetings were first held
in the Ethical Church Hall off Queensway.

Big bearded Alec Craig, the organizer of the verse side of these
meetings, well exemplified the Anglo-Saxon mind with its odd
contradictions and paradoxical loyalties. With his beer-drinker's
paunch, his tweeds and rosy cheeks, he might well have come out
of Chesterton. G. K. could easily have chosen him to illustrate the
point that hops and rude health incline the possessor to orthodoxy;
but this was not Alec's position at all: it was a great deal more
complex.

A civil servant who was hearty, learned and a poet, he had
stigmatized our age in a book of verse, *The Aspirin Eaters*. Earlier
volumes included a study of the banned books of Britain and
another which was entitled *Sexual Revolution*. These two, pointing
back to the crusading days of Dr Norman Haire in the 'twenties
and 'thirties, revealed Alec in the role of emancipationist and
libertarian.

But the Ethical Church, besides respecting reason, sought to inculcate reverence. Alec, at least, had a sense of ritual – a feeling for the numinous artistically expressed. He accordingly enjoyed his Anglo-Catholic High Mass with choral procession. And, better still, left-wing as he seemed in certain of his adherences, he observed a devotion to King Charles the Martyr, and was a member of the White Rose League. No doubt he was like the character 'C' in Eliot's *Dialogue on Dramatic Poetry*: 'I am a member of the Labour Party. I believe in the King and the Islington Empire.'

Alec once urged me to become a member of the White Rose League. He knew that I took Viscount Falkland, Charles I's Secretary for War, as one of my culture heroes, and how I had made a practice of spitting on passing the Lord Protector's statue outside the Houses of Parliament. By the middle 'fifties, however, I had discontinued this unhygienic habit and come to look on Cromwell as a necessary evil. Thus I never enjoyed the liturgical high jinks of a Requiem Mass on 30 January, when the White Rose supporters gather in London, mourn their sovereign and later consume a royal repast.

From 1947 to 1949 Jack Bayliss and I attended most meetings where songs and piano music alternated with readings of verse. Sometimes we were unable to stifle our amusement at the perform-ance of the poets on the platform or the behaviour of certain members of the audience. There was, for example, Iris Orton who always listened with her mouth wide open. A poet was such a sacred being to her that a pair of ears was not sufficient wherewith to witness his charismatic words. Iris was a poet too, and given to wearing a cloak. She was also reputed to believe herself a reincar-nation of Dr Johnson and did, in fact, address Wrey Gardiner as 'Sir' on first being introduced to him – a salutation so very respect-ful that Wrey was both mystified and flattered. Iris, however, was worth her weight in gold to the poet Jimmy Kirkup, whose socks she used to darn whenever he descended on London from his northern fastnesses.

Another splendid character among the supporters was the big plump man who snored. No one could look more amiable, more full of cheer and beaming goodwill. His eyes, behind his glasses, signalled approval, and when each poet started reading his look would become blindly ecstatic. Alas, within ten lines he would be asleep, his nose and mouth performing thunderous feats of orchestration.

At these meetings in the Ethical Church Hall there were regulars and birds of passage. One of the regulars was the aforementioned James Kirkup, a poet later to receive wide fame for his fine poem on a heart operation, written after he had received a grandstand view of this surgical miracle. Jimmy, in those far-off days, was melancholy and pale, with a drawn face quite different from his present well padded ambassadorial mask. He looked like the balletic ghost of a lily and had written extensively about a drowned sailor. When Jack and I first knew him there was still the provincial's residual touch about him. Poetry belonged to *la vie bohème,* so he wore his shirt with the collar open; but London, after all, was the capital city so, along with his open-necked shirt and tweed jacket, he carried a pair of kid gloves. How distant this all seems from the present Jimmy with his Japanese kimono as token of his professorial years in the land of the rising sun and his witty sophisticated sequence of poems on all parts of the human body! Jimmy's religion was likewise personal to him. For a poet, at that time, to be Anglican or Catholic was nothing surprising, nothing against him. Jimmy, however, went one better by joining the Greek Orthodox Church. This, in terms of lifemanship, was certainly a more advanced gesture.

The toughest meeting of the Music and Poetry Circle which I ever witnessed at Bayswater was one in which Roy Campbell made his appearance. Roy was a bit of a rogue elephant and was on the trail of certain leftist poets who had not been his most enthusiastic reviewers. My own first sight of him in action confirmed all the worst rumours I had heard of this marauding poet-scalping figure. There was a good audience that evening since Stephen Spender had been billed. Tall, sensitive, beautiful, he had mounted the rostrum and was about to read. Suddenly, attention was abruptly disrupted by cries and catcalls from the back. Roy had arrived, and, egged on by a poet whose only merit was that his prosody was not as impaired as his precarious balance, advanced down the hall towards the dais, a sort of vengeful boxer-faced seraph, calling on Spender to meet his doom.

Roy climbed the steps and backed Spender, who did not put up his fists, against the wall. Menaced by this literary Carnera, he acquitted himself with passive dignity. Robert Greacen, the Ulster poet, and one or two others threw themselves on Roy, urging him to give over and be a good chap, etc. etc. It was touch and go whether he would allow himself to be called off. Roy could probably have laid out four men before being downed, if he was so minded. Fortunately discretion won the day and he was quietly prevailed upon to leave.

Roy Campbell's politics were primitive indeed. Herbert Palmer described him as 'almost too close a bed-fellow with Nietzsche', and quoted the following lines in support:

> There is no joy like those who fight alone,
> Whom lust and gluttony have never tied,
> Who in their purity have built a throne,
> And in their solitude a tower of pride.

But it would be wrong to think of Roy as proud in the ordinary sense of the word. His attitude was truly one of self-reliance, of one who knows he can trust himself. In many ways he was positively modest. On one occasion, when looking for a job, after his war wounds had earned him a discharge, he was told by an acquaintance to try the B.B.C. Wearing his 'Army great-coat dyed navy blue and a South African soldier's hat undyed', he turned up walking 'with a heavy stick, rubber-ferruled'.[1] Roy went along, hoping for the post of commissionaire, but he was not to be rewarded with that old soldier's dream of a soft job. Broadcasting House refused him this position, making him instead a producer in the Talks Department.

This, in itself, was anomaly enough. Roy was so little of the culture-wallah, so little of the egg-head personality. It is true he had received an education at Oxford (from which seat of learning he had abruptly absented himself), but he insisted on speaking of the ancient universities as 'charley factories', holding them in the utmost contempt. Asked once in a questionnaire, in what way he differed as a poet from the ordinary man, he wrote: 'In nothing at all . . . in which, however, I differ very much from the ordinary poet.'

[1] Rayner Heppenstall, *Portrait of the Artist as a Professional Man*, 1969.

He would tell, for example, how in the south of France he happened on an ample figure seated with his back to him at an easel. The light-coloured curls at the nape of the neck, visible below a painter's broad hat, convinced Roy that the sedentary figure was that of a famous art critic whom he in no way esteemed. He therefore decided to steal up on him and administer a playful tweak in the pants ('the Bloomsbury equivalent of shaking hands',[1] as Roy scornfully described the action) when the person before him blandly turned round, raised his hat and returned to his canvas. Appalled to find himself staring at Sir Winston Churchill, Roy tiptoed sheepishly away.

Born raconteur and mimic as he was, he could render the slightest event, the most trifling observation vivid. I remember hearing him speaking of a nursing sister who had been in charge of a ward in an African hospital where he lay wounded. 'Ah, she was a fine woman, man,' he told us. 'I liked her a lot. I used to show my respect for her by lying at attention whenever she passed.'

Another of his stories which delighted me because of the cunning it showed in him concerned a near-amorous encounter. Roy, fancier of bulls and bull-fights, was paying a visit to some South American state where he was billed as a great celebrity. After appearing in the arena, he was wined and dined at a number of banquets which were national or civic occasions. At one of these he met a woman who was powerfully captivated by him. 'A real mother-of-pearl tanker' was how he described her amplitude. It was very soon made evident to him that this fair creature desired to be slept with. However, here was the rub – or lack of it! Roy was much in love with his wife (the beautiful sister of Epstein's spouse) and wished to keep things that way. At the same time, this woman was a great señora, a person of consequence, an owner of estates. As a Latin-American diplomat explained, 'it was all most difficult'. The lady would be most offended. She had always taken great foreign bull-fighters who visited the country to bed with her. She regarded it as part of the national honours accorded them.

Roy was, indeed, in a ticklish position. The temptress was almost in government service. A little indelicate treatment of her was tantamount to international ill-will. At length he worked up the answer. Accepting her invitation to dinner, which was partaken

[1] *Light on a Dark Horse*, 1951.

tête-à-tête, he paid her compliments throughout the many courses. At the end of the repast, he sat silent and sad till his hostess enquired if all was well with him.

'Well, madam? Indeed, you might ask me. You see before you a most unhappy man. Always I have this devotion to beauty. And now when I see your beauty before me, I think that perhaps I might have been happy. "Might have been " not "may be", madame. That is why all is not well. During the War this thing happened to me. Fighting against that evil man Hitler, I received a wound which left me changed.'

'Say no more,' declared the señora, 'but let me hope we shall always be friends.'

Among Roy's quirks and caprices, there buzzed the bee of anti-semitism. Ironically, like many so afflicted, he numbered Jews among his personal friends. My last recollection of him, in fact, was at the Hampstead flat of Hugo Manning, Jewish poet and friend of Henry Miller. Roy was making his departure and, having said his general goodbyes to the company, sought out his host to bid his adieu. Hugo, too, was a man of great girth and, as they parted, they kissed on both cheeks, Latin fashion, like two husky bears. Roy was off in a couple of days to Portugal where his daughter had married a grandee. Within a year or so, he was killed in a motoring accident, his death being possibly an act of mercy since he believed himself to be suffering from cancer. He was not the sort of man to succumb to long illness or die piecemeal in his bed.

Myself, I first met him at the Institute of Contemporary Arts – not the kind of cultural purlieu which might seem to be his natural habitat. I had just written a review of a volume of his poems in some magazine, and while dissociating myself from his political image (this was during my anarchist spell), I praised the formal qualities of rounded stanza and elegant phrasing with genuine sincerity, allowing my enthusiasm full rein since I was annoyed by the current fashion of still doing his poetry down.

Because I had repudiated his views with some assertiveness, I was a little apprehensive when he sought me out. That face 'of a benevolent ram' (as Rayner Heppenstall so aptly put it) could look extremely nasty when he was bent on 'correcting' some reviewer. However, I was to be spared.

'You were a real pal to me, Derek,' he proclaimed, immediately on Christian name terms. It was only then that I realized how much my small meed of praise could mean to a poet who had received a ten years' rough ride from the left literary Establishment, not for writing badly (he wrote better than all save the best of them), but for stating opinions which they did not like to hear. Of course, he had called down coals on his head. In polemical verse and prose, concerning the Spanish Civil War (in which he had fought on Franco's side), he had equated the various Republican elements with respective sickness, physical and moral. The anarchists, he had pronounced, were largely syphilitics; so I was accordingly relieved he had not sent me packing with a chit to the lock hospital.

In reporting on the Campbell–Spender schemozzle, I spoke of another poet who egged Roy on. This was the late John Gawsworth (i.e. Terence Ian Fytton Armstrong), inveterate hater of modernism in verse, and hence, on this occasion, the aider and abettor of attack on that cause in the person of Stephen Spender. A violent man, fantasist and alcoholic, he merits a mention in this humble narrative.

When Muriel Spark left the Poetry Society, Gawsworth took over as editor of *The Poetry Review*. He had, however, been in the field from the 'thirties onwards; and when Michael Roberts published his influential anthology *New Signatures* (containing some of the early works of Auden, Day Lewis and MacNeice), he had reacted by collecting a symposium which haughtily bore the title *Known Signatures* (1932) and included poems by certain lesser Georgian poets. (It is amusing to reflect that those 'signatures' which claimed only to be 'new' are, now, much better 'known' in the field of verse than the latter.)

Herbert Palmer, who knew Gawsworth well, wrote of him as being 'pre-eminent' as a 'bookman' and 'almost certainly the best informed of any under thirty years of age'.[1] Palmer also remarked to me on Gawsworth's extreme reluctance to assist the much older man in digging his potato-patch after coming to see him one day for lunch and tea.

Gawsworth had a passion for the 'nineties which should have predisposed me in his favour, and he had edited a small collection

[1] *Post-Victorian Poetry*, 1938.

of Theodore Wratislaw's poems, a poet who might be described as the elegant ape of Arthur Symons – to which distinction must be added the fact that he was an hereditary Count of the Holy Roman Empire (a poetic title if ever there was one). Gawsworth had also published a paper of considerable interest on Ernest Dowson in the Proceedings of the Royal Society of Literature; but all these assets could not bring me to like the man.

In appearance, just after the war, with his slightly twisted nose, he bore some resemblance to the present Prime Minister of Rhodesia. There was also some faint suggestion of Hitler about him. Was it in his eyes, I wonder? Like the Führer, he was partially mad. Certainly he had Hitler's bad temper, his sudden rages, his peremptory conduct. One evening, at a party, he gratuitously insulted and threatened Muriel Spark. Howard Sergeant strode over to him and said – one word more and he would knock him down. That was the best procedure with Gawsworth, a bully who understood the language of force.

Like many other bullies he enjoyed harrying women. Somebody in whose house Gawsworth once had a flat, told me how he had heard the poet chasing one of his wives or reigning mistresses about the place, shouting after her: 'Get out! Get out! You vile old bag. Get out and work and make some money! Why the hell else do you think I keep you?' Later, he boasted to my informant that he had gone after her with a meat axe. 'That got the old sow moving,' he proclaimed.

Gawsworth was given to dressing up in different kinds of costume. Once, he had donned the dress of a French admiral of the fleet and was walking past Lucien Freud's house when he believed he observed the artist quietly laughing at him. His response to this fancied slight was to draw his sword from its scabbard and hack down a bough from the magnolia growing in Lucien's garden.

Nor were even his supporters free from his tiresome tantrums. Jack Bayliss, who sat on a committee at the Poetry Society during Gawsworth's editorship, told me how he had nearly been strangled after some meeting by an enraged Gawsworth, who had caught hold of the two ends of his long woollen scarf and pulled. Jack had not said what Gawsworth wanted simply because the latter had failed to make his wishes clear in advance.

It was, of course, Gawsworth's Kingdom of Rodonda which secured him publicity in the national press during his latter down-at-heel years. He had inherited this island in the Caribbean from the strange novelist M. P. Shiel, whose literary executor he became. Every so often, he would hold levées and, as King of Rodonda, bestow titles. Sir John Waller received a peerage from Gawsworth before he came into his own somewhat more substantial baronetcy. John Heath-Stubbs, I believe, was made a bishop (Rodonda's church would seem to have been on Anglican lines with the monarch at its head). Jack Bayliss, too, was granted some honour before obtaining his own O.B.E.

His last years were wretched in the extreme. Drink had taken from him the capacity to work, and he was reduced to selling every scrap of association material – letters from friends, from writers of distinction, manuscript scribbles, the scrapings of the barrel. These had come to be not the perks of his profession but his sole means of subsistence. Added to which he had diabetes and other grievous ills of the flesh.

If ever I found myself in a bar where he was drinking, I felt drawn to leave as soon as possible, since the spectacle of Gawsworth in his cups was not a pleasant one. He would shout, hector and bang the table, his ruined face looking debauched and diseased under longish hair of a peculiar colour.

Then Ian Fletcher got up a fund which would pay for Gawsworth's rent and guarantee him a small sum each week. Unwisely, he was allowed to get his hands on part of this, and proceeded to go on a jag in 'the delectable Duchy'. Arthur Caddick has told part of the tale of this sorry spree in the pages of *The Cornish Review* (Winter 1972), a brilliant piece of humorous writing which presents the squalid plight of the poet in ironic and picaresque terms. One cannot but think of Dylan Thomas's catastrophic days in New York as told by Malcolm Brinnin. This was followed by his visit to an admirer in Italy where he finally took fatally ill, returning to die in Brompton Hospital on 24 September 1970.

What I have written here is, of course, only one side of him. His friends, no doubt, could tell another story. Indeed, I would like to have the impressions of George Fraser or Ian Fletcher, both of whom knew him, I believe, over in Cairo when he was one of that wartime band of poets who described themselves as the Salamanders.

A year or so before he died, I received from America for review a symposium in honour of Richard Aldington[1] and found in it a delightful account by Gawsworth of his relationship with the author of *Death of a Hero*. I had always had a soft spot for Aldington since the time I read this novel in my teens, and was happy to think that these two bitter men (one certainly resentful with good reason) had enjoyed so warm and loyal a friendship, though conducted mostly by correspondence.

The most successful meeting of the Music and Poetry Circle took place at Stanton Coit House. This was situated in a street to the south of Kensington Gardens and was the gift to the Ethical Church of the nineteenth-century humanist Stanton Coit. The whole spirit of the Ethical Church was incarnate in a little volume which Coit had edited. It contained a selection of Great Thoughts, drawn largely from the seventeenth-century divines. This touching of the hem of divinity's gown was a popular sport with these reverent agnostics. The building he bequeathed was known among my friends as Stanford Coitus House.

However popular poetry may be, pornography is a great deal more so. When, therefore, Allen Ginsberg, King of the American Beat poets, came to read from his long poem *Howl*, a good attendance was guaranteed, as its author regarded the right to occasional obscenity as a holy cause. Gregory Corso, Ginsberg's poetic lieutenant, together with a tame professor from Berkeley, made up a supporting cast.

On entering, I found the room was nearly packed. Ginsberg, Corso, the professor and his wife were seated in the front row just below the rostrum. The two poets were well steamed up, waiting to blast off their rocket-missile verse. Both had flasks of whisky in the hip pockets of their jeans and were taking frequent pulls at them. Beat though they were, the ordeal before them clearly constituted a strain. This was before the Swinging 'Sixties; and one did not, before the Chatterley trial, say 'fuck' outright to a female audience.

---

[1] *Richard Aldington: an intimate portrait*, ed. Alister Kershaw and F. J. Temple, 1965.

The professor, bland as butter, spoke his piece and we were off. Soon we were up to our knees in it:

> Who copulated ecstatic and insatiate with a
>   bottle of beer a sweetheart a packet of
>   cigarettes a candle and fell off the
>   bed, and continued along the floor
>   and down the hall and ended fainting
>   on the wall with a vision of ultimate
>   cunt and come eluding the last
>   gyzym of consciousness.[1]

A few odd handbags and umbrellas were clutched somewhat anxiously. As the naughty words came round, again and again, their shock impact was appreciably diminished. It wasn't long before they were sounding like daring but delightful acquaintances; and before the poem was finished, they appeared as undisturbing as familiar old friends. Everyone – spinsters, mums and matrons – clapped. When, in the second half of the programme, Corso told us that he had been to Alcatraz or some such hostelry when he was seventeen, we had exhausted all surprise and could only beam on him as if he had told us he was a Boy Scout.

Corso's youthful period in a penitentiary did not seem to have developed in him certain necessary amorous refinements. He was a small but good-looking young man with mobile Latin (or Semite?) features; but he did not, on the evening in question, seem to know how to ingratiate himself with women.

We had all trooped over to the Bodega, a largish pub on the Gardens side of Kensington Gore, where we proceeded to refresh ourselves with drink and gossip. Before our symposium came to a close, Corso went the round of the nubile girls present, asking them aloud, without circumlocution, whether they would sleep with him. With such attendant publicity, the most obliging damsel in those days said No. Was he not acquainted with the quiet word privily spoken, or was it just a part of the Beat-Circus-in-Britain performance?

'Oh well, I guess I'll have to masturbate again on Hampstead Heath,' he exclaimed in summarizing his erotic plans for the night.

[1] Allen Ginsberg, *Howl*, 1956.

Talking to me later about the American Beat poets, John Heath-Stubbs, whose opinions I always respected though not invariably endorsed, said he thought he preferred them to the poets of the Movement. At least the Americans seemed to sense what poetry was all about though they did not generally know quite what to do with this realization.

Whatever one makes of *Howl* poetically – and it seems to me a powerful but imperfect poem – its sociological testament cannot be gainsaid. In one way, the reverse of the coin to Whitman, it speaks with the utmost hate and horror of what the technological revolution, in conjunction with capitalism, has done to America:

> What sphinx of cement and aluminium bashed open their skulls
>   and ate up their brains and imagination?
> Moloch! Solitude! Filth! Ugliness! ashcans and unobtainable
>   dollars! Children screaming under the stairways! Boys
>   sobbing in armies! Old men weeping in the parks!
> Moloch! Moloch! Nightmare of Moloch! Moloch the loveless!
>   Mental Moloch! Moloch the heavy judger of men![1]

Ginsberg himself has a strong, though often sloppy, imagination; but he is too accommodating to his friends. When he says, in the beginning of his poem, that he 'saw the best minds of his generation' destroyed by their environment, he is writing very uncritically. Few of the Beat Generation had anything like good minds (poor Jack Kerouac was an example). The best minds are hardly ever destroyed by their environments, their own subjugating force being, in fact, one of the reasons why we speak of them as we do. It is mostly the second- and third-rate minds who fall victims to what they cannot understand. Even so, Ginsberg's statement, made before he was thirty, was a generous reference and full of more essential human content than so many Movement poems which had the appearance of marginalia on the pages of some Eng. Lit. syllabus.

[1] *Howl*, 1956.

P

15

A Challenge to Possum

It must have been towards the end of 1949, when Muriel Spark was still living at Vicarage Gate, that the first number of *Nine* appeared, since I remember carefully studying it with her there. Our scrutiny was all the more thorough in that there seemed to hang about it a certain flavour of Fascism. In retrospect, this proved a silly suspicion; but with Pound declared a nut case in order to save him from a trial for treason, the invocation of his name always gave birth to doubts and caused hackles to rise among those who firmly signed themselves 'Democrat'. *Nine* unashamedly flew the Poundian banner, and clearly intended itself as a Neo-classical challenge to Neo-Romanticism.

Edited by Peter Russell, with a supporting cast which included G. S. Fraser and Ian Fletcher, it was in some way like a pale ghost of Wyndham Lewis's *Blast*. It had the same abrasive militant tone, but without that effective zippiness which had marked the earlier magazine. There were good translations from the Latin, the Greek and the Chinese included; but, on the whole, its impact on the Neo-Romantic was that of a red rag to a bull.

Along with some fulsome gratulatory epistles printed in the second number, and one or two of more discriminating goodwill (I remember a good one from David Gascoyne), there appeared a contentious letter by me. I should not, at that time, have written equably in any circumstances, but since I had been attacked in the pages of *Nine* I did not need to curb correction with courtesy. In the fifth number of the Grey Walls Press anthology *New Road* appeared two essays by me: 'Rilke and his exclusive myth' and 'Three directions in French writing'. Both of these came under fire from *Nine*'s critical sharpshooters. It was in the former that George Fraser found matter for a little sport. I had spoken of how, for Rilke, sexual love seemed important for the impetus it gave to poetry, and expressed this notion figuratively by saying that he used the phallus as a peg for the lyre. George picked on this tit-bit and made some play with the tale of the Duke of Wellington who had been told of a rat exhibited in a bottle. 'Damn small rat! Damn large bottle!' the unbelieving Iron Duke had replied. George seemed to think that it must be a massive phallus which could support a lyre. To such comment I retorted that the term phallus, as distinct from the word penis, had been employed to imply a symbolical rather than factual reference to the erotic, concluding that I took George's statement as an excuse for talking cock. Such was, in Jack Bayliss's phrase, an instance of those 'tea-cup warfares stirred up by our latter day critics'.[1]

When we are younger, I suspect, we choose our friends more from some accordance of ideas than when we grow older and more sceptical. This being so, it was not to be expected that the contributors to *Nine* would become bosom pals with the Neo-Romantics. At parties and pubbing, however, a certain amount of intercourse took place, and some of their band I liked or respected.

Peter Russell, the editor, seemed a large boisterous dog. He was enthusiastic and amiable, not at all 'the Enemy' figure which an admirer of Wyndham Lewis might have been expected to adopt as his role. I recall an enormous party which he threw in a flat in Duke Street, and how Muriel Spark and I, together with 'Little Derek (a protégé of Sir John Waller), locked ourselves in a lavatory to enjoy the joint consumption of a half-bottle of whisky which we had been able to capture late in the evening when the drink was running out. More memorable was the occasion when at some other junketing, Peter bodily picked up the attractive half-Japanese poetess Gloria Kemai and bore her away upstairs. This was a feat of note since the lady in question would not lightly permit such entire abduction of her person. She was, indeed, a gentle

---

[1] Preface to *The White Knight*, 1944.

and delightful creature – the goddaughter of H. G. Wells, friend
of her father, a Japanese poet and scholar who committed suicide.
Her mother, who often accompanied her to poetry readings, was
a charming and lovely Englishwoman.

Gloria used to work at the Sylvan Press, a small publishing firm
now no more, and two small books of verse by her appeared under
their imprint: *Never Despair of Gardens* (1948) and *In Wake of
Wind* (1949). My copy of the first of these carries an inscription by
her: 'For Dereyck Stanford. In Memory of "Danish Blue".' The
reference is to a cheese I then favoured and to many symposia
in a little café in Queensway, following poetry meetings at the
Ethical Church Hall in its crypt-like rooms in Bayswater. Even the
misspelling of my simple name pleases me since I take it to be the
result of Gloria believing me to be a more complex character than
I actually am.

Although published in many places in its day, Gloria's poetry
does not appear to survive in any anthology – at least, not in those
I have come across. This seems to me a great pity. Though conceived in a minor mode, it had colour, vividness and an elegaic
economy. Since I do not know of her whereabouts and her publishers no longer exist, I print the following miniature from her
book *Never Despair of Gardens*, believing she would grant me
permission:

Candle-end

> Blue twilit hyacinth, magnolia
> Guessing at summer, lilac in the air
> Like promise, lilies with long throats like queens,
> Roses sweet history we make our own,
> Nights glittering Venetian wine-glasses
> Brimming with stars: beyond the feast the cold
> Tomorrow's, spent delight, collapsing ash,
> Staggering music and the candle-flame
> Gasping at dawn. Will wisdom enter in
> The early hours; or will it be too late?

Peter Russell has recently been rediscovered by William Oxley,
editor of the combative magazine *Littack*, as 'the major neglected

talent of our time'.[1] William has made much of the term 'Vitalism' as applying to the kind of poetry he wishes to promote, and when he asked me to write an assessment of his review I could think of no particular reason why Peter Russell should have been translated to his Vitalist pantheon and could only recall Peter playing at the rape of the Sabine women with Gloria which I supposed was, after all, a rather Vitalist thing to do.

Other *Nine* contributors I got to know were G. S. Fraser (about whom more anon), Ian Fletcher, and Hugh Gordon Porteus, whom Muriel Spark and I sometimes used to meet breakfasting in Lyons restaurant next to High Street Kensington station. Hugh was then working in the Chinese section of the B.B.C., being something of a Sinologist. He had translated a number of Chinese poems and written a Faber Pamphlet on Chinese painting to serve as an introduction to the large exhibition of Chinese art held at Burlington House before the war.

I took to Hugh at once, liking his bright blue eyes, alternately twinkling and sad, and his natural good manners. I admired, too, the frank open manner in which he could speak of his ruined marriage, his wife having gone off with Geoffrey Grigson. Although the latter had singled out Jack Bayliss, Jimmy Kirkup and myself for helpful praise in his anthology *Poetry of the Present*, I had formed no high opinion of his amiable properties, and quite expected Hugh to deliver a broadside upon him. Confronted with our evident sympathy, his verdict on Grigson – 'he was the better man' – evinced a magnanimity of mind away beyond the average run of humanity.

I had come across some of Hugh's writing when he acted as art critic to *Life and Letters* in the 'thirties and formed a high opinion of his critical prose. Then, too, at the beginning of the war I had read his clever but neglected study of Wyndham Lewis, published in 1932. About this he was, as in most things, modest, casually dismissing it as a young man's first book. All in all, he answered as little to the temperamental Fascist as one could look to find, so little self-assertive or insistently doctrinaire.

When Muriel and I took up the theme of *Nine*'s reputed politics, he told us stories of how the left had tried to establish a

[1] *Contemporary Poets*, ed. James Vinson, 1975.

literary closed shop in the 'thirties and of how he had been mobbed
at a party following the appearance of his Wyndham Lewis
volume. In any case, I had always distinguished between Pound's
naïve belief in Mussolini and Wyndham Lewis's curious flirtation with the British Union of Fascists, which was as much a product
as anything of his anti-Communism and his angry contempt for
left-wing aesthetics. The pan-Fascism which Lewis manifested
for a short period was as much a gesture of provocation as a deep
commitment. He and the left were always spoiling for a fight,
and Lewis knew that the Jolly Roger – the Mosley insignia of a
lightning flash within a circle (facetiously known as 'a flash in the
pan') – of the B.U.F. would draw the guns of the left quicker than
any other device.

Lewis, unlike Pound, had a complex intelligence, and the simpli-
fication of Fascism could never have satisfied him. He was
essentially a one-man party, though he sometimes claimed it was
the party of genius. His aggressive outsidership was expressly
proclaimed in his own brilliant *One-Way Song* :

                          Look

    No wind of sickle and hammer, of bell and book,
    No wind of any party, or blowing out
    Of any mountain hemming us about
    Of 'High Finance', or the foothills of same.
    The man I am who does *not* play the game.

Like his master, Hugh was one of those of whom Lewis had
written.

    If so the man you are who lets the cat
    Out of the bag, you're a marked fellow and that's flat.

Peter Russell, I think, had private money, but Hugh, who had
to rely on the salability of his talent in the literary market, found
the continuing left-wing climate of the postwar period a depress-
ing feature. I remember meeting him, a year or so later, in a pub
near Brompton Oratory. With that directness which I admired
in him, he confessed he was tight though neither I nor Muriel,

who was with me, would otherwise have known it. He invited us
back to lunch with him at his flat in a street off the Old Brompton
Road. Out in a little patio, we ate some kind of steak or horse-meat
and drank a bottle of wine. I remember it was a heat-wave day, and
Muriel announced that she must leave because she wanted to take
a bath. Hugh said she could use the bathroom which he shared
with a woman sculptor who had a flat on the next floor. Either the
woman was given to keeping her casts or sculpting tools in the
bath or did not consider questions of hygiene after her own
immersions.

'How could I bath in that?' Muriel whispered to me. 'How can
I tell him why I can't?'

So she said she had changed her mind, and that we would stay a
little longer. It was one of those torrid days of summer, too hot to
work and too hot to sleep, when all one can do is talk and drink.

G. S. Fraser was by far the best critic of my generation, and Ian
Fletcher was his first lieutenant. Later, Ian preferred not to think of
himself as a critic – a claim which his writings could well have
justified – but chose rather to regard himself as a scholar. Here
there was no brooking his merits, his edition of the poems of
Lionel Johnson, published in 1953, laying the basis of his position as the foremost authority on the English 1890s throughout the
world. When *Nine* started, however, this side had not become so
very evident and we thought of him as a poet who had written an
attractive seventeenth-century poem about a pretty female cousin –
that, and the fact that he was George's Number One. We always
spoke of them as 'George and Ian', a literary conjunction which
was respected. George was born in Glasgow and Ian, I take it, was
of Scots descent. In appearance they were quite different, Ian being
tall, lean and somewhat monastic while George was shorter and
broader, a reflective and troubled *homme moyen sensuel*.

The image I have of Ian which seems most characteristic of him
is the following. There was a bevy of us at some party, the hour
was late, and a number had left. Those who remained were growing restless. Should we disband or go somewhere else? The question was being put to the vote.

'For myself,' said Ian, 'I'm perfectly contented to stay talking about books all night.' That was Ian to a 't' – the most complete, most absorbing, all-but-exclusive passion for books I have ever seen manifested in any person.

Much later on, in the 'sixties, when I was myself engaged in 'nineties studies and living in the 'ninetyish district of Bedford Park, Ian gave proof of having found room in his personality for a fresh preoccupation. Bearing off a copy of my newly published *Poets of the Nineties* to America, where he was taking up a visiting professorship, he wrote to say all things were in tumult and he didn't know whether he was married or not.

This I took to mean that he was or would be very shortly and, indeed, so it turned out. A year or so later, while visiting his old mother in Shepherds Bush, in the house which contained his personal library (the largest, most fascinating collection of 'nineties volumes I had ever seen – not having then set eyes upon the collection of Dr G. Krishnamurti), he brought his wife, a former student of his at Reading University, and their little daughter to tea with me at Bedford Park. The small child played on the floor as pretty and good as a little girl from a Millais painting. Ian, as hairless as me on top, had grown impressive sideburns which were quite thick and reddish, though the hair on his scalp had been fair. This gave him a faintly Victorian *pater familias* appearance.

Running his eyes over my dining-room bookcase, he inveighed against Max Beerbohm, calling him a drone who had lived on his people. This invocation of the Protestant work-ethic on the part of the foremost *fin-de-sièclist* struck me as oddly incongruous. In any case, I protested, Max had produced a mass of work, both in writing and drawing, even before he took over from Shaw as dramatic critic on *The Saturday Review* in 1898.

'A few precious essays,' retorted Ian. 'Well, of course, I should have liked to have done just the same thing myself – working only on what pleased me. But there were other people to think of. I had to earn a living.'

The image of Ian sedulously shaping small choice dissertations was not unpleasing: some of the prose in his introduction to Lionel Johnson's poems is remarkably good. But, after all, I could not deeply regret the loss of the aesthete in the pundit of aestheticism. Reading University, whose collection of 'ninties material he has helped to build up, has given him useful conditions for research as well as profiting by his knowledge. He has found, and appropriately fills, his niche.

The same, I feel, cannot be said of George Fraser in his incarceration at the University of Leicester. Good scholars and good teachers are rare enough, but first-rate critics are rarer still. George had two gifts seldom effectively conjoined in those who practise criticism: sensitive powers of perception and a powerful flair for analysis. The critic of distinction requires resources of intellect and sensibility, and George possessed them both in a remarkable degree. Another quality which singled him out was his lucid command of the language of ideas, his workable acquaintance with philosophic notions – something all too seldom found in the British critic, and probably stemming, in George's case, from his Scots blood and education. In America he would have been the Edmund Wilson of his generation, clarifying and assessing in the weekly press the issues of our contemporary literary culture, not stuck away in some provincial city, hobbled or part-hobbled by an English teaching programme, however exacting or unexacting it might prove. Neither has he always received the treatment from publishers which his merits should command. That excellent guide *The Modern Writer and His World* is currently available in Penguin, but Faber have not bothered to reprint his *Vision and Rhetoric* (1960), possibly the finest critical volume on contemporary poets published since the war.

When I first met George I did not much like him; but this, I feel now, was due to my shortcomings. By 1949 he had reneged on the Neo-Romantic theories he had professed so eloquently in *The White Horseman* (1941), and had assumed the Neoclassical stance he displayed in the pages of *Nine* and elsewhere. Then, too, he was my senior by a couple of years; and, though shy and uncertain in many ways, was more intellectually sophisticated and worldly wise than me – both of which characteristics I inclined to attribute to the corruption of this good Scot by the Sassenach metropolis.

George himself may almost be thought to have aided and abetted this view, since he would humorously refer to himself as 'a trimmer'. As I was not then acquainted with Lord Halifax's fine

pamphlet, I did not see how this 'Character of a Trimmer' might
have much to say to the critic who needs to be able to mark and
elucidate points of possible reconciliation as well as points of difference. Then, too, George would humorously heighten the
suspicions which a black-and-white mentality might entertain of
him. Robert Greacen once told me of a distinction which George
had drawn in conversation. There were, he said, two kinds of
Scotsman, at least as concerns their conduct in England. One type
came south rearing for a fight, aggressively anticipating a slight;
while the other looked for peace and sought to please. This latter
type was sometimes spoken of as sycophantic; and to it, George
declared, he himself belonged.

In 1949 he went as British Council lecturer to Tokyo, following
in Edmund Blunden's footsteps; while there he published the first
version of his dissertations to Japanese students under the title of
The Modern Writer and His World. This appeared in England in
1953, obtaining the dignity of inclusion in the Penguin list in
1964. Most manuals of this order – in this case dealing with
twentieth-century Eng. Lit. – are unreadable necessities; fodder
for the student or reference-shelf makeweights. *The Modern
Writer and His World*, on the other hand, sets forth the critic's
report in a series of enjoyable judgements.

While in Japan George made an attempt at suicide, motivated,
no doubt, by anxiety. Apparently, he afterwards declared, all the
males of his line tried this once. His elder brother had attempted
it. Once this attempt had been made and had failed, one could
settle down to a normal life. So George was glad to have got his
shot over and, on returning to England, proceeded to broadcast on
the experience.

For a while he worked part-time on the *Times Literary
Supplement*, wrote frequently in the *New Statesman* and did a
weekly book review for the B.B.C. I suspect that the anxiety, the
lack of security, still worried him deeply; and when in 1958
Leicester University opened its jaws, he disappeared down that
comfortable maw into comparative non-productivity. For a lesser
literary critic, this would have been a good thing. It would have
relieved us of a literary superfluity and allowed us to wish him
well. But George's status was quite other. It is as though Samuel
Johnson had been given an Oxford funk-hole before he was fifty,

thus depriving us of *The Lives of the Poets* written after his seventieth year.

Another place where George Fraser was to be met in his London years was the Old Bell on a Thursday at lunchtime. This tavern, almost at the corner of Fleet Street and Ludgate Circus, had been built for the victualling of Sir Christopher Wren's workmen engaged in erecting the new St Paul's. These midday Thursday meetings, between 1950 and 1952, were not gatherings sacred either to the Neo-classical or the Neo-Romantic muse. George and Edmund Blunden came from the *Times Literary Supplement* in Printing House Square, Kenneth Hopkins from an editorial desk at *Everybody's*. There was Jack Bayliss, then at Macmillan's; Anthony Rye, free-lancing from his flat in Devereux Court; and Eileen Bigland, who had written popular biographies and a book on Russia. I joined them once or twice; once, I remember, with Muriel Spark.

Blunden I had first met at a *World Review* party. I was talking to the art critic Anthony Bertram about a little-known poet, Alan Porter, who had published one book of verse in the 'twenties and then decamped to the United States. Bertram had been with Blunden at Oxford where they were officer-undergraduates after the First World War, and both of them had been friends of Porter. Bertram accordingly sought Blunden out, introducing me to him, and I thought how his lean figure and long, thoughtful, wistful face – that of a distinguished pastoral poet – brought a fragrance as of wood-smoke into the tinkling cocktail scene. Looking at him, I always thought of some ultrasensitive hedger-and-ditcher – a cousin of the Scholar Gipsy perhaps.

Blunden and Bertram told me tales of Porter; I found the former to be a quiet, friendly, gentle spirit. I knew him, too, as a leading scholar of English Romanticism. He had done pioneering work in the rehabilitation of John Clare and delved deep into the relationship between Keats and his publisher John Taylor and other members of the circle that revolved about *The London Magazine* of the 1820s. My own interest, at that time, in such minor Romantics as Darley and Beddoes imbued Blunden with charismatic properties for me. I felt he was the possessor of certain abracadabras and could open magic casements on to prospects of the past.

Among the younger men at the Old Bell, he was natural, sympathetic and quite without airs. When he was working at the *Times Literary Supplement* he helped me by giving me books to notice, not acting on the principle favoured by many review editors that they know what is best for one but sending instead, in almost all cases, just those titles for which I had asked. When, in 1953, he went off as Eng. Lit. Professor at Hong Kong University, I missed his encouragement.

Blunden was an academic, having been a tutor at Merton; Fraser was a literary critic first and a literary journalist second; while Kenneth Hopkins was primarily a poet turned journalist and would put his hand to anything occasion demanded. All shared in common a sense of the *pleasures of literature* which was to be communicated to the reader in the language of 'a man talking to men'. Anyone acquainted with the speech of academic criticism will know that the communicability of pleasure is hardly its first object. Few of the American now old New Critics, or Dr Leavis and his progeny, convey in their writing the genial experience of men who have dined well off the printed page. The suggestion, to go by their anxious or dyspeptic tone, is rather one of indigestion, of how to live with your literary ulcer. Another thing about these men of the Old Bell : all, without exception, were poets.

Kenneth Hopkins, with his mandarin moustaches, had a full-stomached gusto much out of fashion with the critics. His amusing book, *The Corruption of a Poet* (1954), its title taken from an epigram by Dryden : 'The corruption of a poet is the generation of a critic', describes his background as a bright boy in Bournemouth who decided to complete for himself in London his otherwise scanty education. This he did so effectively that he was for years acting as a visiting professor at an American university (getting himself made an 'Honorary Admiral of the Texan Navy' as a sort of cultural bonus) and writing his *History of English Poetry* (1962), a study which takes one back to such rare and readable guides as Earle Welby's *A Popular History of English Poetry* (1923) or Edmund Gosse's *A History of Eighteenth Century Literature* (1889) – works now completely out of favour save with those exceptional readers left with the vestiges of independent judgement.

Not being a staid man of the rostrum but a writer, among other things, of mystery stories, Hopkins could not resist the temptation of creating a supernumerary figure in his otherwise objective account of *The Poets Laureate* (1954). This, of course, did not endear him to a number of highbrow critics who were innocently taken in. English academic scholarship – especially the more imperfect order – does not take lightly to fun from outsiders.

I never knew Kenneth Hopkins save to exchange a few words in passing, but his appearance fascinated me. It was that truncated mandarin moustache, pendant like two abbreviated mousetails planted beneath his nostrils, which so drew my attention. It gave him, in my eyes, a faintly sinister aura. There was something slightly raffish about his looks, not out of place in Fleet Street, as if a trendy mandarin had been superimposed on a star reporter. Look at that cigarette drooping just a little from one side of his mouth, somewhat in the manner of Malraux in the 'thirties, as depicted on the cover of *The Corruption of a Poet*. Though published in 1954, the image recalls prewar days and makes me think of the journalists with their belted raincoats in Auden's *The Dog Beneath the Skin*.

This raffishness is borne out by Hopkins's autobiography. I have always been powerfully interested in people who are shameless and – better still – in those who confess their shamelessness, a quality strangely akin to honesty. Those who pursue a goal and do not have their way made smooth for them must profess their case more assertively, more ruthlessly, than those more fortunately accommodated. The manner in which Hopkins admitted to gatecrashing and badgering the Powys brothers is enough to set the sensitive's teeth on edge; but 'needs must' is the first command of all successful survivorship.

Hopkins's friend Anthony Rye was a very different figure. When he wore his soft black hat he looked like a country gent emulating Hannen Swaffer, or reminded me, perhaps' more suitably, of Bosinney in *The Forsyte Saga*, whose soft grey hat, in that bastion of Forsyte toppers, was mistaken by Aunt Hester for a cat asleep on a chair. Even Tony's broken long nose could not obscure his air of distinction. His old-fashioned upper-class voice added to this impression; though his views, which were pacifist, lent no support to the Establishment as would more naturally have befitted his *haut bourgeois* background.

Like Blunden, whose protégé in some ways he was, Tony's

poetry was primarily pastoral. His book of verse *The Inn of Birds* (1947) was beautifully illustrated by him, the volume being dedicated to Blunden. Tony was to publish a second book of rustic pieces by the title of *Poems from Selborne* (Gilbert White's village which had been his family's country retreat since before the Great War) in 1961. Indeed, it was not till the middle of the 'sixties that I got to know him properly through his attendance, with Jack Bayliss, at the West Country Writers' Conference, first at Plymouth and later at Bath; but in September 1974 I was happy to gather with some forty others for a party to mark his seventieth birthday held at Anne Mallinson's Selborne Bookshop. We drank Veuve du Vernay and read celebratory poems to salute the seventieth birthday of this bard of Selborne. Not many poets could boast, like Tony, that their well-selling poems could be seen and purchased in the local pub, as his could be at the Queen's Hotel.

In revising these pages for the press, I was forced to substitute 'could' for 'can'. Tony died suddenly in August 1975, a fortnight after my wife and I had been visiting him and his wife Constance. In 1970 he had published *Gilbert White and His Selborne*, and himself lies buried in the churchyard of that village which was as important to his writing and drawing as was Cookham to Stanley Spencer's painting.

Eileen Bigland was the only woman among that bevy of Old Bell writers. She had a roguish eye, a ready wit, and a raised glass: I think of her always with this last property as if, like her merry laugh, it was a regular attribute. My own copy of *The Inn of Birds* bears the name 'John Bayliss'. Beneath it, in Tony Rye's fine hand, it is inscribed 'To Eileen, With affection and esteem from the author, December 13th 1951'. This is followed by a postscript: ' – and you should have had it before!'

Eileen had taken over Jack's flat at Chiswick when he first went to Rhodesia as a publications officer in Government service. There she left her copy of the book which he kept till giving it to me. She also left the flat in a state of chaos – perhaps something to do with all those empty sherry bottles which had not been discarded. Peace to her spirit: she is now no more.

The above section about the Old Bell has been included to prove that all the poetic converse of the 'fifties was not bedevilled by disagreements between the Neo-classicals and the Neo-Romantics. However, since this chapter was intended to portray the conflict and differences between the two groups, it is only right that the reader should be reminded of them at the finish. Mindful of T. S. Eliot's admonition concerning the way in which he envisaged the ending of the world, I have decided to terminate these memoirs with a bang – a bang with Eliot right at the centre.

Ever since he had declared his commitment to classicism, royalism and Anglo-Catholicism Eliot had been under suspicion by those who saw things differently. At a rather silly *New Verse* level, he had drawn the fire of one of Grigson's brigade when he had visited Salazar's state during the Spanish Civil War:

> As a POET you visit today
> The NICE Portuguese.
> You can help England so in that way;
> I DO hope you please.
>
> You WILL watch Spain's terrible border;
> Take care where you tread.
> How AWFUL for England if you were
> Shot down for a 'RED'.[1]

On a higher plane of comment – no names, no packdrill – Herbert Read expressed his rejection of one of Eliot's three props, when he wrote at the time of the Surrealist Exhibition in 1936:

Classicism, let it be stated without further preface, represents for us now, and has always represented, the forces of oppression. Classicism is the intellectual counterpart of political tyranny. It was so in the ancient world and in the medieval empires; it was renewed to express the dictatorships of the Renaissance and has ever since been the official creed of capitalism. Wherever the blood of martyrs stains the ground, there you will find a doric column or perhaps a statue of Minerva.[2]

---

[1] W. T. Nettlefold, 'Fan Mail for a Poet', *Poetry of the Thirties*, ed. Robin Skelton, 1964.
[2] 'Surrealism and the Romantic Principle', *The Philosophy of Modern Art*, 1951.

Strong stuff this, from the man who had been Eliot's lieutenant on *The Criterion*. No wonder that all the anarchists and Neo-Romantics who looked to Read for a lead had conceived a hearty distrust of Possum and those who resorted to his name to justify their own position.

What I am about to relate has already been described by Dannie Abse in his riotous autobiography *A Poet in the Family* (1974). Dannie was there and I was there; and although I would endorse his every word, it is certain that each of us would place his accents differently or make his own individual comment. I reviewed Dannie's book a year or so ago, but have not referred to it in writing my account. I did, however, discuss it with Tony Rye a week or so before describing the incident here. Tony had also been present at the happening (though I did not see him at the time) and his recollections served to revive the scene in my mind.

The occasion was a poetry reading at the Institute of Contemporary Arts. Herbert Read was in the chair, and a host of members, poets and their friends filled all the chairs in the auditorium, leaving a number standing at the back. The evening proceeded without hap until Emmanuel Litvinoff, a tall dark Jewish poet, started to read a poem which rebuked Eliot for his anti-semitism. The poem constituted a dignified and eloquent protest against words written by Eliot on more than one occasion – words the more reprehensible because of their casual yet dismissive nature. To these words I will turn shortly.

As Litvinoff's poetic indictment rang out, a tense feeling intruded on the hush. Then some murmuring started, to cease almost immediately. Eliot was standing at the back of the audience, though he had not been present when the programme began. Had someone tipped him off, someone knowing what Litvinoff planned to read?

To Eliot's everlasting credit, he commented that it was 'a very good poem'. 'Only that, and nothing more' – Possum had spoken. With Eliot's presence recognized, the murmuring, now louder, broke out anew. Some were applauding the poem; others protesting about it. 'That young Sun-God' Stephen Spender (as Tony Rye remembered him from that night) was now on his feet defending his 'Tom', obviously believing him a more suitable object for his knight-erranting than the memory of all those exterminated Jews.

That, in itself, was remarkable enough. Spender had Jewish blood in his veins; and in no way shared Eliot's Conservatism or his Christianity. An ex-Communist, who was now a pink Liberal, Spender might have been thought to represent all that Eliot intellectually disapproved of. Why, then, this eagerness to support him, to attest before the audience what looked like the betrayal of his own people?

I have said that this was remarkable enough, but it did not constitute the sum of surprises which that evening held for us – another revelation which might seem singularly out of character. Spender's speech was followed by more confused shouting; and Emmanuel Litvinoff immediately began to answer Spender. Herbert Read, that champion of free speech, now decided to claim the office of the Chair to call the meeting to order (which he had every right to do) and also to insist that Litvinoff sit down, which struck many of us as a very different thing. He had permitted Spender to make his declaration in defence of Eliot. Why, then, should Litvinoff not have the right to reply? Could it be that Read, the egalitarian, felt what must be accorded to Spender as a figure of considerable status need not be allowed for Litvinoff, a younger and then but little known man? Or was it that Read, who did not object to disagreeing with Eliot in print (see the former's little essay in his book *In Defence of Shelley* 1936), felt it ungentlemanly not to interfere in any vocal attack on him? The two men were, after all, friends and colleagues though not on such close terms as they had been in the 'twenties and early 'thirties. Whatever Read's motive for suppressing Litvinoff, it was felt by many to come very oddly from a man who had testified on behalf of the anarchists in court during the war when they had been persecuted for speaking in Hyde Park and spreading disaffection among members of the Forces.

'Let him speak! Let him speak!' came calls from the floor again and again; but Read remained adamant. A number of Neo-Romantic poets then got up and left, I and Muriel Spark among them, for although Muriel had seldom a good word to say for the Jews, she was the first to protest or defend them if others in any way slighted their name.

The question now arises here (though it has been raised and answered before) of how far Litvinoff was justified in impugning

Q

Eliot for his antisemitism. Well, there are passages in the poems which must be offensive to Jewish people:

> But this or such was Bleistein's way:
> A saggy bending of the knees
> And elbows, with the palms turned out,
> Chicago Semite Viennese.[1]

In the same piece, speaking of Venice, the poet remarks that

> The rats are underneath the piles.
> The Jew is underneath the lot.
> Money in furs.

Other Jewish characters who feel the poet's disapprobation are Sir Ferdinand Klein from the same poem (nothing is said about him save that he is entertained by Princess Volupine, which Eliot presumably thinks damning enough) and 'Rachel *née* Rabinovitch' (from 'Sweeney Among the Nightingales' who 'Tears at the grapes with murderous paws'.

These amiable references are not exactly shining examples of Christian *caritas*. There could, it is true, be another explanation: namely, that they are the product not of life but of literature. Lady Churchill once remarked that Sir Winston had really no idea of the real world in which he lived. He had never, she declared, even ridden in a bus. Now it might be thought unlikely that the author of *The Waste Land* was not conversant with the twentieth-century scene on which his great poem so frequently draws. Yet consider the number of quotations within it; the way in which writers from the past have been pressed into service to speak for the present. Till the middle 'thirties, Eliot was much concerned with Elizabethan and Jacobean drama; and the figure which the Jew cuts in this – with a few exceptions – is hardly praiseworthy. Could Eliot have taken over the period's paper-cut-out image of the villain?

Another second-hand source of his antisemitism was, almost certainly, the writings of Charles Maurras (founder of *Action Française*), whose work was closely studied by him. Was there something in his nature which led him never to trust the evidence of his

[1] 'Burbank with a Baedeker: Bleistein with a cigar', *Poems*, 1920.

senses but only attain to certitude if he found the 'proof' in print? All this may sound incredible; but Eliot was too complex a man to be judged by standards of normality.

And, beyond the poems, there is that other unfortunate statement in prose about the undesirability of too many 'free-thinking Jews' which adorns his *Notes towards a Definition of Culture*, as if the Semitic element in our population were principally responsible for rationalism, atheism and agnosticism, and not such true-blooded Anglo-Saxons as Tom Paine, William Goodwin, Charles Brad-laugh, and Thomas Huxley. But why should I seek to 'explain' Eliot or in any marginal manner excuse him, when, on this issue, I believe him guilty? For me, he remains the greatest poet of our time; but I see, as I saw then, no valid reason to accord his every opinion the authority of infallibility.

To the outward eye, and objectively speaking, this incident at the I.C.A. was no more than one of those literary shindies which occasionally enliven the writer's sedentary life. Looking at the affair in a more subjective fashion, I feel it could be seen to symbolize the defeat of the Neo-Romantic generation. Many of its members were certainly discomforted on this particular evening. Herbert Read, their leader, appeared to have betrayed them, siding with Spender who, for all his personal attractiveness, was seen by them (somewhat unfairly, it must be admitted) as representing, still, the poetics of the 'thirties. Eliot, unmarked by this vulgar brick-sling-ing, maintained as ever his place of glory; our era's supreme inviolable poet, but, as some thought, the source of negative-minded doctrine.

Nor was it a simple case of the libertarians against the authoritarians; the earlier connection between Neo-Romanticism and Anarchism no longer existed as it had tended to do in the first half of the 'forties. I wrote a severe critical article on Alex Comfort's *Art and Social Responsibility* some time in 1948. (In the same number of the *Poetry Review*; Comfort contributed a notice of my poems *Music for Statues*, saying he did not go for my verse but proclaiming me to be a good critic, which at least gave some credence to my judgement of him).

By 1950 I had completely ceased to subscribe to Read's philo-sophic Anarchism but regarded all he wrote with respect and looked to him still for instruction in the field of artistic theory. To this day, I remember the excitement which *The True Voice of Feeling,* his 'Studies in English Romantic Poetry' created in me when it appeared in 1953. Conservative and pro-Christian as I then was, I felt no compulsion to enroll myself in Eliot's cohorts. There were, after all, many other types of Christian persuasion and Conservative opinion than those which he represented. Indeed, the more that religious thought occupied my attention, the more strongly I repudiated Eliot's own position.

I remember, for instance, a pamphlet he published at the time when the proposed union of the Methodistical Church of South India and the Church of England was about to take place. The Anglo-Catholics – of whom Eliot was one – were making admonitory noises with talk of heresy. Some (not Eliot) threatened to leave if the union became an actual fact; Hugh Ross Williamson and other perfervid spirits did so and joined the Church of Rome. For these men, who included married priests with families whose gesture meant a loss of livings, I had the highest respect. Eliot's own cautious reservations – his eternal 'if and perhaps and but' – affected me quite differently. I saw only the legalistic kind of theology which I instinctively disliked, and an attack on that 'comprehension' which many have taken to be the hallmark of the Anglican Church as the professed Church of all the nation. An enthusiast, at that time, for the Ecumenical Movement, I regarded Eliot as an obstacle to a more generous-spirited Christian unity.

In 1957, however, there occurred an event which changed his image in my eyes. His first wife had died in 1947, and ten years later he married his secretary Miss Valerie Fletcher, many years younger than him. With this action, he seemed to have put off the hair-shirt aura which he so sedulously – and, no doubt, sincerely – cultivated. Something as commonplace as mere human happiness now appeared a matter not unworthy of attention. He was photographed on holiday with Mrs Eliot looking almost embarrassingly boyish and happy; and I remember him seated with his wife at a press conference held after the performance of the première of his play *The Elder Statesman* in 1959 at the Edinburgh Festival, obviously feeling consoled and comforted by her presence at what was not a very sympathetic interview with journalists from many countries. These proofs of humanity and fallibility warmed me towards him, and I wrote of his play more appreciatively than most of my generation. It satisfied me deeply in a way in which *Murder in the Cathedral*, save for its poetry, certainly did not.

Later I had a chance to write a book on the notion of God and religion in Eliot's writings, which I lost by being too aggressively honest. Having been approached by an American publisher, I replied that I would undertake the work only if granted the freedom to treat my subject as contentiously as I chose. Since then I have regretted this silly insistence. It would have been good for me to have disciplined myself to a careful study of his thought on these matters. Even in 1939, just a month after the outbreak of war, I had read his lectures on *The Idea of a Christian Society* with deep intellectual pleasure, though I was then at a far greater distance from his standpoint than I was in the 'sixties. It is true that his early attempt to integrate Christianity and culture in the specific act of literary criticism as represented by *After Strange Gods: a primer of modern heresy* (1934) had always riled me – but then we do not read serious literature merely to be confirmed in our own self-limitations. From all of which, it will be inferred that I feel rather closer to Eliot today than I did on that stormy evening at the I.C.A.

The development and changes which my own thought was undergoing was something apparent in other Neo-Romantics, though their own re-orientation may have differed greatly from mine. Even on the occasion of the I.C.A. conflict, no simple theoretical line of political or philosophical nature could be drawn between the forces of Neo-Romanticism and Neo-classicism.

It was left to Alex Comfort to sum up what he took to be the demoralization and corruption of his one-time colleagues and partisans. The poem is ironically entitled 'Maturity' :

> Let them turn to the bottle
> the Yogi and the rope,
> some of them go to Uncle Joe,
> some of them to the Pope –
>
> one by one grown prosperous
> of excellent intent
> they set their names on the pay roll
> of God and Government;

one is turned evangelist,
another is turned Knight :
let them go wherever they wish –
we will stay and fight.[1]

That 'we' might almost have been the Royal Plural. Indeed, it was
necessary for purposes of morale since of that literary generation
Alex was perhaps the last in the field to profess the old faith still
in this decisive fashion.

It is not only in Keats's 'Ode to a Nightingale' that the hungry
generations tread one another down. It is, unfortunately, a law of
life, of animal life especially, and of that higher reflection of it: a
law of the creative imagination.

The Neo-Romantic generation had enjoyed their twenty-year
innings. Now was the turn of other teams waiting none too
patiently in the pavilion. First, there were the Angry Young Men
– a mixed batch of assorted novelists and publicists which included
John Wain, Kingsley Amis, John Braine and Colin Wilson. Next
there came the Movement poets, gathered together for the first
time in Robert Conquest's *New Lines* anthology, a volume which
appeared in 1956 and whose style and attitude led G. S. Fraser to
speak of an ousting of the bohemians by the academics. Lastly,
there appeared the Kitchen Sink dramatists – John Osborne, Shelagh
Delaney, Arnold Wesker and Harold Pinter – with new social
standards to formulate and the baby's potty as an important em-
blematic stage prop.

It was time for the Neo-Romantic eleven to draw stumps and
declare.

[1] *Haste to the Wedding*, 1962.

Index